Great Books
for Boys

Great Books for Boys

More than 600 Books
for Boys 2 to 14

Kathleen Odean

Ballantine Books
New York

A Ballantine Book
Published by The Ballantine Publishing Group

http://www.randomhouse.com

LIBRARY OF CONGRESS CATALOGING-IN-PUBLICATION DATA
Odean, Kathleen.
  Great books for boys : more than 600 books for boys
2 to 14 / Kathleen Odean.—1st ed.
    p. cm.
  ISBN 0-345-42083-7 (alk. paper)
  1. Boys—Books and reading.   I. Title.
Z1037.O24   1998
028.1'6241—dc21   97-45926
                                              CIP

Manufactured in the United States of America

First Edition: March 1998

10 9 8 7 6 5 4 3 2 1

Dedicated with love to Autumn, Isabel, Rosalie, Graham,
Andrew, Naomi, Shayla, Tyler, Noah, and Dana
and to my students past and present

Contents

CONTENTS

CONTENTS

Acknowledgments

I want to thank the following people who helped make this book possible: my fellow librarians and other friends in the children's book world, for their thoughts about boys' reading and their dedication to children and books; the teachers at Moses Brown School who shared their excitement about books with me; the staff at the Barrington Public Library, for their help in obtaining so many books; my editor, Andrea Schulz, and my agent, Lisa Ross, for their encouragement; my friends Martha Wellbaum, Elizabeth Overmyer, Mary Lee Griffin, Donna Good, Debby Neely, and Pam Jenkins, for sharing their ideas and their love of children's books; and my husband, Ross Cheit, for his love and support.

Introduction

"Men may still grow up to inherit the earth but they give up a great deal on the way."
—Angela Phillips, *The Trouble with Boys**

One of the things that many boys give up on their way to manhood is a love of reading. If they are lucky, at one point boys find books exciting and enjoyable. As young children, they see adults or older siblings reading and want to try it themselves. Books begin to be a rewarding part of their lives—providing both entertainment and education. But as boys move toward adolescence, all too many quit reading for pleasure because it's not cool and a reader risks being labeled a "sissy" or "nerd."

Yet in an age in which information is increasingly the key to success, and our shrinking planet requires a wide understanding

*Angela Phillips, *The Trouble with Boys* (New York: Basic Books, 1994), p. 2.

1

of other people and cultures, the ability to read well is essential. Parents who understand the importance of reading worry that their sons read too little and save their enthusiasm for other pastimes. It is troubling that, in standardized testing, boys consistently score lower in reading than girls do. Boys make up two-thirds of special education classes in the United States, a much higher figure than in some other countries. Just as girls need encouragement in math and science, boys clearly need to be better motivated to read and care about books.

Unfortunately, as writer Bruce Brooks observed in his essay "Real Boys Read Books," our society makes it hard for boys who like to read, especially as they get older.

> Nobody ever came upon a girl reading a book and said, "What the hell are you *doing?*" Nobody ever said to a girl, "Why don't you put that thing down and go outside and play some ball?". . . But these are exactly what most boys hear from fathers and brothers and other guys, most every time they let somebody catch them reading a book.*

If, as a society, we conveyed the same enthusiasm about reading that we do about, for example, sports, boys would be reading far more than they do now. Instead, boys see that athletic excellence is widely admired while love of reading is not. As Brooks's title suggests, boys get the discouraging message that "real men don't read."

Another strength that many boys lose as they get older is the ability to express a range of emotions. Competition and achievement become all-important while traits like empathy lose ground. In *The Courage to Raise Good Men*, family therapist Olga Silverstein observes, "Boys from all

*Bruce Brooks, *Boys Will Be* (New York: Hyperion, 1993), p. 64.

INTRODUCTION

ethnic and economic groups are pressured to compete, be aggressive, gain status and power, and do it at the expense of those against whom they are competing. . . ."† Silverstein writes persuasively about the importance of changing the way boys are raised, to avoid the "emotional shutdown" that society forces on most boys.‡ It bothers many parents when their young sons absorb the idea that males shouldn't show affection, which leads them to refuse to kiss or hug even close relatives. Older boys learn to hide emotions like unhappiness and fear, to avoid being teased or bullied. The images children see in the media only reinforce those behaviors. Males on television and in movies are associated with violence and power, not shown expressing a full range of emotions.

We are raising more girls who expect to work outside the home and be financially responsible as well as to take care of families and relationships, but we continue to raise most boys as if their responsibilities as adults will end with their paychecks. We try to teach them to be competent and competitive, but we don't emphasize compassion and cooperation. Yet, in my experience, many boys *wish* that they were expected to be affectionate, compassionate, and more open about how they feel. They know they are being eased—or pushed—out of those roles as they get older, whether they want it or not. Once when I had a class of fourth-graders in the library and I asked a girl to do a task for me, a kind and thoughtful fourth-grade boy asked me in a baffled tone, "Why don't grown-ups expect boys to be helpful?" His question made me reexamine my attitude toward boys and look at how our expectations affect them. Boys are as eager to give and get

†Olga Silverstein and Beth Rashbaum, *The Courage to Raise Good Men* (New York: Viking, 1994), pp. 111–12.
‡Ibid., p. 223.

affection as girls are, if only we would keep that option open for them.

It must also be baffling for boys to watch as many girls continue to cry when something hurts, and to tell their friends and parents when they are afraid or anxious without feeling like a failure, while those avenues become closed to boys. The pressure to hide emotions is isolating, and leaves boys wondering why they feel the way they do and if their feelings are normal.

What can parents do to help their sons grow up without losing so much of importance, including a love of reading, on the way? Trying to change societal values about males is a difficult process that won't happen quickly. But in the meantime, parents can provide their sons with a more expansive vision of what boys can be and what sort of men they can become. One practical step for parents to take is to give their sons well-chosen books that will keep reading *fun*, as well as showing fictional boys discovering values that go beyond competition and stoicism. Skillfully developed characters show different ways to be strong and mature. In *Ironman* by Chris Crutcher, for example, the main character realizes that learning to control his anger is far more difficult for him than training for a triathlon. Listening to the confidences of an unhappy friend, grieving for a loss, resisting peer pressure, defining one's own values—these are different facets of maturity, but how often do boys see these modeled by men on the screen or in their lives? Books can help fill in those gaps.

At the same time, reading can introduce new ideas and feelings, other ways of looking at life, that prompt a reader to develop compassion for others. Books offer models of friendship and love, showing that boys can be close to each other, to girls, and to caring adults, in settings where affection is seen not as a weakness but as an invaluable strength.

Criteria: Exciting Books, Expansive Viewpoints

More than four thousand books are published for children each year, yet boys—and the adults who care about what boys read—maintain that it is hard to find books that boys like. This belief has been echoed by Robert Lipsyte, Bruce Coville, and Gary Paulsen, writers who are popular with boys. Paulsen speaks of a time when he "was horrified that there was so little being done for boys," because, he was told, publishers believe that boys don't read. Paulsen decided to fill that gap: "I just assumed if you did something that appealed to boys, there would be boy readers."*

Although some of them may be hard to find, books that appeal to boys and satisfy their needs and interests *do* exist. In gathering together more than six hundred such books, I have looked for those that meet at least one of two main criteria. First, I chose genres or topics that particularly appeal to boys, based on research about boys' reading preferences and on my sixteen years of experience as a children's librarian. Second, I looked for books that rise above others in how well they capture the complexity of boys' lives. These outstanding books reflect boys' feelings and experiences in their three-dimensional characters and believable plots. Too often, books geared toward boys, including many sports books and horror novels, present shallow, stereotypical male characters and rely on sensational or predictable plots. Boys deserve better-written, richer reading.

*Gary Paulsen, quoted in "The Maximum Expression of Being Human" by David Gale, *School Library Journal*, June 1997, p. 27.

INTRODUCTION

Of course, a wide variety of books interest different boys, but some characteristics have especially broad appeal. Humor is a winner with all age groups. I looked for books for younger children in which the words and pictures work together to create the humor. I include some folktale parodies with clever twists on familiar tales, popular with many children. Older readers like modern novels in which the witty narrator describes how he deals with the ups and downs of daily life.

Stories of adventure also rank high. For younger boys, this can mean a picture-story book with a heroic main character who faces monsters or travels someplace new. Survival stories by Gary Paulsen, Jean Craighead George, Will Hobbs, and Avi satisfy older boys looking for a gripping read. The related category of mysteries and ghost stories also appeals to many elementary and middle school students, so I've assembled a strong list of those for different age groups. For those often voracious readers who like fantasy, I've annotated many great books, often describing the first in a satisfying series.

Children who like to have information incorporated into their fiction especially enjoy historical fiction and sports books. The settings for historical fiction range from prehistoric times to as recent as the 1950s. Although many historical novels have a wartime setting and may include some violence, I looked for books that emphasize the devastation of war rather than glorify violence.

Sports books, which tend to be very popular with some boys, can lure children who don't usually turn to books for pleasure. In addition to novels on many different sports, I looked for biographies of favorite stars, books to improve techniques, and some sports history.

Informational books, which I address at length below, appeal to children who may not necessarily enjoy fiction. Dinosaurs, magic tricks, snakes, firefighters, airplanes, monsters, the *Titanic*, science experiments—children have a multitude of interests, and I've tried to include books on many of them. Students with serious tastes will find challenging nonfiction on supercomputers, the Holocaust, Pompeii, the Mississippi flood, and more, as well as biographies on Albert Einstein, Barbara McClintock, Frederick Douglass, and Martin Luther King, Jr. As many adults realize, biographies can be as exciting as fiction. I've known reluctant readers who loved reading about spies or other real-life adventurers. Younger readers can enjoy heavily illustrated biographies like that of black cowboy and rodeo performer Bill Pickett, which reads like a compelling novel, with plenty of pictures to add historical setting and atmosphere.

My second aim was to find outstanding books populated by fully rounded characters whose stories reflect feelings and issues that affect boys. In 1992 writer Robert Lipsyte suggested that boys don't read because "current books do not deal with the real problems and fears of individual boys."* I have sought out books that *do* deal with real problems through characters readers will recognize and relate to. Convincing characters feel sadness and pain, just as real boys do, and suffer all the more when they are expected not to show it. They want families who love them and express that love. They want friends to talk to about their concerns as well as to share adventures.

The books I describe in this guide can reveal to boys the welcome truth that others feel as they do, that they are not alone in their problems or confusion. Fictional characters struggle with the same problems as readers, sometimes literally, sometimes figuratively. This can be true on a very simple level for young children, with a bear in a picture book who needs a

*Robert Lipsyte, "Listening for the Footsteps: Books and Boys," *The Horn Book*, May/June 1992, p. 292.

friend, or on increasingly complex levels for older readers, such as a fictional middle school boy coming to terms with his parents' divorce.

Any good novel, even a humorous one, will incorporate real feelings. Children enjoy reading about other children like themselves, who get into scrapes but mean well. Fantasy, though set in an imaginary world, can also be deeply relevant, addressing the ever-present question of what it means to be brave. Most boys struggle with issues about courage and fear, and have to reach their own conclusions about what those qualities mean. This is a recurring theme in novels for adolescents who struggle with peer pressure and living up to their parents' expectations.

Friendships and relationships with siblings play a big role in children's lives. I found books that show that friendship is not automatic or necessarily easy, something children don't always realize. Many picture-story books focus on these themes, reassuring readers that others share their problems and challenges. For adolescents who may also be interested in romance, even if they only joke about it in public, books are a safe place to begin to explore the meaning of romantic love.

I was disturbed at the overwhelming presence of two themes in the novels I read: problems with bullies, and problems with fathers. Bullies played a major role in book after book, even the humorous ones, which I didn't find in researching books about girls. Bullies appear to be a universal threat for boys, making life miserable or frightening for their victims. While some novels with bullies show a boy who overcomes the problem, or a bully who reforms, most books realistically acknowledge that there are no easy solutions. To counter the sad reality about bullies, I have included many books about strong friendships between boys and among groups of children.

Fathers, including those who are absent, emerge again and again as powerful forces in the lives of fictional boys. Often the fathers portrayed in novels are emotionally distant, overly demanding, or violent, which unfortunately reflects the experience of many boys. To offer a balance to the novels about harsh or absent fathers, I looked for books that show caring older men, including fathers, grandfathers, and teachers. Picture-story books often have simple plots in which a boy and an older male relative have a quiet, happy time together. Novels tend to be more complicated, but often offer portraits of fathers or teachers who have a profound positive influence on a boy's life. I also looked for boys in nurturing roles, even those as simple as the boy in *If You Give a Mouse a Cookie*, who finds himself in charge of an energetic mouse. In novels, an older boy may enjoy taking care of younger siblings or children in the neighborhood.

Biographies can offer images of courageous, accomplished men and women who may inspire readers to develop their own talents or pursue a certain career. Biography subjects such as Nelson Mandela, John Muir, and Alexander Graham Bell embody qualities of greatness that children rarely see in the mass media, where often financial success equals greatness. Many parents would like to replace that equation with more meaningful definitions of heroism.

While some children are drawn to biographies, others find that poetry speaks to them in ways that other writing doesn't. Good poetry, which says so much in so few words, has a natural appeal for children. Many adults who disliked the elusive, intellectual poetry they had to analyze in English classes will be pleasantly surprised to find that poetry written for children is easy to like. The lighter verses revel in wordplay, and catchy rhythms and rhymes. The more serious ones depend on apt images about familiar objects and experiences that prompt the listener to look at the world in a fresh way. Most of the poems are short and accessible, perfect for reading aloud just a few at a time.

Surprisingly, poetry lovers are not always the best students or the most avid readers. Poetry can engage reluctant readers who may not want to tackle a whole book but *can* read a whole poem and enjoy it. A librarian at an urban high school recently told me that poetry is the most popular section in her library—in a school with low test scores located in a troubled neighborhood. I've described several anthologies and some collections of individual poets in the hope that they will be dipped into with no goal but sheer joy. Libraries offer many more poetry books than most bookstores, although owning a favorite poetry collection can be a lasting pleasure.

Don't Underestimate Nonfiction

To some adults, if a book isn't fiction it doesn't count as reading. These parents and teachers should take a fresh look at informational books and what they have to offer readers. True, many of the best children's books are novels, which expand children's imagination and love of language, but nonfiction books can also stretch the mind. Adults may not realize how greatly nonfiction has improved since they were young. Far from dull and dusty, today's best informational books are imaginative, enriching, and beautifully written, with stunning photographs or excellent illustrations, on a wide assortment of topics.

Even children who think they don't like books have subjects they want to know more about. They may never have made the connection between, say, baseball and books: biographies of stars, tips on playing better, photographs of their favorite teams. I know many boys, and some girls, who gravitate straight to the nonfiction shelves in the library once they realize what such books can offer. I have seen children who were bored or intimidated by the sight of so many books change their tune when they were led to shelves of books about planes or snakes. While these students may also enjoy the novels their teachers read to them or that they read in language arts classes, on their own time they want books about nature, sports, or other "real things." We need to respect and encourage these interests.

For this reason, I have created specific nonfiction sections in addition to those for fiction and biographies. There is a wealth of nonfiction available for children, which my list can only begin to show. I've described books by some of the best nonfiction writers, such as Russell Freedman, Patricia Lauber, James Giblin, Jim Murphy, Judith St. George, Seymour Simon, and Bianca Lavies, whose writing is as elegant and well crafted as wonderful fiction. I've also included a small sample of outstanding experiment books by Vicki Cobbs and Bernie Zubrowski, but, again, there are many more good experiment books to choose from by these writers and others. For parents of children with a thirst for knowledge, I recommend two guides devoted to children's nonfiction: *Eyeopeners* and *Eyeopeners II*, by Beverly Kobrin, which list hundreds of nonfiction books chosen by an enthusiastic and knowledgeable writer.*

It is especially important for children who prefer nonfiction to have access to a library. While novels are often reprinted as affordable paperbacks, most good nonfiction isn't. Because library nonfiction sections are arranged by subject, a child who has a particular interest can go to that area and browse with great pleasure among the choices.

If your child prefers information to stories, consider reading a nonfiction book aloud. Many children want to know more about a subject discussed in a book that is too hard for them to read themselves. A young airplane fan would love to hear *To Fly the Hot Ones*, while *Mistakes That Worked*, short essays about inventions based on mistakes, would have wide appeal for young listeners.

When thinking about nonfiction, don't be limited to books. Magazines, the sports pages of the newspaper, instruction manuals, and even baseball cards also qualify as reading

---

*Beverly Kobrin, *Eyeopeners! How To Choose and Use Children's Books about Real People, Places, and Things* (New York: Viking, 1991).

material that develops a positive attitude toward the written word. In fact, instructions for making a model or installing software can be unusually challenging. Sports pages not only enhance the sports fan's enjoyment of games, they also introduce statistical information that children don't usually encounter elsewhere. Magazines geared to a special interest may appeal to children who find long books intimidating, or who aren't ready to commit a lot of time to reading but could ease into it with short articles. I have listed recommended magazines in the back of the book, with age designations.

What About Girls and Books About Girls?

Girls will find many books they'll enjoy listed in these pages. My companion guide, *Great Books for Girls*, offers more suggestions of books *about* girls, which some readers prefer, but many girls are open to reading about male protagonists if they like the story. Since I did not include nonfiction in my first guide, girls may want to check out those sections for ideas on informational books and poetry.

I have included a number of books in which the main character is a girl or woman, many drawn from *Great Books for Girls* with the annotations rewritten to emphasize aspects that will appeal to boys. While accepted wisdom has it that boys won't read books about girls, I have found that to be less true than many people think. Young boys rarely object to an exciting book about a girl, such as *JoJo's Flying Side Kick*, a picture-story book about a girl who earns her yellow belt in tae kwon do. What boy wouldn't like *The Samurai's Daughter*, a folktale in which the daughter learns samurai skills and uses them to kill a sea monster and rescue her father? And I have yet to hear a boy object to the Magic School Bus books because the amazing Ms. Frizzle is female. Second-graders at my school who like mysteries read the Cam Jansen series about a girl detective who has a male sidekick, while third-graders enthusiastically go through the Ramona books by Beverly Cleary. The list goes on.

Gearing books to a boy's interests is important in suggesting books for older boys, whether the main character is male or female. Boys who love fantasy will read *The Hero and the Crown*, in which the main dragon killer is a young woman, because it's about sorcerers and dragons. A boy obsessed with World War II will be fascinated by *In Kindling Flame*, the biography of Hannah Senesh, who parachuted behind enemy lines as part of the Jewish Resistance.

Another way to encourage boys to read about girls is through books in which a boy and girl are friends. In *Climb or Die*, a brother and sister must save their parents by climbing a mountain to get help. As they work together to survive danger, their respect for each other increases. The plot of *Witch Week* throws together three boys and two girls who are coming into their magical powers in a country where witches are burned, and they must cooperate to avoid being caught.

Older boys are often increasingly interested in girls and would like to read about them if they could do so without being teased. Teachers can help create an atmosphere in which boys feel as safe reading about girls as girls do reading about boys. One year I read a hilarious book called *Anastasia Again* by Lois Lowry aloud to a group of fifth-graders. The children, boys and girls alike, laughed day after day at how Anastasia deals with her family's move to the suburbs. When it was clear that everyone liked these books, it was easy for the boys to check out others in the series without worrying about what their classmates would say. (You'll find one of the latest entries in the series, *All About Sam*, in the Books for Middle Readers "Humorous Stories" section.)

Just as most adults don't think twice about offering girls books with male protagonists, let's give boys a chance to put themselves in the minds of girls and women through fiction and biography, without being accused of being weak.

15

Encouraging Boys
to Read

As a whole, our society conveys that reading is not a valued activity for boys. What can parents and educators do to compensate for this societal failing? First, all children need to see the adults around them reading books, magazines, or newspapers. Research has shown that seeing their parents read is a strong motivating factor in children learning to read and caring about books. Children want to be like adults, so they take their cues from the grown-ups around them.

Another vital step is to read aloud to boys, even when they can read to themselves, for as long as they will keep listening. (In the final chapter I give tips for those who aren't comfortable reading aloud.)

It's important to realize that some older boys require privacy about their reading. They have absorbed the message that reading isn't cool, so they keep a low profile with their books and don't respond well to any fuss about reading. In the same vein, some children, as they get older, quit taking book suggestions from their parents. Instead of direct insistence, parents can try leaving appealing books and magazines lying around the house and see what happens.

Teachers can have a powerful influence on boys' enthusiasm for reading and their choices in books. For example, it might seem unlikely that boys on the East Coast would get excited about a book concerning a Michigan girl who deals with bullies and makes her dreams come true. Yet when a friend of mine who teaches fifth grade read the book *Yolonda's Genius* aloud to her class, the boys as well as the girls dashed to the library, hoping to find a sequel. This is only one of many examples of teachers expanding their students' reading tastes and creating an atmosphere where books are considered exciting.

Like adults, children choose books to read based in part on recommendations from friends. In a classroom where children have a chance to recommend books to each other, a well-liked or respected student can influence what other children read. Scouting troops, church groups, and other gatherings of children can use this principle to promote reading. Some public libraries sponsor reading clubs for children and adolescents, where members talk about specific books and sometimes issue lists evaluating the books they read as a group.

Children like control, and they don't have very much of it. Adults decide when children will go to school and go to bed, what foods they will eat, and so on. Independent, out-of-school reading is a good area in which to let a boy make decisions for himself, even if it means he is choosing books that seem too easy or too difficult for him. The reading he does in school will be on grade level, but he may seek comfort in books for younger children or may turn to advanced books because his interests outstrip his reading abilities. I had a student who liked to read and whose mother read aloud to him often, but in the library he usually chose books above his reading level, filled with photographs of cars and motorcycles, which reinforced his good feeling about books with no harm done. This impulse is not much different from adults leafing through glossy magazines, barely skimming the text. Not all reading has to be geared toward a serious goal. In fact, if it is, many children lose interest.

Parents worry about children who, left to their own devices, want to read only series books, such as the popular Goosebumps series. The advantage is that the child is reading and developing a positive feeling about books, which is crucial.

Unfortunately, the writing is poor in many series, including Goosebumps, and the excessive number published may crowd out better books that children are capable of reading. Most children will eventually outgrow their attachment to a series, but in the meantime, one approach is to introduce similar but better-written books—perhaps reading them aloud at first. For example, a Goosebumps reader might like books by John Bellairs, such as his short series that begins with *The House with a Clock in Its Walls*. The plot, about a boy who raises a spirit from the dead and needs his warlock uncle to help him control it, is right on target, but the writing is much better than that of the average Goosebumps. I have arranged the fiction in the guide by genres, such as mystery and ghost stories, sports stories, fantasy, and others, which facilitates finding alternatives to unchallenging series books.

Making the Choices

I read or reread every book on this list, and have read many of the shorter ones and some of the novels aloud to children. A number of the novels have also been read aloud by classroom teachers I know, with great success. Still others I've given to older children to get their reactions.

The guide is a *selection* from the many good children's books in print, and is far from exhaustive. I had to make choices among the high-quality books available, trying to achieve a balanced whole, so inevitably many fine books are omitted, which should not be interpreted as rejection. To satisfy the different tastes of listeners and readers, I looked for books with different flavors: funny, scary, action-packed, reassuring, serious, inspiring. The themes include adventure, friendship, problem solving, family relationships, and just plain having fun. Most of the books were published in the last fifteen years, although I also included some old favorites that parents may recognize from their own childhoods.

In the area of picture-story books, I looked for different art styles, since these books are one of the few places many children see art. The styles range from oil paintings to collage, watercolors to photographs. In terms of writing, they vary from extremely brief stories to longer texts for older children. Some rhyme, some invite the child to answer questions, some are as beautifully written as fine poetry.

I looked for novels with excellent prose, fully developed characters, and strong plots. Even voracious readers will find a rich selection to choose from. Since I wanted to include a lot of authors, I could describe only a few books by such fine writers as Marc Talbert, Rosemary Sutcliff, Paul Fleischman, and Paula Fox, among others. Boys who enjoy a book from this guide may want to look for other books by the same author.

In all the categories, I tried to include a diversity of cultural groups to reflect the many backgrounds of children in this country. As discussed above, I also looked for books with strong female characters, sometimes as the main character, sometimes as a friend in fiction books or the subject of an intriguing biography. I tried to avoid sexist content and have made a note of it in the few cases where it seemed important to include a book even though it has some female stereotypes, usually because of when it was written. For example, I feel strongly that children should meet the real *Winnie-the-Pooh*, not the inferior Disney version, even though this classic includes only one female, the overly protective Kanga. (Some parents choose to deal with this by changing other characters to female when they read the book aloud.)

Parents may be surprised not to find more of the old classics, such as *The Adventures of Tom Sawyer*. In my experience, parents are familiar with classics and don't need guidance to find them, or the children will read them in English classes. I have found that the old, unabridged classics appeal most to children when their own parents remember the books fondly. For example, a boy whose father loved *Treasure Island* will read it to feel closer to his father. Otherwise these books typically don't attract children as much as more recent novels do.

How to Use This Guide

The guide is divided into five main chapters—"Picture-Story Books," "Folktales," "Books for Beginning Readers," "Books for Middle Readers," "Books for Older Readers"—and a chapter on resources for parents. Each book entry gives the author, title, illustrator, publishing information, an age range, and a description. The publishing information lists the original year of publication and the name of the current hardcover and paperback publishers. I have included only books that are in print as this guide is going to press, which means they are available for purchase.

If the book has sequels or related books, I list those at the end of the annotation. I also mention whether a book has won a Newbery or Caldecott Medal. These are annual awards given by the American Library Association to the most distinguished children's books of the year. The Newbery Medal is for writing, and the Caldecott for illustration. Each year several other outstanding books are named Newbery or Caldecott Honor Books.

The books listed in "Picture-Story Books" typically consist of thirty-two pages with pictures on every page. Most but not all have a short text. At many libraries these are labeled "E," which technically stands for "easy," but often a sign is posted that reads "E is for Everyone" because these books span such a wide age range. Many of them have surprisingly sophisticated vocabulary—don't be deceived by their length. Preschoolers and early readers will enjoy listening to picture-story books read aloud, and as they become stronger readers, children will enjoy these books on their own. The books in this category for older readers can serve as excellent starting points for a discussion or as models of concise, poetic writing.

Most of the "Folktales" are single tales with pictures on every page, although some are gathered into collections with just a few illustrations. They also speak to a wide age range and are good for reading aloud. I have drawn a number of my selections from traditional Western tales that are part of our cultural heritage, and so important for children to know. Others come from different cultures and show how certain themes are shared by tale tellers around the world.

The "Books for Beginning Readers" are for children who are learning to read and those who are ready for short chapter books, typically children ages six to eight, although the age of beginning readers varies a great deal. The books in this section may suit older children, particularly those reluctant readers who find long books intimidating. The list includes Easy Readers, Short Novels, Biographies, and Nonfiction, most of which have many illustrations. Easy Readers are specifically aimed at children who are at an early stage of reading, who may be sounding out words and relying on pictures to supply clues about the story. The books under Short Novels are for children who have a wider sight vocabulary and greater fluency. The Biographies range from heavily illustrated thirty-two-page books to sixty pages with much more text. Nonfiction is divided into several areas of interest.

The chapter "Books for Middle Readers" gives ideas for children ages roughly nine to eleven, while "Books for Older Readers" covers ages twelve to fourteen. Within these two chapters, the lists include fiction divided by genre, biography, and nonfiction books divided by categories. Within the chapters, there are variations in the age ranges, which are indicated in each annotation: one book in "Middle Readers" might be listed for ages 8–11, and another for 10–13. In "Books for

Older Readers," many of the choices are more challenging than those for Middle Readers. For example, *Fallen Angels* by Walter Dean Myers is a long, powerful novel about the Vietnam War, with vivid descriptions of violence and sorrow that are most appropriate for adolescents. However, some of the books in this section are also appropriate for those younger readers who are ready for long books and challenging vocabulary. The annotations indicate unusually sophisticated themes, content, or writing style.

Most parents will want to browse through the appropriate sections, read book descriptions, and decide what sounds good. Do not be limited by the age ranges, which are loose guidelines, and don't confine yourself to only one chapter. Early elementary school children who are strong readers, and reluctant older readers, present real challenges for parents. Look at the sections before and after your child's age for ideas. The annotations can also alert you to books in an older category that you might want to read aloud.

Older children may want to browse through the guide themselves, reading the annotations and choosing books that sound appealing. Voracious readers are always looking for new ideas, and less enthusiastic readers may have a strong sense of topics that interest them.

Again, remember that older children still benefit from listening to books read aloud. Often parents will conclude that once a child can read to himself, reading aloud serves no purpose, but this is far from true. Even most older children understand far more words hearing them spoken than they can recognize on the page. Think of the conversations you have with a child, full of long words. Books tend to use even more complex vocabulary than occurs in conversation, so reading aloud introduces new words in context. Later, when your child runs across such a word on the page in his own reading, he will have heard the word before and have a sense of what it means. Especially in nonfiction, children have informational interests that outstrip their reading ability; help satisfy their thirst for knowledge by reading them well-written nonfiction books.

Even if reading aloud did not enhance vocabulary and knowledge of grammar, it would be worth continuing past the early grades because it is such pleasurable time spent with a child. In today's hectic world it offers a quiet, positive interlude together, a way to wind down at the end of the day. It also offers the perfect chance to discuss values and opinions about issues raised in the books.

Many of the books are so wonderful that you should consider reading them on your own. While the choices are many, here are recommendations of three longer books that adults would appreciate on more than one level: *Bridge to Terabithia* by Katherine Paterson, *The Giver* by Lois Lowry, and *The Wright Brothers* by Russell Freedman. The annotations indicate other outstanding books. You may have more success recommending a book to a child if you have already read it and can describe it enthusiastically. As mentioned earlier, the sight of parents reading is one of the strongest incentives for children to read.

The last chapter gives tips on reading aloud and information about locating books through bookstores and libraries. Sometimes it's fun to pair a book with a field trip, a craft, or another activity. With this in mind, I have listed some ideas of possible tie-ins to specific books. I have also compiled a number of tips on how to encourage your son to read, based on my experience and the ideas I've gathered from parents and librarians. I have included an annotated list of children's books about sex and growing up as well, something every boy should feel free to read about.

24

My Hopes

"No kind of writing lodges itself so deeply in our memory, echoing there for the rest of our lives, as the books that we met in our childhood. . . ."
—William Zinsser, *Worlds of Childhood**

My goal in this guide is to lead boys to books that will echo in their memories and influence their lives, as so many books have for me. I hope to help them develop a lifelong love of reading through books that celebrate language, put new ideas in their heads, and speak directly to their hearts.

Traditionally we have raised boys as if their heads were more important than their hearts, and girls, the other way around. Surely it is time to develop both aspects of all children. Just as girls are expanding into realms previously reserved for males, boys need to become competent in long-undervalued realms such as creating a warm home, nurturing children, and taking responsibility for relationships.

To accomplish this, boys need more expansive images of what it means to be a boy and a man than they typically see around them. I hope the books I've selected will offer them finer visions of what they can be, while decreasing their sense of isolation. And I wish all children the incomparable joy of losing themselves in a great book and, through it, expanding the world in which they live.

*William Zinsser, ed., *Worlds of Childhood* (Boston: Houghton Mifflin, 1990), p. 3.

1

Picture-Story Books

Picture-story books are a pleasure for everyone, but they draw their largest audience from preschoolers and children in the early elementary grades. Typically thirty-two pages long, these books can be read in one sitting, making them perfect for bedtime or for entertaining a group of children. Most of the books in the following list are geared toward children three to seven. (Note that the age ranges in this section indicate ages for listening, not independent reading.) But do not be strictly limited by the age-range suggestions. A two-year-old book lover will probably enjoy having many of the books marked for ages three to six read to him, while eight- and nine-year-olds may enjoy reading those same books to themselves.

The best thing about reading these books with children is sharing their enjoyment of the story and pictures. Reading together can be a peaceful, cozy escape from a busy world. Besides the emotional pleasures, the educational benefits of reading picture-story books with your children cannot be overstated. Children absorb new vocabulary, hearing it in context and storing it away for the day when, as readers, they come across it in print. Listeners begin to understand the basic structure of stories and enjoy the beauty of well-written prose. Beginning writers can use these tightly crafted books as models for brief stories. For adults as well as children, the illustrations are a special treat. Poring over the superb artwork in many of these books is like going to a museum without leaving home.

Be sure to check other sections of the guide for more book suggestions for young children. Most of the folktales in Chapter 2 are also thirty-two pages long and heavily illustrated, while the collections at the end of that chapter contain folktales suitable for reading aloud to children four and older. The "Easy Readers" in Chapter 3 are short, illustrated books that can be read in one sitting, geared to preschoolers as well as beginning readers. For example, the Frog and Toad books and the series about Henry and Mudge are wonderful for reading to young children. Chapter 3 offers possible read-alouds in the list of novels and biographies. Many of the biographies are short, with pictures on nearly every page. Young children will also enjoy some of the nonfiction books in Chapter 3, on pets, trucks, sports, and much more.

When reading to young children, remember that the object is to have a good time. Read only as long as your child is enjoying it, then save the rest for another session.

Picture-Story Books

Alexander, Lloyd. *The Fortune-Tellers*. Illustrated by Trina Schart Hyman. 1992. Hardcover: Dutton. Paperback: Penguin. Ages 5–9.

Illustrations brimming with life set this story in a town in Cameroon, where a young carpenter seeks advice from a fortune-teller. Alert readers will notice how crafty the fortune-teller is in his predictions, such as "Rich you will surely be, on one condition: that you earn large sums of money," and assuring the carpenter he will be famous "once you become well known." Thrilled, the carpenter leaves, then returns with more questions and finds the room empty. The landlady comes in, believes the fortune-teller has turned himself into a young man, and the carpenter finds himself with a new career, telling fortunes in the way his was told. The fortune-teller's unlikely fate is shown on the final pages. The superb, ornate pictures and amusing story are a perfect combination.

Allard, Harry. *Miss Nelson Is Missing!* Illustrated by James Marshall. 1977. Hardcover: Houghton. Paperback: Houghton. Ages 4–8.

The kids in Room 207 are the worst behaved in the whole school, and never listen to their good-natured teacher Miss Nelson. But everything changes when Miss Nelson doesn't arrive one day and the substitute is the wicked Miss Viola Swamp, who dresses in black and shows no mercy. "If you misbehave, you'll be sorry," she hisses, and the kids believe her. As day after miserable day passes with no sign of Miss Nelson, the kids get worried. When she finally returns, she finds a class of well-behaved, grateful children. She won't tell them where she's been, but the observant reader will notice clothes at her home that look a lot like Miss Swamp's. Absurdly funny pictures will delight readers as much as the popular story does. Followed by *Miss Nelson Is Back* and *Miss Nelson Has a Field Day.*

Allard, Harry. *The Stupids Step Out.* Illustrated by James Marshall. 1974. Hardcover: Houghton. Paperback: Houghton. Ages 3–7.

For sheer silliness, no one beats the Stupid family. Any child listening to the stories and looking at the pictures feels smarter than Buster and Petunia Stupid and their parents. When the Stupids decide to "step out" one day, they take a bath first—with their clothes on, and no water in the tub. Mr. Stupid puts stockings on his ears, and Mrs. Stupid wears their cat for a hat. The dog, Kitty, drives the car. After a silly day on the town, they return, put on their clown suits, and go to bed, with their feet on the pillows and their heads under the covers. Comic illustrations give readers even more to laugh about. A surefire hit, and one in a short series.

Angelou, Maya. *Kofi and His Magic.* Photographs by Margaret Courtney-Clarke. 1996. Hardcover: Clarkson Potter. Ages 5–9.

Outstanding photographs and an imaginative design make this book a pleasure to look at. Children will be drawn to the cover photograph of a laughing seven-year-old boy wearing colorful Kente cloth. "Hi," the story opens. "My name is Kofi, and I am a magician." Kofi lives in West Africa, where he attends school, carrying his desk outside when it isn't raining. He travels in his imagination to other places in Africa, shown in the photographs, but always returns home in the end, where he invites readers to visit him in their imaginations. An unusually appealing introduction to a boy in another culture.

Asch, Frank. *Bear's Bargain.* **1985. Hardcover: Simon & Schuster. Paperback: Simon & Schuster. Ages 2–6.**

This story of friendship starts with Bear and Little Bird shaking hands over their bargain: to teach each other something important. Little Bird wants to learn how to be big, and Bear wants to learn to fly. But Little Bird's work with tiny barbells doesn't make him grow, so Bear concocts another scheme, carving Little Bird's picture on a pumpkin. When the pumpkin grows huge, so does the picture, to Little Bird's joy. Teaching Bear to fly the traditional way doesn't work either, so Little Bird thinks of another solution, one that will make readers smile. A gentle story—with simple, appealing pictures—about friends who want to make each other happy. Also see *Bear Shadow*, *Mooncake*, and others in this series.

Babbitt, Natalie. *Bub or the Very Best Thing.* **1994. Hardcover: Harper. Paperback: Harper. Ages 3–7.**

What, the young King and Queen wonder, is the *very* best thing to give their toddler Prince? Since they don't agree, the Queen asks others in the castle what they think while the King looks through books for the answer. As the Queen, the Prince, and their golden retriever go through the castle, they collect a variety of answers such as "vegetables," "sleep," "sunshine," and "a song." The Queen has her doubts about each answer, and when she meets the King, finds he has fared no better. Their final consultant is the Cook's Daughter, who is surprised at their ignorance—"What! Don't you know?"—and asks the Prince himself, who answers, "Bub." Only the Cook's Daughter knows what he means, but it is the best answer of all.

Charming illustrations, humorous details, and witty text make this a pleasure to read.

Bang, Molly. *The Paper Crane.* **1985. Hardcover: Greenwillow. Paperback: Morrow. Ages 3–7.**

The deed of a kind stranger saves a restaurant owner and his son from poverty in this story that reads like a folktale. When a road is built that bypasses the restaurant, customers quit coming, until one night a poorly dressed man appears. The owner generously makes him a meal for free, and the guest responds by giving the boy an origami bird that comes to life and dances when someone claps. The bird attracts customers, and even after the stranger returns and flies away on the crane, the restaurant prospers, thanks to its new reputation. Elegant cut-paper and collage illustrations suit the spirit of this mysterious tale about kindness.

Bannerman, Helen. *The Story of Little Babaji.* **Illustrated by Fred Marcellino. 1996. Hardcover: Harper. Ages 3–7.**

Some readers will recognize this story as a retelling of *The Story of Little Black Sambo*, with beautiful new illustrations and without the negative stereotypes. In this tale, a well-loved boy named Babaji receives new, colorful clothes from his parents. "So he put on all his Fine Clothes, and went out for a walk in the Jungle." There he encounters four tigers who threaten to eat him, but each takes a piece of clothing instead and prances around in it. Luckily for Babaji, who is left in his underpants, the four tigers meet and argue about who is the grandest, taking off the clothes to fight. The boy recovers his treasured clothing while the tigers chase each other so fast that they all melt. Children will enjoy this small, beautifully designed book and its outstanding watercolors.

Barton, Byron. *Airport.* **1982. Hardcover: Harper. Paperback: Harper. Ages 2–5.**

Simple words and large, colorful pictures introduce children to different aspects of an airport. Starting as passengers arrive in cars and buses, the book shows people at check-in, sitting in the waiting room, boarding the plane, and fastening their seat belts. Interspersed with these pictures are illustrations of the plane getting checked and loaded, pilots preparing in the cockpit, and finally the plane taking off. A double-page cross section of the plane's interior shows the cargo hold, fuel tanks, and the cockpit. Children who are about to fly or those interested in large vehicles will enjoy this brightly illustrated book.

Bemelmans, Ludwig. *Madeline's Rescue.* **1953. Hardcover: Viking. Paperback: Puffin. Ages 3–7.**

Children and their parents love the feisty Madeline, smallest of her classmates at a Paris boarding school. When her fans hear the words "To the tiger in the zoo/Madeline just said," they call out "Pooh, pooh!" In this escapade, the adventurous Madeline falls into a river and is rescued by a dog. The girls take the dog back to school, name her Genevieve, and delight in her talents as she goes to class with them. Alas, members of the school board visit one day and make the mutt leave. Madeline, her classmates, and their kind teacher Miss Clavel search high and low for the dog, with no luck. Fortunately, Genevieve returns on her own, and provides a puppy for each girl. Bemelmans's sprightly pictures of the lively Madeline won the Caldecott Medal. One in a series.

Bliss, Corinne Demas. *Matthew's Meadow.* **1992. Paperback: Harcourt. Ages 6–12.**

This story has a mystical quality rarely found in a children's book. Every year at blackberry time Matthew goes up to a meadow that his grandmother cleared for him before she died. There, a red-tailed hawk teaches the boy a deep understanding of nature. Matthew learns to listen to nature so carefully that he can hear each milkweed seed make "a beautiful sweet sound, like a note from a harp." Over the next several years, the hawk helps the boy expand his sight, his sense of smell, and his abilities to feel and to taste. He comes to notice and appreciate everything in nature and, much later, comes up with a fitting way to thank his grandmother. Light-filled watercolors complement the lengthy, lyrical text in this contemplative book for older children.

Borden, Louise. *The Little Ships: The Heroic Rescue at Dunkirk in World War II.* Illustrated by Michael Foreman. 1997. Hardcover: McElderry. Ages 6–10.

In this outstanding picture-story book for older children, a girl accompanies her father to help evacuate soldiers at Dunkirk in 1940. The girl, who has grown up in a British fishing village, knows enough about boats to help her father sail their fishing boat, the *Lucy*, across the English Channel to the beach where half a million British and French soldiers are waiting to escape the Germans. The *Lucy* is a fictional part of a real armada of 861 ships, in which the little ships ferried soldiers from the beaches to the bigger ships, and took men back to England. Told by a brave child, this thrilling story of heroism comes alive in a personal way, graced with sweeping watercolors full of action.

Bornstein, Ruth. *Little Gorilla.* 1976. Hardcover: Houghton. Paperback: Houghton. Ages 2–5.

This deceptively simple book speaks so directly to children that it has endured for more than two decades. Large illustrations in jungle greens and oranges show that animals throughout the jungle, from Lion to Old Hippo, love Little Gorilla. "Then one day something happened . . . ," the same thing that happens to all children: Little Gorilla began to "grow and Grow and GROW." After a few pages that don't show Little Gorilla, he suddenly appears, now so big that he fills a double-page spread. But, happily, everybody comes to a birthday party for him, "and everybody still loved him." A reassuring theme, presented in effective pictures and simple words.

Bradby, Marie. *More Than Anything Else*. Illustrated by Chris K. Soentpiet. 1995. Hardcover: Orchard. Ages 4–8.

More than anything else, the nine-year-old African-American narrator wants to learn to read. His dream seems impossible in West Virginia in 1865, but he thinks of it all day long as he, his father, and his brother dig salt for a living. His hopes soar at the sight of a black man reading a newspaper aloud one evening, and when he confides his dream to his mother, she manages to get a book for him. It's difficult to learn on his own, so the boy seeks out the man with the newspaper, who starts to teach him how to read, a beginning that brings the boy great joy. Drawn from the life of Booker T. Washington, this historical story, with handsome watercolors that evoke the era, is a tribute to the power of reading.

Brown, Marc. *Arthur's. Eyes*. 1979. Hardcover: Little, Brown. Paperback: Little, Brown. Ages 3–7.

Although he has recently soared in popularity because of the PBS television show, the aardvark Arthur has been around for years in stories that deal with children's problems. In this early book in the long series, Arthur is having trouble seeing, which holds him back in school until he gets glasses.

At first he is happy to be able to see well, but when his friends tease him, Arthur tries to lose his glasses. The consequences are embarrassing when he enters the girls' bathroom by mistake. But when he learns that his teacher wears reading glasses, Arthur feels proud to be like him. A gentle story with comical pictures, this will interest those who wear glasses and those who don't, thanks to Arthur's wide appeal.

Brown, Marc. *D.W. Rides Again!* 1993. Hardcover: Little, Brown. Paperback: Little, Brown. Ages 2–5.

The aardvark D.W., younger sister of Arthur, has a mind of her own, sometimes to Arthur's distress. In this story, D.W. doesn't want to waste any time in learning how to ride a bike. She considers training wheels beneath her, and practices until she can get rid of them. When their father takes D.W. out to test her new skills, he ends up in a creek while she stays safely on her bike. In her typical wisecracking fashion, D.W. offers him her training wheels now that she has finished with them. Simpler in text and smaller in format than the Arthur books, the D.W. books are high in child appeal.

Brown, Marc, and Laurene Krasny Brown. *The Bionic Bunny Show*. 1984. Hardcover: Little, Brown. Paperback: Little, Brown. Ages 4–8.

This slapstick picture book puts television shows about superheroes into perspective. The rabbit Wilbur plays the Bionic Bunny on television, fighting robbers and saving the day. But in real life, Wilbur is so clumsy and weak that shooting the show is full of disasters. Tricks of filming are revealed as the director tells the camera operator to make Wilbur look larger, and Wilbur falls into a swimming pool that on television looks like the ocean. Comic strip squares show the television action, in contrast to the full pictures that show real life. Children will giggle at the broad humor while they learn a little something about the facts behind the illusions of television.

Browne, Anthony. *Changes*. 1990. Hardcover: Knopf. Ages 3–7.

When Joseph's father leaves one morning to fetch the boy's mother from the hospital, "he'd said that things were going to change." Joseph notices strange changes right away. First, the kettle grows ears and a tail. Then his slipper grows a wing, the sofa grows an alligator face, and the easy chair starts turning into a gorilla. Outside, the changes continue, turning a normal world into a surrealistic landscape that is slightly sinister. Images of birth, such as a soccer ball that turns into an egg and gives birth to a flying bird, foreshadow the final scene, when Joseph's parents return with a newborn baby. The large, elegant illustrations incorporate obvious and subtle changes, to the delight of the careful viewer. An unusual, highly effective picture book.

Browne, Anthony. *Willy and Hugh*. 1991. Hardcover: Knopf. Paperback: Random House. Ages 3–7.

The small ape Willy feels like he has no friends. Bright, stylized pictures show him walking past groups of happy friends who don't want him in their games. Slouching down a sidewalk, discouraged, Willy is bowled over by Hugh, a huge ape who is jogging and doesn't see him. To Willy's surprise, Hugh is truly sorry and the two start a tentative friendship. In the park, Hugh intimidates a scary-looking ape who is after Willy, and at the library, Willy takes away a spider that frightens Hugh. The small format, witty illustrations, and themes of importance to children make this a satisfying picture book. Followed by *Willy the Wimp* and others.

Brusca, María Cristina. *On the Pampas.* **1991. Paperback: Henry Holt. Ages 4–8.**

Horse and cowboy fans will enjoy this story about a girl's summer on her grandparents' ranch in Argentina. She and her cousin spend their days grooming and riding horses, sometimes swimming with them in the creek. A cowboy teaches them to use a lasso, a difficult feat that takes a lot of practice. The cousins love to ride on the pampas, as the plains are called, having adventures and practicing their new skills. Before the girl leaves for school, her grandmother gives her a silver gaucho belt to honor her new accomplishments. Action-filled watercolors show details of ranch life in this appealing memoir. Followed by *My Mama's Little Ranch on the Pampas.*

Bunting, Eve. *Smoky Night.* **Illustrated by David Diaz. 1994. Hardcover: Harcourt. Ages 7–10.**

This serious picture book for older children about a boy and his mother during riots in Los Angeles can lead to discussions about urban problems and racial tensions. Powerful paintings set against collage backgrounds convey danger and anger as looters steal and the alarm of fire is raised. Daniel and his mother flee their building with their neighbors, without time to find their cat, Jasmine. In a hopeful ending, a firefighter appears at their church hall shelter with Jasmine and another cat, and the two cats bring together neighbors who had ignored each other in the past. Notable for tackling a difficult topic and for its innovative, dramatic artwork. Winner of the Caldecott Medal.

Bunting, Eve. *The Wall*. Illustrated by Ronald Himler. 1990. Hardcover: Clarion. Paperback: Houghton. Ages 7–11.

In this moving story, a young boy and his father visit the Vietnam Veterans Memorial in Washington, D.C., and find the boy's grandfather's name on the wall. The boy sees the flowers, flags, and even a teddy bear that people have left, and after his father makes a rubbing of the grandfather's name, they leave the boy's school photograph near the wall. Although the boy is glad to think his grandfather might somehow recognize him, as he walks away he thinks, "But I'd rather have my grandpa here." A simple story with quiet, evocative pictures that convey respect for veterans and sadness about war.

Burningham, John. *Mr. Gumpy's Outing*. 1971. Hardcover: Henry Holt. Paperback: Henry Holt. Ages 2–7.

Mr. Gumpy, who lives by a river, goes out for a boat ride one morning and takes on passenger after passenger, giving directions on how they should behave. When a girl and boy ask to come along, he says, "Yes, if you don't squabble." To the pig, Mr. Gumpy says, "Yes, if you don't muck about," and to the cow, "Don't trample about." All goes well as Mr. Gumpy poles the crowded boat until they all ignore the directions, and the boat tips over. Wet but unharmed, they swim to shore and head across the fields to have tea at Mr. Gumpy's. The lovely, large pictures culminate in nine animals and three people sitting around a table having fruit, cake, and tea. Also read the equally delightful *Mr. Gumpy's Motor Car*.

Carle, Eric. *The Very Hungry Caterpillar*. 1970. Hardcover: Philomel. Paperback: Putnam. Ages 2–7.

In this modern classic, a tiny, hungry caterpillar is born on a Saturday morning. He looks for food, and each day eats more. "On Monday he ate through one apple. But he was still hungry. On Tuesday he ate through two pears, but he was still hungry." By Saturday, he eats through a remarkable array of desserts. After a stomachache, he spins a cocoon and, after a time, emerges as a beautiful butterfly. The text's pacing makes it perfect for reading aloud, and the illustrations are priceless. Small holes are punched in the pages where the caterpillar has eaten through food, which delights young children, who are also thrilled when the colorful butterfly appears on the final pages. Not to be missed.

Carrick, Carol. *Patrick's Dinosaurs*. Illustrated by Donald Carrick. 1983. Hardcover: Clarion. Paperback: Houghton. Ages 3–7.
Dinosaur fans will especially enjoy this story about a boy with a vivid imagination. Patrick goes to the zoo with his older brother, Hank, who explains as they look at the elephants that a brontosaurus was heavier than ten elephants. Suddenly Patrick sees a brontosaurus looking straight at him. When they canoe on the zoo lake and Hank mentions that a diplodocus could stay underwater like a submarine, Patrick spots a huge shadow under the water: Could it be a diplodocus? Their ride home on the bus introduces more fierce dinosaurs that send Patrick dashing for the safety of home. Only Hank's final reassurance that dinosaurs are extinct makes the imaginary creatures disappear. Followed by *What Happened to Patrick's Dinosaurs?*

Charlip, Remy. *Fortunately*. 1964. Hardcover: Four Winds. Paperback: Aladdin. Ages 2–7.
One day—fortunately—Ned got invited to a birthday party, but—unfortunately—the party was hundreds of miles away. "Fortunately a friend loaned him an airplane. Unfortunately the

motor exploded." So starts Ned's series of fortunate and unfortunate incidents and near misses before he finally reaches the birthday party. Each double-page spread of a fortunate event appears in cheerful colors, while those about unfortunate happenings, such as encounters with sharks and tigers, are in black and white. Listeners immediately catch on to the book's alternating use of "fortunately" and "unfortunately," and join in as the pages turn. A rollicking journey with a happy conclusion.

Clifton, Lucille. *Everett Anderson's Friend.* **Illustrated by Ann Grifalconi. 1976. Hardcover: Henry Holt. Ages 3–7.**

Noted poet Lucille Clifton has created a series of engaging books about an African-American boy named Everett Anderson. In this story about friendship, told in verse, Everett Anderson is excited that he will have new neighbors, then disappointed that they are girls. Not only are they girls, but they are good ballplayers and fast runners: "No, girls who can run/are just no fun/thinks Everett Anderson." But when he forgets his key, one of the neighbor girls invites him into her apartment to play and they become friends. Graceful, spare line drawings add to the sense of character and mood in this thoughtful story. Other books include *Everett Anderson's Goodbye, Everett Anderson's Nine-Month Long,* and more.

Cohen, Miriam. *Will I Have a Friend?* **Illustrated by Lillian Hoban. 1967. Hardcover: Macmillan. Paperback: Aladdin. Ages 3–7.**

Jim is worried about his first day at a school where the other children already know each other. Will he have a friend? He watches the other children as they confidently play and talk with each other. He makes a few attempts at joining in, and finally is rewarded by a friendly conversation with another boy about a toy truck. Jim leaves for the day with his father, happy about his new friend. The warm pictures are timeless, showing a multicultural class in a room full of toys and art projects. This simple story cuts to the heart of children's concerns, as do the many other books about Jim and his classmates that follow this one.

Cole, Babette. *Princess Smartypants*. 1987. Hardcover: Putnam. Paperback: Putnam/Sandcastle. Ages 3–7.

Princess Smartypants first appears on the cover of this funny book zipping along on a motorcycle with her alligator perched behind her. Her parents want the princess to marry even though she loves her single life. Nine princes, all with silly names, try to win her favor, to no avail after she sets them difficult tasks at which they fail. But one day Prince Swashbuckle appears and proves equal to every task. Has the princess found her true love who will persuade her to get married? Not a chance. With a magic kiss, Princess Smartypants turns the dashing prince into a toad and returns to her happy life in the castle. A twist on traditional stories, this has zany illustrations that underscore the comic text.

Cowcher, Helen. *Tigress*. 1991. Hardcover: FSG. Paperback: FSG. Ages 4–8.

Rich colors saturate the large paintings in this story with an environmental theme. Near a wildlife sanctuary, herdsmen graze their animals while women come to gather firewood. When a tiger kills a stray camel, the herdsmen consider poisoning the camel meat to kill the tiger. But a sanctuary ranger consults with them to come up with a plan that will protect their herds while it saves the tigers. Wild explosions of firecrackers send the tigers deep into the sanctuary, far from the men and their livestock. Dramatic close-ups of tigers draw in listeners, while the clever solution offers them important messages about problem-solving and preservation.

Coy, John. *Night Driving*. Illustrated by Peter McCarty. 1996. Hardcover: Henry Holt. Ages 4–8.

Exquisite black-and-white drawings of big, rounded cars and old-fashioned roadside diners evoke a time past. A father and his son are driving through the night on their way to the mountains. In the quiet of the evening they share stories and play word games, spot a deer, and stop for doughnuts at a truck stop. They talk about baseball and stars, and the father teaches his son cowboy songs that they sing together. Their warm relationship is palpable, although their talk is mostly of ordinary things. An elegant book design highlights the beautifully executed pictures in this nostalgic story.

Crews, Donald. *Shortcut*. 1992. Hardcover: Greenwillow. Paperback: Morrow. Ages 3–7.

Award-winning artist Donald Crews based this story on an incident from his own childhood. Seven cousins are late going home one night, so they take a shortcut down a railroad track, knowing they might be overtaken by a freight train. Sure enough, they soon hear "Whoo-Whoo," words that are printed bigger and bigger on each page. They dash back toward the road, only to find the train right behind them. An effective series of pictures evoke the train and its "klakity-klakity-klakity-klak" vibrating past the children who have jumped off the tracks. "We walked home without a word. . . . And we didn't take the shortcut again." Excitement is packed into the short text and clever illustrations.

Cummings, Pat. *Clean Your Room, Harvey Moon!* **1991. Hardcover: Bradbury. Paperback: Simon & Schuster. Ages 4–8.**

Harvey Moon plans to spend his Saturday watching television, but his mother has a different idea. In the "voice of DOOM," she tells him that "Today . . . is the day you clean your room!" The rhyming text and comical pictures convey his attempts to bring order to a messy room. As the hours click by, and Harvey thinks of the television shows he's missing, he seems to be making progress. But no, he is simply stashing his many possessions under his bedspread. His mother cannot be fooled, though, and the work—not the television set—will go on after lunch. Messy children will be able to relate to Harvey, while any reader will enjoy the bright pictures of this African-American boy and his huge task.

de Paola, Tomie. *The Art Lesson.* **1989. Hardcover: Putnam. Paperback: Putnam. Ages 3–7.**

Tomie de Paola's characteristically neat, attractive pictures introduce a young boy named Tommy who loves to draw. He draws his friends and family, and posts pictures all over his house. He follows advice from his older cousins in art school, who tell him "not to copy and to practice, practice, practice." But in school, the teacher insists that he use only eight crayons instead of his wonderful box of sixty-four, the children get only one piece of paper per art class, and the new art teacher tells the children to copy her drawing. Luckily, the understanding art teacher strikes a compromise with Tommy that gives him some room for creativity. Young artists will especially enjoy reading about a child like themselves.

DiSalvo-Ryan, DyAnne. *Uncle Willie and the Soup Kitchen*. 1991. Paperback: Mulberry. Ages 5–9.

In this gentle story, the narrator accompanies his great-uncle Willie to the soup kitchen where he volunteers. The outgoing old man works with several other people to prepare food, welcome the guests, and clean up afterward, tasks his nephew shares when he visits. The boy is uncomfortable thinking about homelessness and worrying about the soup kitchen's guests, but he gets into the spirit of things as the place gets crowded and busy. By the end, he is hollering in the same friendly manner his uncle uses. Engaging illustrations depict the cheerful kitchen and the warm relationship between the boy and his uncle. A quiet book that will get children talking and thinking.

Dorros, Arthur. *Abuela*. Illustrated by Elisa Kleven. 1991. Hardcover: Dutton. Paperback: Puffin. Ages 3–7.

On a glorious day, a girl imagines that she and her Abuela, her grandmother, fly together above New York City. They swoop down on the Statue of Liberty, wave to friends in their neighborhood, and race sailboats, with Abuela's star-studded skirts billowing out to catch the wind. Brightly colored, intricate collages convey the shared joy of the girl and her grandmother, and show the bustle of the city through many carefully wrought details. The simple text includes Spanish words and phrases, defined in a glossary at the back. In the sequel, *Isla*, the two fly over the Caribbean island where Abuela grew up. Two exciting journeys with outstanding original illustrations.

Emberley, Ed. *Go Away, Big Green Monster!* 1992. Hardcover: Little, Brown. Ages 2–6.

This book is brilliant in its simplicity, design, and understanding of children. It begins: "Big Green Monster has two big yellow eyes" on a page that is black except for cutout holes that show yellow eyes. Using cutouts, each page adds a feature to the monster: long nose, big red mouth, squiggly ears, and more. When the monster is complete, the text declares, "YOU DON'T SCARE ME!" and the plot reverses direction, eliminating each feature page by page. The final page, which is black, declares that the monster won't come back "Until I say so." The young reader has the pleasure of being frightened, while having control over the monster's appearance. A highly satisfying picture book.

Erdrich, Louise. *Grandmother's Pigeon*. Illustrated by Jim LaMarche. 1996. Hardcover: Hyperion. Paperback: Hyperion. Ages 4–8.

A brother and sister are in for a surprise when their mysterious grandmother rides off on the back of a porpoise and leaves them a nest of birds' eggs. When the three eggs hatch, the children feed the little pigeons with an eyedropper. Their mother calls in an ornithologist, a gray-haired woman who is shocked to identify the birds as an extinct species, the passenger pigeon. Now the boy and his sister have to decide whether to turn their new pets over to scientists to be studied or to set them free. Large, light-filled illustrations combining mystery and reality add to the book's charm.

Fleischman, Paul. *Time Train*. Illustrated by Claire Ewart. 1991. Paperback: Harper. Ages 3–7.

On a field trip, a group of modern schoolchildren and their teacher take the Rocky Mountain Unlimited train west from New York and enjoy a most unusual trip. When they reach Philadelphia and the streets are crowded with horses and buggies, the children realize that they are starting to travel back in time. Civil War soldiers walk through the train, and herds of buffalo gather near the tracks. When they reach their destination, the children are thrilled to see their first dinosaur and to study the dinosaurs' habits, while climbing on one and playing ball with another. They return home happy and exhausted, after one of the best field trips ever. Large, richly colored paintings capture the exciting nature of the trip and the children's exuberance. Great fun, especially for dinosaur fans.

Fleming, Denise. *In the Tall, Tall Grass*. 1991. Hardcover: Henry Holt. Paperback: Henry Holt. Ages 2–7.
"In the tall, tall grass,/crunch, munch, caterpillars lunch"— so opens this outstanding book. A child watches the progress of a caterpillar through the grass, where it passes hummingbirds that dart, dip, and sip; bees that strum, drum, and hum; and other small animals described in the brief, rhyming words that are cleverly incorporated into the pictures. For example, when the bats "swoop," the word itself is shaped like a wing. The innovative art technique employs colored paper pulp in a gorgeous palette with an appealing texture. A joy to look at and read aloud, this is followed by the equally wonderful Caldecott Honor Book *In the Small, Small Pond*.

Fleming, Denise. *Time to Sleep*. 1997. Hardcover: Henry Holt. Ages 2–6.
Striking illustrations in glorious autumn colors fill the large pages of this engaging book. As it opens, Bear sniffs the air and realizes that it is time to crawl into her cave and sleep, but first she must tell Snail. Huge Bear finds tiny Snail and says, "It is time to seal your shell and sleep." But first Snail must tell Skunk, who tells Turtle, who tells Woodchuck, who tells Ladybug. Ladybug then wakes up Bear to tell her to go to her cave to sleep, to which Bear grumbles, "I *am* in my cave. I

was asleep." So Ladybug crawls under a nearby log and, on the final page, all the animals wish each other good-night. A wonderful combination of picture and text, this is perfect for bedtime or anytime you want to feast your eyes.

Fleming, Virginia. *Be Good to Eddie Lee.* **Illustrated by Floyd Cooper. 1993. Hardcover: Philomel. Ages 4–8.**
Luminous paintings create a dreamy green and gold setting in this thoughtful story about Eddie Lee, who has Down's syndrome, and his neighbor Christy. Hanging out on a summer day, Christy agrees to go to the pond with another neighbor, JimBud. They pass the friendly Eddie Lee, who wants to go with them, but they treat him harshly and send him away with hurt feelings. Once at the pond, the two are scared when Eddie Lee approaches them loudly through the bushes, but Christy's attitude changes as Eddie Lee shares his appreciation of the pond's beauty, treats a salamander gently, and takes her to a special secret place. Although a bit sentimental, the gentle story makes its point well, that the Eddie Lees of the world have a lot to offer other children given the chance. Sun-dappled illustrations of Eddie Lee, with close-ups of his expressive face, give depth to his likable character.

Fox, Mem. *Tough Boris.* **Illustrated by Kathryn Brown. 1994. Hardcover: Harcourt. Ages 3–7.**
The dashing pirate Boris has traits typical of pirates, described in few words: "He was tough. All pirates are tough." The large pictures show a story not told by the text, in which Boris and his crew dig up a buried chest by following a treasure map. Little do they know they are being watched by a boy who sneaks onto their ship. One pirate finds a violin, which Boris takes from him, and the boy secretly takes from Boris. Caught, the boy saves himself by playing the instrument for the scary

pirates. Throughout the story, Boris has enjoyed the company of his green parrot, and at the surprising end, when the parrot dies, Boris cries, as the text assures us "All pirates cry."

Freeman, Don. *Corduroy*. 1968. Hardcover: Viking. Paperback: Puffin. Ages 2–6.

The bright-eyed teddy bear Corduroy lives in a department store's toy department. One day a girl wants to buy him, but her mother says no, and points out that Corduroy is missing a button from his overalls. Surprised, the bear waits until the store closes and sets off to find a new button. He unexpectedly steps onto an elevator, which he assumes is a mountain. Next, after mistaking the furniture department for a palace, he thinks he has found his button tied onto a mattress. His attempts to get it off end in a loud crash and a friendly encounter with the store guard. After his night's adventure, Corduroy wakes up to the smiling face of the girl who has come to take him home. This simple story, with its apt pictures, has captivated children for decades with its humor and warmth. Followed by the equally delightful *A Pocket for Corduroy*.

Gove, Doris. *One Rainy Night*. Illustrated by Walter Lyon Krudop. 1994. Hardcover: Atheneum. Ages 4–8.

Soft-edged paintings depict a boy and his mother out on a rainy night collecting small animals for the nature center where she works. With the father, who doesn't like to get wet, in the car, the boy and mother in their yellow slickers search along a road with the car's headlights shining behind them. The boy quickly catches small toads and an orange newt, and his mother happily picks up a big water snake. A baby box turtle and a fat red salamander add to the findings. All will be kept for a few weeks, then released on another rainy night, when the mother and son will look for others to replace them.

Large, glowing paintings and an unusual story make this book appealing, especially to animal lovers.

Greenfield, Eloise. *She Come Bringing Me That Little Baby Girl.* **Illustrated by John Steptoe. 1974. Hardcover: Harper. Paperback: Harper. Ages 3–7.**

This modern classic, dedicated to "Black brothers and sisters who love and take care of each other," explores a young boy's feelings when his parents bring home his new baby sister. Kevin is disappointed that she is a girl, and disgusted with all the attention she is getting. "It was really making me sick." But when his mother says that she is counting on him to help take care of the baby, and then astounds him by saying that she herself was once a baby girl, Kevin changes his attitude. He laughs to think of his mother as a baby, and his uncle Roy as a boy taking care of her. Then he runs off to get his friends, to show them his baby sister. Dark, emotionally charged paintings combine with the well-honed prose to create a timeless picture book.

Greenspun, Adele Aron. *Daddies.* **1991. Hardcover: Philomel. Ages 2–6.**

Inviting black-and-white photographs convey many aspects of fatherhood in this brief photo-essay. On each page, a few words describe things that fathers do: hold babies, read stories, give hugs and kisses, and share their knowledge. The large photos show a multicultural array of fathers with their young and older sons and daughters in an assortment of settings. Avoiding a greeting-card slickness, the book captures good feelings among real-looking people. The overall tone is warm and happy, with a few sadder moments included, in a celebration of caring fathers.

Griffith, Helen V. *Grandaddy's Place*. Illustrated by James Stevenson. 1987. Hardcover: Greenwillow. Paperback: Morrow. Ages 4–8.

At first, Janetta doesn't like her grandaddy's run-down farm, which she is visiting for the first time with her mother. The animals don't seem friendly and she feels shy with her grandfather. But it turns out that Janetta and her grandaddy have the same dry wit, and he tells good stories. After his tall tale about a star coming down and riding his donkey, Janetta asks, "Was the mule all right?" "It was thoughtful for a few days, that's all," Grandaddy answers. A fishing trip together solidifies their friendship, and by the end, Janetta wonders how her grandfather ever got along before she came. Effective pen-and-watercolor illustrations provide the perfect match to the warm, humorous story. Followed by *Georgia Music*, *Grandaddy and Janetta*, and *Grandaddy's Stars*.

Guarino, Deborah. *Is Your Mama a Llama?* Illustrated by Steven Kellogg. 1989. Hardcover: Scholastic. Paperback: Scholastic. Ages 2–6.

A young llama named Lloyd goes about asking his friends, "Is your mama a llama?" The different animals answer by giving clues about their mothers, such as "She's got big hind legs and a pocket for me. . . . So I don't think a llama is what she could be." The listener has a chance to guess what kind of animal it is before the mother animal appears. Playful pictures show the animals in outdoor settings, ending with a nighttime picture of Lloyd and his mother together. The rhyme bounces along, with answers just easy enough for young listeners to guess. A lot of fun.

Harley, Bill. *Sarah's Story.* **Illustrated by Eve Aldridge. 1996. Hardcover: Tricycle. Ages 4–8.**

When Sarah's teacher instructs her students to think of a story to tell the next day, Sarah protests, "But I don't know any stories." By the next morning, she still hasn't thought of one, but on the way to school Sarah hears an ant calling her name and telling her to follow him into a hole. She gives it a try and—*fwop!*—gets sucked into the hole. Once inside, she meets a queen ant who sends her on an errand that involves a beehive. Sarah finally gets to school and, still claiming she has no story, relates her experiences with the ants. Engaging watercolors, with many funny details, create a disheveled, stubborn girl and a decadent television-watching queen ant.

Harris, Robie H. *Happy Birth Day!* **Illustrated by Michael Emberley. 1996. Hardcover: Candlewick. Ages 2–6.**

Many children like to hear the story of their birth. This large book, which tells such a story in a mother's voice, starts, "I'll never ever forget the moment you were born." It continues through the baby's first day, with wonderful close-ups of the crying baby and the glowing parents. Friends and relatives come, and "Everyone was so happy and so excited to finally meet you!" Each small action of the new baby is noted with pleasure—yawns, burps, sneezes, hiccups. The baby nurses, has more visitors, and finally falls asleep. Bathed in an atmosphere of love, the story celebrates the birth of all babies through its warm illustrations and joyful text.

Havill, Juanita. *Jamaica Tag-Along.* **Illustrated by Anne Sibley O'Brien. 1989. Hardcover: Houghton. Paperback: Houghton. Ages 3–7.**

What older sibling hasn't occasionally resented a younger one tagging along? Ossie, who is off to play basketball with friends, doesn't want his younger sister, Jamaica, to come. She follows anyway and tries to join the game. Annoyed, Ossie tells her to go away. Jamaica starts building a sand castle, and when a little boy wants to help, she in turn is annoyed with him. But when his mother's comment—"Big kids don't like to be bothered by little kids"—shows Jamaica the similarity to her own experience, she invites the boy to play. Finished with his game, Ossie wants to join in, too, and Jamaica lets him "tag along." Handsome watercolors underscore the realistic experiences of Ossie and Jamaica. One in a series.

Heide, Florence Parry, and Judith Heide Gilliland. *The Day of Ahmed's Secret*. Illustrated by Ted Lewin. 1990. Hardcover: Lothrop. Ages 4–8.

Light-filled illustrations depict a boy named Ahmed driving a donkey cart through Cairo to deliver canisters of butane gas. The prose and pictures bring the sights and sounds of the bustling city to life as he goes down streets filled with "carts and buses, dogs and bells, shouts and calls and whistles and laughter." He encounters friends and proudly carries the heavy canisters in to his customers. He thinks impatiently about a secret he will reveal to his family that evening, and in a dramatically lit picture, he shares the news about his exciting new accomplishment, which readers will appreciate. Splendid watercolors sweep across the pages to create a bustling city.

Henkes, Kevin. *Chester's Way*. 1988. Hardcover: Greenwillow. Paperback: Morrow. Ages 3–7.

Chester and Wilson are mice with a careful approach to life; they always eat the same thing for breakfast and always carry miniature first-aid kits in their back pockets—"Just in case." When the exuberant Lilly moves into their neighborhood, they are not taken with her. *She* always carries a loaded squirt gun in her back pocket—"Just in case." Chester and Wilson go out of their way to avoid her, until the day when Lilly, dressed in one of her many disguises, saves them from some bullies. Grateful, Chester invites Lilly over for lunch and the three new friends find some things in common and other things they can teach each other. Skillful watercolor-and-pen pictures add to the personalities of the mice in this outstanding book. Also try *Julius, the Baby of the World*, in which Lilly deals in her own inimitable way with a new baby brother.

Henkes, Kevin. *Lilly's Purple Plastic Purse*. 1996. Hardcover: Greenwillow. Ages 3–8.

The personable mouse Lilly introduced in *Chester's Way* loves her teacher Mr. Slinger for good reason. He is witty and kind, and wears terrific colorful clothes. One day, however, Lilly's excitement about her new purple plastic purse, which plays a "jaunty tune" when it is opened, overcomes her desire to please her teacher. When Mr. Slinger finally has to take the purse away for a while, Lilly takes her mild revenge by putting a hostile picture of him—labeled "Big Fat Mean Mr. Stealing Teacher"—in his bag. She regrets it when she reads the note he sends home with her: "Today was a difficult day. Tomorrow will be better." And sure enough, the repentant Lilly does have a much better day the next day. The story shows a keen understanding of children, the pictures are brilliant, and Mr. Slinger is worth his weight in gold.

Henkes, Kevin. *Owen*. 1991. Hardcover: Greenwillow. Ages 3–7.

This delightful book takes on the common theme of a child who is attached to his blanket. Owen loves his blanket, Fuzzy, and plans to take it with him when he starts school. His loving but frustrated parents cannot persuade him otherwise. Their neighbor Mrs. Tweezers suggests that the Blanket Fairy should come, but Owen sees through that trick. Her next idea is the vinegar trick, but Owen loves Fuzzy even with a vinegary smell. Mrs. Tweezer finally asks Owen's parents, "Haven't you ever heard of saying no?" They haven't. Instead, Owen's mother comes up with a clever solution that makes everyone happy. The well-honed writing is perfectly suited to the pictures, which echo the rhythm of the text and add funny, cozy details. An outstanding Caldecott Honor Book that children and parents love.

Hines, Anna Grossnickle. *Daddy Makes the Best Spaghetti.* **1986. Hardcover: Clarion. Paperback: Houghton. Ages 2–7.**

In this simple story, a young boy accompanies his father on a trip to the grocery store before they go home and make spaghetti together. Small-scale pictures show them at work in the kitchen, then enjoying dinner with the mother when she comes home from work. While the boy helps his mother clean up, his father runs the boy's bath, then bounces into the kitchen in a shower cap and a towel cape: "Ta da! Ta daaaa! . . . Bathman!" He flies his son into the bathroom and helps him wash, after which the mother reads a story and both parents kiss him good-night. A warm portrayal of a father and son enjoying chores together.

Hoban, Tana. *Look Again!* **1971. Hardcover: Simon & Schuster. Ages 3–8.**

This clever book of photographs is designed to make children look and think. It begins with a blank page that has a square cut out of the middle. Through the square, the reader sees part of a photograph of something in nature: a dandelion, a zebra's head, a turtle's underside. The challenge is to identify from the small clue what the larger, mostly concealed, photograph shows. Readers turn the page to get the answer. This kind of guessing game appeals to many children, who enjoy trying to figure it out and then testing the book with a friend. One of many excellent photograph concept books by Tana Hoban.

Hoffman, Mary. *Henry's Baby*. Illustrated by Susan Winter. 1993. Hardcover: Dorling Kindersley. Ages 3–8.

On the cover of this wonderful book, a boy wearing sunglasses and a jeans jacket is striking a casual pose while a toddler tries to get his attention, next to the lines "As babies go, George was nice. It was just that a baby didn't really fit Henry's image. Tough. Cool. *Interesting*." Henry longs to be part of a group of cool boys at his new school. He succeeds in making friends with them, but avoids having them to his house because of George. When he finally has them over, he is amazed that the other boys love playing with George and want to come back to play with him again. Large, expressive illustrations give each child a distinctive personality. Readers will sympathize with Henry's dilemma while absorbing the welcome message that "cool" boys can like babies.

Howard, Elizabeth Fitzgerald. *Papa Tells Chita a Story*. Illustrated by Floyd Cooper. 1995. Hardcover: Simon & Schuster. Ages 4–8.

In this beautifully illustrated story that reads like a tall tale, Papa tells his daughter Chita about one of his escapades during the Spanish-American War. As a black soldier serving in Cuba, Papa volunteered to deliver an important secret message. Soft-edged pictures exaggerate the dangers of his mission, showing an alligator's mouth and an eagle's claw, both larger than Papa himself. He succeeds despite the hazards.

After hearing the story, Chita tries on her father's soldier's hat, ammunition belt, and medal for bravery. An author's note talks about black soldiers who served in the war and the origin of this particular story.

Hunter, Anne. *Possum's Harvest Moon.* **1996. Hardcover: Houghton. Ages 3–7.**

In this gentle story, Possum wants to give the last party of the season, under the beautiful harvest moon. But when he invites his neighbors to his Harvest Soiree, they turn him down. The mice are gathering seeds, the crickets are tired from a summer of singing, and the raccoon is too busy eating. Forlornly, Possum sits alone in his party hat with a pile of berries ready to feed guests. But as the moon rises, the animals pause: "It was a moon that made them dream of dancing, of eating and singing. Toes twitched and voices hummed." Gathering their friends, they hurry to Possum's party, where they have great fun until it is time to sleep for the winter. Large, luminous drawings show Possum's preparations and his success in this cozy tale.

Hurd, Thacher. *Mama Don't Allow.* **1984. Hardcover: Harper. Paperback: Harper. Ages 3–8.**

Vivid colors and funny comments in cartoons fill this book about a swamp band that outwits some alligators. When the possum Miles gets a saxophone for his birthday, his parents make him practice outside. While walking through town making a racket, he finds three other musicians, and they head to the swamp to practice, calling themselves the Swamp Band. To their surprise, the "sharp-toothed, long-tailed, yellow-eyed alligators" like their music and invite them to play at the Alligator Ball on a riverboat. The elegantly dressed alligators dance all night, but afterward they plan to cook up some Swamp Band Soup, until Miles outwits them. A crowd-pleaser, this book includes the music and words to the folk song "Mama Don't Allow" so children can sing along with the Swamp Band.

Hutchins, Pat. *The Very Worst Monster*. 1985. Hardcover: Greenwillow. Paperback: Morrow. Ages 3–7.

Sibling rivalry takes on a different face in this book about a monster family. Hazel is tired of everyone predicting proudly that baby Billy will grow up to be the Worst Monster in the World. She can do every monsterlike thing he can, such as bend iron bars, growl, and scare the postman, but no one pays any attention to her. After Billy wins a contest for the Worst Monster Baby in the World, Hazel takes things into her own hands and shocks her parents with what she's done. All ends well, though, for these green-skinned, pointy-eared monsters. Children love the funny pictures and premise of this popular story. One in a short series.

Isadora, Rachel. *Max*. 1976. Hardcover: Macmillan. Paper-back: Macmillan. Ages 3–7.

Humorous black-and-white pencil drawings and a short text tell the story of Max, a talented baseball player. Every Saturday he plays ball in the park, walking his sister to her ballet class on the way. One day when he goes inside to watch, Max starts to imitate the dancers' movements and the teacher invites him to join in. Dressed in his baseball uniform, Max stretches at the barre, tries to do the splits, and bounces into the air for the leaps. He is not as graceful as the students, but he has a great time. Having warmed up so well, he hits a home run in his game and does a ballet leap to celebrate. The last picture shows his new routine: warming up for baseball at dancing class. Although the baseball team has no girls, the ballet class has a male student in this still timely, charming book.

Jeram, Anita. *Daisy Dare*. 1995. Hardcover: Candlewick. Paperback: Candlewick. Ages 2–5.

The mouse Daisy can't resist a dare, and her three admiring friends—two boys and a girl—keep her trying new feats. She climbs tall trees to get apples. She walks high walls while they trail along below, and she even eats a worm. Agreeing to a truly dangerous dare, Daisy steals a bell from the collar of a gigantic cat and almost gets caught. But safe in a cozy house, Daisy basks in the admiration of her friends, who lift her onto their shoulders, and admits that she, too, is scared— sometimes. A brief but exciting text and cheerful pictures make this a winner with young listeners.

Johnson, Angela. *Julius*. Illustrated by Dav Pilkey. 1993. Hardcover: Orchard. Ages 3–7.

Julius is an Alaskan pig who comes to live with Maya and her parents. He and Maya have a riotous time together, dancing and swinging and slurping peanut butter. Maya's parents are not always happy with Julius, who messes up the house and makes a lot of noise, but Maya cannot imagine a better friend than the lovable, huggable Julius. Bold pictures full of wild designs and bright colors convey the excitement that Julius adds to Maya's home. Children will find the idea of living with the exuberant Julius irresistible.

Johnson, Angela. *The Leaving Morning*. Illustrated by David Soman. 1992. Paperback: Orchard. Ages 2–7.

Luminous paintings and poetic writing come together in this story about an African-American family moving to a new

58

home. A boy and his older sister gaze sadly out of their apartment window at the misty morning, then turn to look at the
packed boxes in the room. A sequence of pictures depicts the
family's good-byes to friends and neighbors, while a final picture in their apartment shows the children and their parents
sitting on the floor, visually creating a circle that expresses
their love. "I sat between my mama and daddy, holding their
hands." After that reassuring scene, they wave good-bye to
their apartment from the street below. A thoughtful book that
acknowledges the sadness of leaving, but also speaks about
going to "someplace we'd love."

**Johnson, Stephen T. *Alphabet City*. 1995. Hardcover:
Viking. Ages 4–8.**
Remarkable oil paintings that look like photographs illustrate this clever alphabet book. Each page has a painting of a
letter formed by an object in a city. The "A" is the end of
a sawhorse, the "B" is created by the twists in a fire escape, the
"C" occurs in the curve of a cathedral window. Children love
looking closely to find the letter in the urban scene, and are
inspired to look for letters in their own surroundings. For
example, the "Y" from the book can be found in lights along
many highways, and "O"s are everywhere. This wonderful
lesson in visual literacy is a Caldecott Honor Book.

**Jones, Rebecca C. *Matthew and Tilly*. Illustrated by Beth
Peck. 1991. Paperback: Puffin. Ages 3–7.**
A friendship between a white boy and a black girl thrives
in an urban setting where they ride bikes, sell lemonade, and
play games. Dark, impressionistic paintings show the city
streets and residents, and the two children at play. But, as in
all friendships, the two squabble one day when Matthew
breaks one of Tilly's crayons, and they exchange hurtful

words. The pictures reflect the rift, showing the children far apart, then alone and lonely. Luckily, it takes only a little smile on Tilly's part to prompt Matthew to say he is sorry, and they walk off together, close again. Through this simple story, children will recognize feelings from their own lives and rejoice when it all works out well.

Joyce, William. *Bently & Egg*. 1992. Hardcover: Harper. Paperback: Harper. Ages 4–8.

An old-fashioned charm characterizes the words and pictures of this unusual book about Bently Hopperton, "a young and rather musical frog who loved to draw." Clad in a dapper outfit, complete with pince-nez, Bently agrees to look after his duck friend Kack Kack's egg. But to his distress a boy steals the egg, which Bently has painted, and the frog must follow to get it back. He uses a balloon to rescue the egg, escapes from a garden party, and sails a toy boat across a pond, composing little songs to keep up his spirits. In the happy ending, Bently enjoys his new fame for saving the egg and his newly hatched duck friend. Stylish illustrations and a heartwarming story make this book a joy.

Keats, Ezra Jack. *The Snowy Day*. 1962. Hardcover: Viking. Paperback: Scholastic, Viking. Ages 2–7.

One of the best picture books ever published, *The Snowy Day* is a timeless story about a boy named Peter who wakes up one morning to find it has snowed during the night. He spends his day enjoying the snow, making tracks, a snowman, and snow angels. That night, Peter dreams that the snow melts, but he wakes up to enjoy another day of snow. The book has a memorable combination of a simple, lyrical story and exquisite illustrations. The bright collage pictures convey Peter's sheer happiness in the snow, the thrill of sliding down a steep hill, and the joy of waking up to a snowy day. Winner of the Caldecott Medal. Other wonderful books about Peter include *Whistle for Willie* and *Peter's Chair*.

Keller, Holly. *Island Baby*. 1992. Hardcover: Greenwillow. Paperback: Morrow. Ages 3–7.

A caring older man named Pops tends to wounded birds on a Caribbean island with the help of young Simon, who feeds the birds and cleans their cages. As Simon walks home near the ocean one day, he spies a small bird with a broken leg floundering in the water. With Pops's help, Simon catches the baby flamingo and names it Baby. In the following days, he helps care for it until the time when, sad but proud of his work, Simon sets the recovered bird free. The large pages are filled with bright colors, tidy drawings, and whimsical bird borders. An attractive book that presents an old man and a young boy united in nurturing birds.

Kellogg, Steven. *The Mysterious Tadpole*. 1977. Hardcover: Viking. Paperback: Dutton. Ages 3–8.

The fun begins when Louis gets a tadpole for his birthday from his uncle McAllister in Scotland. At first it lives in a jar like any other tadpole. But soon it outgrows the jar, then the sink, then the bathtub. Louis sneaks it into an indoor school pool for the summer, where he teaches it to dive and fetch large things. When school starts again, Louis needs a new home for his huge pet or it will have to go to a zoo. Luckily, Louis consults his friendly librarian and they come up with a glorious plan to keep the tadpole near Louis. Zany, frenetic pictures underscore Louis's delight, his parents' long-suffering patience, and the pink-spotted, gigantic tadpole's sweet nature. This appealing fantasy continues to be popular year after year.

Kimmel, Eric. *Hershel and the Hanukkah Goblins*. Illustrated by Trina Schart Hyman. 1989. Hardcover: Holiday House. Paperback: Holiday House. Ages 4–9.

A man named Hershel enters a village on the first night of Hanukkah and finds no menorahs lit. When he learns it is because of goblins that haunt the synagogue, Hershel offers to get rid of the goblins by spending eight nights in the synagogue and lighting the Hanukkah candles. Each night a progressively scarier goblin shows up and Hershel outwits it. But on the final night the king of the goblins comes, a truly scary figure who fills the doorway with his height and wings. In a stroke of brilliance, Hershel tricks the powerful creature into lighting the candles himself. The excellent artwork is frightening yet funny in places, with surefire appeal to children who like to scare themselves, then have a happy ending. A Caldecott Honor Book.

Klinting, Lars. *Bruno the Carpenter*. 1996. Hardcover: Henry Holt. Ages 3–7.

Any child interested in building things will love this book. The beaver Bruno is a carpenter with a very messy workshop. He manages to find the plans he wants, and begins an unspecified project. Each tool is shown and named before he uses it, starting with his T-square and ruler, going on to his crosscut saw, jigsaw, hand drill, and more. As the beaver makes progress—including a mistake that he fixes—listeners will guess that his project is a toolbox to help clear up the chaos in his workshop. The final two pages show the toolbox plans, with specifics about the wood, screws, and nails. A beautifully designed book, likely to inspire some children (and parents) to try carpentry. Also enjoy *Bruno the Tailor*.

Krauss, Ruth. *The Carrot Seed*. Illustrated by Crockett Johnson. 1945. Hardcover: Harper. Paperback: Harper. Ages 2–5.

This classic picture-story book uses a short text and small pictures to tell the story of a young boy who plants a carrot seed, takes good care of it, then waits impatiently for it to grow. His parents and older brother tell him the carrot won't come up, but he persists, and in the end, a huge carrot proves he was right. The small format suits the story, as do the uncluttered pictures in browns and yellows. This deceptively simple story that conveys an important message to young children about hope and persistence has been a favorite for more than fifty years.

Leaf, Munro. *The Story of Ferdinand*. Illustrated by Robert Lawson. 1936. Hardcover: Viking. Ages 3–7.

Ferdinand grows up to be the strongest bull in the field, but he has no interest in fighting. He prefers to sit under a tree and enjoy the flowers, and when his mother realizes that he isn't lonely, she lets him "just sit there and be happy." But one day, men arrive to find the strongest bull for bullfights in Madrid. By chance, Ferdinand is stung by a bee as they are watching, and his fierce response convinces the men that he is a fighter. They take him to Madrid, where the bullfighters parade proudly into the ring only to find a quiet bull who is enjoying the perfume of flowers in the ladies' hair. Lawson's expressive black-and-white pictures add to Ferdinand's personality in this well-loved story where peace triumphs over violence.

Lionni, Leo. *Tillie and the Wall*. 1969. Hardcover: Knopf. Ages 3–6.

Tillie's friends and neighbors never think twice about the big wall at the edge of their land. But the youngest mouse, Tillie, who is an explorer at heart, needs to know what is on the other side. She tries every method she can think of to scale the wall, finally hitting on a solution when she sees a worm tunneling under it. She, too, digs a tunnel and emerges to find ordinary mice on the other side. After they have celebrated her feat, she leads them back to meet her community. From that day on, Tillie is honored as the one "who first showed the way." Young children will appreciate a book in which the youngest character proves the bravest. Charming collage illustrations in a large format add to the book's appeal.

Lobel, Arnold, selector and illustrator. *The Random House Book of Mother Goose*. 1986. Hardcover: Random House. Ages 2–7.

Outstanding illustrator Arnold Lobel has compiled and illustrated more than three hundred nursery rhymes, some well known, others more obscure. His delightful pencil-and-watercolor pictures amplify every rhyme, adding personality and humor with animals and humans in old-fashioned clothing acting out the verses. The nursery rhymes are grouped roughly by themes such as love, weather, and journeys. This wonderful collection is bound to become a family favorite. Be sure to introduce your young children to this or one of the many other collections of rhymes that are part of our culture.

Locker, Thomas. *The Mare on the Hill*. 1985. Hardcover: Dial. Paperback: Puffin. Ages 5–9.

Dramatic oil paintings dominate this story about two boys and the mare their grandfather has bought. Through the seasons on their picturesque, hilly farm, the boys slowly win the trust of the mare, which had been mistreated by a previous owner. Finally, after a year, a roaring storm brings the mare down close to the barn where, one morning soon afterward, she gives birth to a foal. Sweeping vistas show the horse racing through green pastures, grazing under glorious autumn trees, and standing near the red barn under stormy skies. Children's books rarely feature magnificent, formal paintings like these, which glow with a love of nature.

Macaulay, David. *Black and White*. 1990. Hardcover: Houghton. Ages 5–9.
Four different stories take place on each double-page spread of this unique book. One features a boy alone on a train trip, another is about two children and their parents, a third is about commuters waiting for a train, and the last concerns a robber and some cows. Children will pore over the pictures, which require careful viewing to appreciate all four stories. By the end of the book the stories have become intertwined in a number of ways. Things in black and white link the pages' four quarters—newspapers, the robber's mask and eyes, and the cows. An unusually clever book full of visual humor and challenges. Winner of the Caldecott Medal.

Mahy, Margaret. *The Boy Who Was Followed Home*. Illustrated by Steven Kellogg. 1975. Paperback: Dial. Ages 3–8.
An ordinary boy named Robert is thrilled one day when he sees a hippopotamus following him home from school. When he shoos it away from the house, it settles happily in a large goldfish pond. The next day, four hippos follow him home, to Robert's further delight. But when, just a few days later, twenty-seven hippos fill the goldfish pond, Robert's parents call in a witch to get rid of them. After she gives Robert a

magic pill, she is interrupted by Robert's father before she can explain the pill's disadvantage. The hippos leave, but Robert is in for a happy surprise when the "disadvantage" appears. Kellogg's breezy, cheerful pictures suit the eccentric story that will leave children wishing they had Robert's good luck.

Mahy, Margaret. *The Great White Man-Eating Shark: A Cautionary Tale.* Illustrated by Jonathan Allen. 1989. Hardcover: Dial. Paperback: Puffin. Ages 3–7.

In this quirky story, a boy named Norvin wishes he had the beach at Caramel Cove all to himself, so that he could "shoot through the water like a silver arrow," something he excels at. Oddly, Norvin looks a lot like a shark, so he constructs a plastic dorsal fin, straps it on, and swims through Caramel Cove. Everyone runs screaming from the water, leaving the cove to Norvin for days. When swimmers return to the water, Norvin pulls his trick again. This time the joke is on him, in a funny twist that reveals his trick. Exaggerated cartoonlike pictures will have readers laughing out loud.

Marshall, James. *George and Martha.* 1972. Hardcover: Houghton. Paperback: Houghton, Scholastic. Ages 3–8.

George and Martha are priceless. In the first of "Five Stories about Two Great Friends," Martha, clad in a gigantic checked skirt, makes pots of split pea soup and serves them to George, who hates it but doesn't want to hurt her feelings. One day she catches him pouring the soup into his loafers, tells him that "Friends should always tell each other the truth," and bakes cookies instead. The other stories continue with small problems solved in the spirit of friendship. The appealing pictures of these large hippos in their dapper clothes and cozy houses are full of humorous details. The first in a wonderful series that every child should get to know.

Marshall, James. *Old Mother Hubbard and Her Wonderful Dog.* **1991. Hardcover: FSG. Paperback: FSG. Ages 2–7.**

Hilarious illustrations refresh this old nursery rhyme that begins: "Old Mother Hubbard went to the cupboard" and continues with many verses about her dog's talents. The incomparable James Marshall creates a dog like no other, with a deadpan expression, witty side remarks in balloons, and a remarkable wardrobe. Each verse, on a double-page spread, is illustrated with the old woman and dog in different costumes, from the Wild West, the flapper era, and other settings. Chickens and mice pop up in many of the pictures, voicing their astonishment about a dog who can stand on his head, play the flute, and ride a goat, among other tricks. An original, colorful interpretation of a jaunty rhyme.

Martin, Bill, Jr., and John Archambault. *Barn Dance!* **Illustrated by Ted Rand. 1986. Hardcover: Henry Holt. Paperback: Henry Holt. Ages 2–7.**

This toe-tapping rhyme starts off strong and keeps on going. On a moonlit farm, rabbits jump over a sleeping dog on their way to the barn dance. A boy who spies them from his bedroom window follows in his pajamas to the barn, where all the animals are dancing to the scarecrow's fiddling. The boy joins them: "Out came the skinny kid, a-tickin' an' a-tockin'." Expansive watercolors show the antics of pigs, donkeys, chickens, and goats kicking up their heels until dawn. This book bounces along in a spirit of great fun like a rollicking square dance.

Martin, Bill, Jr., and John Archambault. *Chicka Chicka Boom Boom.* **Illustrated by Lois Ehlert. 1989. Hardcover: Simon & Schuster. Ages 2–7.**

This felicitous combination of rhyme and picture quickly

becomes a favorite with young listeners. Letters of the alphabet are personified as children playing together and climbing a coconut tree. "Chicka chicka boom boom/Will there be enough room?" When all twenty-six letters have been named, and the last four are on their way up the tree, "BOOM! BOOM!" The tree bends, and the brightly colored letters all fall out. Along come their adult, or uppercase, counterparts: "Mamas and papas/uncles and aunts/hug their little dears, then dust their pants." Once the mess is straightened out, the little ones secretly begin to climb the tree again. The jubilant, brightly colored pictures celebrate the text in this guaranteed winner that will quickly have children chanting along.

Martin, Bill, Jr., and Michael Sampson. *Swish!* **Illustrated by Michael Chesworth. 1997. Hardcover: Henry Holt. Ages 4–8.**

In this fast-paced picture book, a basketball game has come down to the final minute. The rhyming text gives a play-by-play description as the girls dribble, pass, shoot, and rebound. When the Cardinals tie the game with a basket, a huge "SWISH" crosses the page. Then "44 to 44,/only 16 seconds more./Blue Jays rushing,/gotta score." With another "SWISH," the Blue Jays make their jump shot, and the Cardinals take a time-out. Will they try a three-point shot to win? Energetic watercolors capture the drama of the game and the intensity of the players. One of the few picture books on basketball, this is great fun.

Martin, Rafe. *Will's Mammoth.* **Illustrated by Stephen Gammell. 1989. Hardcover: Putnam. Paperback: Putnam. Ages 2–6.**

Magical illustrations celebrate a boy's fascination with

woolly mammoths and his refusal to believe that mammoths have disappeared. Knowing better than his parents, he ventures out into a snowy day and finds one. With a cry of joy, he climbs on the mammoth's back and begins his journey. They encounter more mammoths as well as saber-toothed tigers, bears, wolves, and early human cave-dwellers. The lovable mammoth picks a purple flower for Will, who treasures it as he falls asleep that night. Gammell's extraordinary illustrations, splashed with drops of paint, sweep across the large pages. The brief text is beautifully hand-printed in bright colors, a part of the book's elegant design. The appealing cover illustration of Will on his mammoth will attract readers to this prehistoric adventure.

Mayer, Mercer. *A Boy, a Dog, and a Frog.* **1967. Hardcover: Dial. Paperback: Dial. Ages 3–8.**

This wordless book packs a lot of humor into its little black-and-white pictures. One day a small boy and his dog set off with a net and a pail to a pond. When they spy a frog, the boy tries to catch it with his net, but he ends up in the pond with the pail on his head. The frog, who has a delightfully expressive face, looks as if it is about to start chuckling. The pursuit continues, only to end with the dog under the net and the disgruntled frog watching from a lily pad. Yet when the boy and dog leave, the frog looks progressively sadder, until it starts to follow them. It hops into the house, follows the wet trail to the bathtub, and with a smiling face, leaps up to greet its new friends. Many more funny books follow in this series.

Mayer, Mercer. *There's an Alligator Under My Bed.* **1987. Hardcover: Dial. Ages 3–7.**

The narrator of this brief story believes that an alligator lives under his bed. "But whenever I looked, he hid . . . or something." Tired of being scared, the boy devises a clever plan to lay a trail of goodies from his bed down the stairs and into the garage. Sure enough, when he hides and watches, an alligator emerges, eats the food along the trail, and crawls into the garage. The boy slams the door, then remembers to leave a note for his dad with an explanation and the comment "If you need help, wake me up." Large, colorful pictures depict a bright-eyed boy clad in red pajamas and a huge green alligator. This engaging book is similar to *The Nightmare in My Closet* and *There's Something in My Attic* by the same author.

McLerran, Alice. *Roxaboxen.* Illustrated by Barbara Cooney. 1991. Hardcover: Lothrop. Paperback: Puffin. Ages 5–8.

Exceptional paintings full of desert colors portray Roxaboxen, a make-believe town created by a group of children many years ago. Marking off streets with stones, they each had a plot to furnish with wooden boxes for tables and chairs, broken pottery for dishes, and pieces of desert glass to create "a house of jewels." Any sort of wheel served as a car and any long stick was a horse. Wars broke out, and "the raids were fierce, loud with whooping and the stamping of horses!" Roxaboxen continued until the children grew too old and moved away, but they never forgot. The final evocative picture shows one of them, fifty years later, standing among the stones left from that magical place. A true story from the childhood of the author's mother, this beautifully written and illustrated book celebrates the power of the imagination. Not to be missed.

McMillan, Bruce. *Eating Fractions.* 1991. Hardcover: Scholastic. Ages 3–7.

Simple fractions have never been so fun. Through cheerful

photographs of two children cooking and eating, the concepts of "whole," "halves," "thirds," and "fourths" take on real meaning. They cut a small pizza in fourths, and divide corn on the cob into halves, and then eat them. Small drawings and words in large print reinforce the information in the photographs. Two final photos show the children sharing their strawberry pie with a dog, and the appendix gives four simple recipes followed by notes for parents. The large color photographs of a black boy and a white girl sharing fun and food add to the high quality of this useful, enjoyable book.

McPhail, David. *Edward and the Pirates*. 1997. Hardcover: Little, Brown. Ages 3–7.

Edward loves to read and especially loves adventure stories. When he reads about Robin Hood, he becomes part of the story and rescues Robin Hood himself. He carries the shield for Joan of Arc and comforts Admiral Peary's sled dogs at the North Pole. Reading *Lost Pirate Treasure* brings about his strangest adventure of all, when pirates invade his bedroom one night and demand he give them the book, which may tell where treasure is buried. Edward stalwartly refuses, because it is a library book—"You'll have to wait till I return it." Just as a pirate starts waving his sword, in charges Edward's mother on a horse, followed by his father with a bow and arrow. Bloodshed is avoided when Edward offers to read the book aloud to the pirates, who cannot read. A wonderful story with large, shadowy pictures that reflect Edward's imagination.

McPhail, David. *Pig Pig Grows Up*. 1980. Paperback: Dutton. Ages 3–7.

Pig Pig, who has decided that he likes being a baby, refuses to grow up. He sleeps in a crib, although he can barely fit, and eats baby food while crammed into a high chair. His mother is tired of his silly behavior, but gives in when he starts sobbing. Cartoonlike pictures of the pink-cheeked porkers will have readers giggling as Pig Pig acts out an impulse many children have felt. But things change one day when Pig Pig's mother collapses after pushing him in a stroller to the top of a hill. The stroller careens downward, and when Pig Pig sees he is about to crash into a real baby, he hops out and averts disaster. Enjoying his hero status, Pig Pig insists on pushing his mother home. This funny book is part of a short series.

Meddaugh, Susan. *Hog-Eye*. 1995. Hardcover: Houghton. Ages 3–7.
In the fine tradition of pigs who fool wolves, this story tells of a young pig who is captured by a wolf and cleverly escapes. As the book opens, she is telling her family of her escapade, and describing the danger in dreadful terms, but the pictures show a somewhat different story. The wolf's "terrible, gloomy cave," for example, appears as a bright, neat house. The wolf plans to make the pig into soup, but she persuades him that she knows a great recipe and sends him out to find the ingredients. The final ingredient is a plant with three leaves that gives the wolf a terrible rash. In his agony of itching, the wolf lets the pig escape. The sprightly, cartoonish pictures are integral to the wonderful humor. Great fun.

Miller, Margaret. *Whose Shoe?* 1991. Hardcover: Greenwillow. Ages 2–6.
Children who like guessing will love this book. Each sequence of pages shows a photograph of a shoe with the question "Whose shoe?," followed, after turning a page, by the answer and two more photographs. For example, the jogging shoe pages give the answer "Runner," with photographs of a woman running on one page and a young boy running on

another. The clear, color photographs show a diversity of age, race, and gender, with touches of humor, such as huge clown shoes and a young girl in waders fishing for plastic fish. Another outstanding concept book that is fun to read.

Mochizuki, Ken. *Baseball Saved Us.* **Illustrated by Dom Lee. 1993. Hardcover: Lee & Low. Paperback: Lee & Low. Ages 6–10.**

In 1942, during World War II, the U.S. government moved American citizens and others of Japanese descent into internment camps, an action for which the government has since apologized. This moving picture book for older children tells a fictional story of one such camp, where the discouraged men take heart by playing baseball with their sons. While they play, they try to ignore the guards who constantly watch over them. But in a dramatic moment, the young narrator makes his first home run by channeling his anger against the guards into his swing. Finally back home after the war, he is still plagued by prejudice, and once again turns his emotion into a home run. Richly textured illustrations convey a story that introduces a shameful chapter in American history.

Moss, Lloyd. *Zin! Zin! Zin! A Violin.* **Illustrated by Marjorie Priceman. 1995. Hardcover: Simon & Schuster. Ages 3–8.**

In this joyful introduction to ten orchestra instruments, a witty rhyme bounces along from instrument to instrument as orchestra members assemble and tune up. Whimsical illustrations show musicians who resemble their instruments in intriguing ways. The flute player is a tall, thin woman with coloring similar to that of her flute, while the trumpet player's skirt flares out just as her instrument does. The rhyme culminates in a performance before an enthusiastic audience. Children will enjoy the dog, mouse, and two cats that appear in many pictures but are never mentioned in the text. This Caldecott Honor Book is a delightful celebration of music.

Nash, Ogden. *The Adventures of Isabel.* **Illustrated by James Marshall. 1991. Paperback: Little, Brown. Ages 3–8.**

"Isabel met an enormous bear/Isabel, Isabel didn't care" begins this upbeat poem about the fearless Isabel. In hilarious illustrations and a bouncing rhyme, she conquers the bear, a witch, giant, doctor, and nightmare, and sets an example for the adoring children who surround her in the book. In the final pages she teaches them to "banish a bugaboo" by yelling "Boo to you!"—a phrase soon adopted by listeners. The green-skinned witch and truly hideous giant add to the fun of this outstanding book about a brave girl. Certain to be a favorite.

Nolen, Jerdine. *Harvey Potter's Balloon Farm.* **Illustrated by Mark Buehner. 1994. Hardcover: Lothrop. Ages 5–9.**

In this offbeat story, a girl describes Harvey Potter and the farm where he grows colorful balloons in his fields. Harvey Potter has a strange look, due to his thick, reflecting eye-glasses, and an even stranger way of tending his fields. It seems in keeping with his mysterious appearance and unusual crop that Government men come one day clothed in white-hooded coats to check up on him. To the narrator's relief, the balloon farm passes inspection. She has grown to like Harvey Potter, who "didn't ask you no questions about why you weren't this or that. He just let a person be." A satisfying twist in the plot ends this quirky tall tale, notable for its originality and its striking illustrations.

Numeroff, Laura Joffe. *If You Give a Mouse a Cookie.* Illustrated by Felicia Bond. 1985. Hardcover: Harper. Ages 2–7.

"If you give a mouse a cookie, he's going to ask for a glass of milk. When you give him the milk, he'll probably ask you for a straw." And so the pattern goes, with a charming little mouse clad in overalls making request after request to a good-natured boy. The boy, bemused by his parentlike role of looking after his enthusiastic new friend, fulfills each request. Unexpectedly the mouse ends up cleaning the house, before settling in for a story and drawing a picture. The picture leads to the cycle starting over with another cookie and glass of milk. An irresistible combination of story and picture not to be missed. A similar book is *If You Give a Moose a Muffin.*

Opie, Iona, editor. *My Very First Mother Goose.* Illustrated by Rosemary Wells. 1996. Hardcover: Candlewick. Ages 2–5.

Noted folklorist Iona Opie has brought together more than sixty well-chosen familiar and lesser-known Mother Goose rhymes. In an oversized format, with large print, the rhymes are interspersed with wonderful pictures. Wells's characteristic lovable rabbits mingle with well-dressed pigs, cats, and plump people. She gives new images to old poems, such as rabbits in an old-fashioned roadster who are driving an urbane pig for "To market, to market, to buy a fat pig." Everything about this large book is funny or cozy. Young children will want to hear it and look at it again and again.

Osofsky, Audrey. *My Buddy.* Illustrated by Ted Rand. 1992. Hardcover: Henry Holt. Paperback: Henry Holt. Ages 4–8.

Its unusual subject matter distinguishes this book and will intrigue many readers. The two main characters are the narrator, a boy who has muscular dystrophy and uses a wheelchair, and his Service Dog, Buddy. Buddy can perform remarkable tasks for the boy, such as turning on light switches, opening doors, and fetching things. The substantial text explains the rigors of the training camp where the boy and dog learned to work together, no easy accomplishment. The light-filled watercolors show the two at home and at school, shopping and playing ball. With its interesting details, this book provides a positive picture of a disabled boy and his dog.

Patrick, Denise Lewis. *The Car Washing Street*. Illustrated by John Ward. 1993. Hardcover: Tambourine. Ages 3–7.

Matthew, a young African-American boy, likes to wake his father on Saturday mornings so they can go out and watch their neighbors wash cars. They sit on the steps of their apartment building drinking orange juice, listening to a neighbor's boom box, and soaking in the hot sun. Just as they are about to go inside, one man accidentally splashes water on another, who splashes back, and a good-natured water fight gets started. Matthew and his father join in the action with their hose, even though they don't have a car, until finally everyone is cool from the water and tired from the fun. The acrylic paintings, with the bold colors and flat planes, add to the congenial feeling of this book.

Pinkney, Brian. *The Adventures of Sparrowboy*. 1997. Hardcover: Simon & Schuster. Ages 3–7.

Pinkney effectively uses a comic book format in this snappy story about an African-American paperboy. Henry sometimes gets discouraged reading the negative headlines in the newspapers, and wishes life held more heroes like those in the comics. A double-page spread shows a comic strip about "Falconman," who can fly through the air and performs good deeds. To Henry's surprised delight, he finds himself taking off from the ground—*zap!* In his superhero role, he has a chance to save two boys from a vicious dog and to take a bully to task. Action-packed pictures, with just enough text to keep the story going, will delight comics fans and satisfy anyone looking for a young superhero.

Pinkney, Brian. *JoJo's Flying Side Kick*. 1995. Hardcover: Simon & Schuster. Ages 3–7.

Despite children's strong interest in martial arts, few picture-story books deal with them. In this popular book, a resourceful girl named JoJo needs to perform a flying side kick to win her yellow belt in tae kwon do. She psychs herself up by getting advice from a friend, her grandfather, and her mother, who advise her to yell loudly, practice her footwork, and visualize herself accomplishing her goal. Then JoJo puts all the advice together in her own creative way and succeeds. A spectacular picture shows her flying through the air to break a board with her kick. Powerful artwork adds to the story's energy in this winner about a child who masters her fears and meets her goal.

Pinkwater, Daniel. *Aunt Lulu*. 1988. Hardcover: Macmillan. Paperback: Aladdin. Ages 3–7.

"Melvin, Louise, Phoebe, Willie, Norman, Hortense, Bruce, Susie, Charles, Teddie, Neddie, Eddie, Freddie, and Sweetie Pie" are the names of Aunt Lulu's sled dogs, which she recites often in this quirky book. As a librarian in Alaska, Aunt Lulu drives a dogsled to deliver books to gold miners, who are thrilled to get books they've requested on pirates, wolves, freezing to death, and sweet little kittens. But Aunt Lulu is bored and decides to return to her hometown in New Jersey. When she starts to say good-bye to her dogs, they look so sad she agrees to take them with her. One of the final pictures shows Aunt Lulu and her dogs, all wearing pink-framed sunglasses, happy to be in New Jersey. An offbeat story that is great fun to read aloud.

Pinkwater, Daniel Manus. *The Big Orange Splot*. 1977. Hardcover: Hastings House. Paperback: Scholastic. Ages 3–8.

Children are entranced by this unusual tale of nonconformity. As the story opens, Pinkwater's bright, childlike illustrations show the street where Mr. Plumbean lives, where all the houses are the same, boxy and dull brown. One day a bird carrying a can of orange paint—"no one knows why"—drops it on Mr. Plumbean's house and makes an orange splot. To the horror of his conformist neighbors, instead of painting over the splot, Mr. Plumbean paints his house in an explosively colorful way, then landscapes the boring yard with palm trees, a hammock, and an alligator. One by one the neighbors (unfortunately, only males) try to talk him out of his scheme, but after the talks, they transform their own houses to fit their dreams: a ship, a castle, a hot-air balloon, and more. The short, polished text reads aloud beautifully, and the pictures will inspire children to imagine houses that "look like all their dreams."

Pomerantz, Charlotte. *The Piggy in the Puddle*. Illustrated by James Marshall. 1974. Hardcover: Macmillan. Paperback: Aladdin. Ages 2–7.

"Mud is squishy, mud is squashy/Mud is oh so squishy squashy" reads one of the bouncy rhymes in this rollicking story. A pig has jumped into the middle of a mud puddle, to the distress of her family. She defies their orders to get out, telling her father, "Squishy-squashy, squishy-squashy-NOPE!"

Amusing cartoonish pictures show the well-dressed pig family finally giving in to the inevitable. When they can't get her out of the mud, they jump in to join her. A romp of a book, full of wordplay and irresistible rhythms, this may well become a family favorite.

Raschka, Chris. *Charlie Parker Played Be Bop*. 1992. Hardcover: Orchard. Paperback: Orchard. Ages 2–8.

This joyful tribute to jazz saxophonist Charlie Parker is a distinctive pleasure. Extraordinary pictures combine with a brilliant rhythmic text to echo Parker's recording of "A Night In Tunisia." "Boomba, boomba . . . Boppity, bibbitty, bop. BANG!" In an allusion to "Bird," Parker's nickname, various objects on birds' feet dance through the pages to the pulse of the words. Large, smoky illustrations of Parker and his sax seen from various angles provide a balance to the more whimsical creatures who fill the other pages. While hard to describe, this creative book appeals enormously to children, who end up chanting its words just for fun. Give it a try, even if you don't know Charlie Parker's music.

Raschka, Chris. *Yo! Yes?* 1993. Hardcover: Orchard. Ages 3–8.

Bold creativity characterizes this award-winning book about interracial friendship. An outgoing black boy and a shy white boy meet and finally connect, each appearing on opposite pages until the final pages when they get together as friends. The friendly boy makes overtures with simple words like "Yo!," "Hey!," and "What's up?" to which the shy boy admits he has "No fun" and "No friends." To the shy boy's surprise and delight, the other offers him friendship, and the two boys jump high to celebrate their good feelings. Children quickly learn the very brief text, and love to read along with enthusiasm. Powerful in its simplicity, this unusual book taps feelings about loneliness and hope. A Caldecott Honor Book of originality and insight.

Rathmann, Peggy. *Good Night, Gorilla*. 1994. Hardcover: Putnam. Ages 2–7.
This nearly wordless picture book will charm children right away when a gorilla steals the keys from a zookeeper, follows him, and lets the other animals out of their cages one by one. The gorilla, elephant, lion, hyena, giraffe, and armadillo, plus a little mouse carrying a banana, follow the zookeeper to his house and into his bedroom. But when the zookeeper's wife turns out the light, all the animals say "Good night," to her surprise, and she leads them back to the zoo. Little does she know the gorilla and mouse follow her back to the bedroom again. The clever pictures, which have the timing of a comical silent movie, intensify the joke.

Rathmann, Peggy. *Officer Buckle and Gloria*. 1995. Hardcover: Putnam. Ages 3–7.
When the police dog Gloria starts to accompany the kind but dull Officer Buckle on his trips to speak to schoolchildren, the safety officer notices that the children pay more attention than they did before. Each time he checks to be sure Gloria is behaving, she looks up at him innocently. But when his back is turned, Gloria can't resist acting out Officer Buckle's safety tips in increasingly funny ways. In her wildest rendition, for the tip "Don't swim during electrical storms," Gloria hangs in the air with her fur standing on end. Children listening to the book have the pleasure of knowing more than Officer Buckle does. Humorous details, starting with funny safety tips on the

endpapers, fill the pictures. A notable combination of concise text and superb pictures, this won the Caldecott Medal.

Rice, Eve. *Benny Bakes a Cake*. 1981. Hardcover: Greenwillow. Ages 2–6.

In this brief, appealing story, preschooler Benny is having a birthday. Simple colored-pencil pictures show him helping his mother mix a cake, all the while making sure that Ralph, the family dog, is good. They read a book while the cake bakes, ice it, and then get ready to go on a walk, only to discover that Ralph has knocked the cake onto the floor and started eating it. Poor Benny cries while his mother calls his father and they solve the problem. Listeners will smile when the still-teary Benny hears a knock at the door and opens it to find his father with a big cake from the bakery. Eve Rice, who has a gift for writing and illustrating stories for very young children, knows just what will hold their attention. A charming book for parent and child.

Ringgold, Faith. *Tar Beach*. 1991. Hardcover: Crown. Paperback: Crown. Ages 3–7.

Boldly colored paintings, bordered by quilt squares, show Cassie Louise Lightfoot as she flies above her apartment building and over the George Washington Bridge, marveling at "its sparkling beauty." In the lyrical text, she describes her life in New York City. On hot nights, her parents play cards and she sleeps on Tar Beach, the apartment house roof. She dreams of the day when her African-American father can own a building, unhindered by racial bias, and her family can have all they need. And she teaches her younger brother to fly, closing her story with the words "The next thing you know, you're flying among the stars." A Caldecott Honor Book.

Roop, Peter. *The Buffalo Jump*. Illustrated by Bill Farnsworth. 1996. Hardcover: Northland. Ages 5–9.

Based on historical fact, this long picture book features a boy named Little Blaze, who is a member of the Blackfoot tribe. He is angry that his father did not choose him to be the buffalo runner, who stampedes buffalo over a cliff called the buffalo jump. Instead, his older brother, Curly Bear, has the honored role. But when Curly Bear is leading the buffalo toward the jump, he slows down and stumbles, with the buffalo right behind him. With no concern for danger, Little Blaze saves his older brother and helps him lead the buffalo on the right path. Realistic paintings, full of browns and yellows, show the dramatic Western landscape and the brave boys. An afterword provides historical information about buffalo jumps.

Rounds, Glen. *Cowboys*. 1991. Hardcover: Holiday House. Paperback: Holiday House. Ages 2–7.

Rough, energetic drawings and a handful of sentences create an intriguing picture of a cowboy's life. A newly hired cowboy is shown trying to catch and saddle a horse, "but sometimes that's easier said than done." The bucking horse throws him, but the cowboy climbs back on and rides out onto the range with the others, where they look for stray cattle and deal with a wild stampede. After rounding up the cattle and driving them into the corral, his day ends with supper. The wide format of the book suits the expansive lines of the horizon in the treeless, dusty country where this cowboy works. The hand-lettered text is nicely integrated into the pictures, which are sure to appeal to cowboy and horse fans.

Say, Allen. *Grandfather's Journey*. 1993. Hardcover: Houghton. Ages 5–8.

Arranged like a photograph album, exquisite framed

watercolors follow the life of the narrator's grandfather and pay fond tribute to both the United States and Japan. The grandfather journeyed from Japan to travel around the United States when he was a young man. "Huge cities of factories and tall buildings bewildered and yet excited him. He marveled at the towering mountains and rivers as clear as the sky." He married and raised a family in California but returned in his older years to Japan, where his daughter married and gave birth to the narrator, who shares his grandfather's love of both countries. A quiet, evocative book, gloriously illustrated, this won the Caldecott Medal.

Say, Allen. *The Lost Lake*. 1989. Hardcover: Houghton. Paperback: Houghton. Ages 4–8.

The narrator, who has gone to stay with his father in the city one summer, finds it boring. He dreams of mountain lakes, fishing, and canoeing, and tapes on his walls pictures of beautiful places. When his father, who has been absorbed in his work, finally notices the pictures, he arranges a camping trip, to the boy's great joy. At first, the trip seems ruined, as they find Lost Lake overrun with campers. But they keep hiking, hard as it is, and reach a beautiful and pristine area. The camping trip brings them closer, and the father starts to listen to his son for the first time all summer. Their slightly awkward, realistic relationship will ring true for many readers, who will enjoy the story and its exquisite watercolors.

Scieszka, Jon, and Lane Smith. *Math Curse*. 1995. Hardcover: Viking. Ages 8–12.

Here is a zany tribute to the power of math. When the narrator's teacher says one Monday, "YOU KNOW, you can think of almost everything as a math problem," daily life suddenly seems to be filled with numbers, fractions, geometry, and much more. Jokes mingle with serious math problems at a frantic pace. Collage pictures incorporate geometric shapes, charts, lots of numbers, rulers, money, and monsters, while the text includes boxed math problems, equations, and multiple-choice tests. Although a bit overwhelming for some, this is a highly original picture book for older children that adds up to a lot of fun.

Sendak, Maurice. *In the Night Kitchen.* **1970. Hardcover: Harper. Ages 2–7.**

This original work practically sings in words and pictures. A boy named Mickey falls out of his bed and into "the light of the night kitchen," a campy place where three bakers who look like Oliver Hardy are baking for the morning. The action is set against a background of starlight, with a skyline of buildings made from kitchen items—jam jars, saltshakers, eggbeaters, and more. The bakers mix Mickey into the batter, but he pops out, fashions himself a plane out of dough, and fetches milk for them by diving into a huge bottle. "Milk in the batter! Milk in the batter! We bake cake! And nothing's the matter!" The pictures are irresistible, and the rhythmic words echo in the reader's head long after the book is closed. A Caldecott Honor Book.

Sendak, Maurice. *Where the Wild Things Are.* **1963. Hardcover: Harper. Paperback: Harper. Ages 3–7.**

"The night Max wore his wolf suit and made mischief of one kind and another . . ."—so begins this tour de force among picture-story books. After the incorrigible Max is sent to bed without his supper, a forest grows in his room, an ocean tumbles by, and Max takes off in a boat to where the wild things are. Max tames these huge, cuddly creatures, immortalized by the brilliant illustrations. But once he is king, Max longs "to be where someone loved him best of all," so he sails back home. The combination of honed text and extraordinary pictures has made this book into a modern classic. Although some children and parents find the wild things too scary, most embrace Max's imaginative voyage and his happy return. Winner of the Caldecott Medal.

Shannon, George. *Climbing Kansas Mountains*. **Illustrated by Thomas B. Allen. 1993. Hardcover: Bradbury. Paperback: Aladdin. Ages 3–7.**

Soft-edged illustrations draw a picture of life in a small Midwestern town in this gentle story. One hot summer afternoon, the narrator's father says to him, "Sam, time you and I went to climb a Kansas mountain." Although Sam doubts they will find a mountain in their flat surroundings, he is pleased to have his father to himself with no brothers along. After driving through the familiar town, they arrive at Sam's father's workplace, the town grain elevator—the closest thing the town has to a mountain. They climb up "as high as eight houses stacked like blocks," to an amazing view that changes how Sam looks at his world. The warm, quiet relationship between father and son pervades the story and the lovely illustrations.

Shaw, Nancy. *Sheep in a Jeep*. **Illustrated by Margot Apple. 1986. Hardcover: Houghton. Paperback: Houghton. Ages 2–6.**

"Beep! Beep!/Sheep in a jeep on a hill that's steep" opens this short romp about some silly sheep piled into a red jeep. Relying on words that rhyme with "sheep," the well-crafted text tells its story in words that children can soon repeat themselves. The sprightly colored-pencil illustrations give the sheep personalities and introduce other animals not mentioned in the text. Some hefty pigs, complete with tattoos, save the yelping sheep when their jeep gets stuck in mud, but more foolishness leads to another mishap. No matter—nothing can discourage the sheep for long. An absolute must for young children, this is the first in a series.

Siebert, Diane. *Train Song*. Illustrated by Mike Wimmer. 1990. Hardcover: Harper. Ages 2–7.

Expansive paintings of railroad cars from the past are paired with a brief text that echoes the sounds of a train chugging along. "Creaking/clanking/air brakes squeal/ moaning/groaning/steel on steel." Train lovers will appreciate the different cars pictured and the workers, such as the engineer and conductor. The essence of the book is the beauty of the countryside and the train, captured in lush illustrations and heard in the musical words. Those who enjoy this will also like *Plane Song* and *Truck Song* by the same author.

Sis, Peter. *Komodo!* 1993. Hardcover: Greenwillow. Ages 3–8.

"I have loved dragons as long as I can remember," says the narrator, shown in his dragon-filled bedroom. He is thrilled to learn that his parents are going to take him to the Indonesian island of Komodo, home of Komodo dragons, which are monitor lizards that grow up to nine feet long and three hundred pounds in weight. The boy imagines meeting the Komodo dragon in an empty glade, but when they finally reach the island, it is overrun with tourists waiting for one dragon to emerge from his shelter. While they wait, the boy sneaks off and has the encounter he had dreamed of. Sis's beautifully wrought illustrations cast a magical spell that suits the simple story.

Slobodkina, Esphyr. *Caps for Sale: A Tale of a Peddler, Some Monkeys and Their Monkey Business.* 1940. Hardcover: Addison-Wesley. Ages 2–6.

This time-tested picture book about a man and some mischievous monkeys is a delight to read aloud, with refrains that inspire children to join in. "You monkeys, you," the peddler says, shaking his finger at some monkeys who have taken the caps he sells. "You give me back my caps." In response, "The monkeys only shook their fingers back at him and said, 'Tsz, tsz, tsz.' " The peddler finally gets his caps back when he throws his cap down in disgust, and the monkeys in the tree, each wearing one of the caps, imitate him. Expect the irresistible phrase "you monkeys, you" and the finger-shaking response to become part of your family folklore.

Soto, Gary. *Chato's Kitchen.* Illustrated by Susan Guevara. 1995. Hardcover: Putnam. Paperback: Putnam. Ages 5–8.

One day, a tough, low-riding cat named Chato invites his new mice neighbors in the barrio over for dinner, planning to have the mice themselves as the main course. Cautious, but wanting to be neighborly, the mice ask if they can bring a friend. Chato assumes this will mean six mice for dinner, and enthusiastically prepares fajitas, enchiladas, and more with his cat pal Novio Boy. But when the mice arrive, the cats are shocked to see that their friend is a dog. The bold, rich pictures full of comic details are the perfect accompaniment to the funny story. A glossary in the front clues readers in to Spanish words, while a menu explains the food names.

Soto, Gary. *The Old Man & His Door.* Illustrated by Joe Cepeda. 1996. Hardcover: Putnam. Ages 4–8.

The key to this appealing story, which is laced with Spanish words, is the similarity between *el puerco*, which means "pig," and *la puerta*, which means "door." As an old man is washing his dog, his wife tells him that she is leaving for a neighbor's barbecue, and that, when he comes, he should bring *el puerco*. Distracted by the soapy dog, the old man barely listens, and when he leaves, he takes a door instead of a pig. On the way, he finds several uses for the door—to console a crying child, to protect himself from bees, and more. Each good deed is rewarded, and even though he arrives at the barbecue without the pig, he brings the rewards and a good story. Using resonant colors that echo Mexican folk art, the illustrations create a good-natured old man on a comic journey.

Spinelli, Eileen. *Boy, Can He Dance!* **Illustrated by Paul Yalowitz. 1993. Paperback: Aladdin. Ages 4–8.**

The age-old theme of a son who doesn't want to follow in his father's footsteps takes on a fresh look in this toe-tapping tale. Tony's father is a successful chef in a big hotel, just as his father was. But Tony doesn't want to cook; he wants to dance. Colored-pencil pictures with wonderful texture show Tony dancing everywhere—in his crib when he was young, on the school bus, on the beach. When his father takes Tony to the hotel to learn the trade, Tony dutifully starts squeezing lemons, but he can't keep his feet still, and the lemons end up everywhere. An unexpected solution saves the day and puts Tony on a stage, dancing to his heart's content. The creative design and quirky pictures enrich this satisfying story about following one's dream.

Steig, William. *Amos & Boris.* **1971. Hardcover: FSG. Ages 4–9.**

Amos, a mouse, builds himself a boat, names it the *Rodent*, and sets off to sea. Gazing at the sky one magical night, he is so overwhelmed with the "beauty and mystery of everything" that he rolls off the ship and it sails away without him. A kind whale named Boris rescues Amos and agrees to take him home. In the weeklong journey, the two become great friends. Boris admires "the gemlike radiance of the mouse" while Amos admires "the abounding friendliness of the whale." They part sadly, with Amos offering his help if Boris ever needs it. Many years later, Boris is stranded on the beach where Amos lives, and the mouse has a chance to repay his kindness. Steig's love of language and his cartoonlike illustrations are a complete delight.

Steig, William. *Doctor De Soto*. 1982. Hardcover: FSG. Ages 4–8.

Rarely is a thirty-two-page picture book named a Newbery Honor Book, but Steig's crisp writing won that award for this story of a mouse dentist who outfoxes a fox. Doctor De Soto is so skillful that he has many patients, including pigs, cows, and donkeys. When a miserable fox begs him to cure a toothache, De Soto and his wife, who assists him, reluctantly agree, although they do not normally treat foxes. They pull out his tooth, dripping with blood, and tell him to return the next day for a replacement. As he leaves, the fox wonders "if it would be shabby of him to eat the De Sotos when the job was done." Meanwhile, the De Sotos suspect that he means them no good and hatch a clever scheme to save themselves. Witty pictures match the excellence of the writing.

Stevenson, James. *"Could Be Worse!"* 1977. Hardcover: Greenwillow. Ages 3–8.

No matter what annoying thing happens to Mary Ann or Louie, their grandpa's reaction is always "Could be worse." But after Grandpa overhears the children conclude that he never says anything interesting because nothing interesting happens to him, he just happens to have an incredible adventure to tell them about at breakfast. Cartoonlike pictures show the old man encountering one dire danger after another, from the abominable snowman to a "giant something-or-other." He is attacked by a huge blob of marmalade, gets stuck in the ocean, and finally escapes on a floating piece of toast. Stevenson's characteristic watercolors provide the details of the absurd adventures in this first of a series of stories about Grandpa and his wild times.

Sutcliff, Rosemary. *The Minstrel and the Dragon Pup*. Illustrated by Emma Chichester Clark. 1993. Hardcover: Candlewick. Paperback: Candlewick. Ages 5–9.

In an unusually long story for a picture book, a minstrel finds a dragon pup and nurtures it as it grows to the size of a pony. But then a villain kidnaps the dragon, and the minstrel, unable to find it, grows sadder and sadder. At long last, he comes to a king's palace where the two friends are reunited, and the minstrel's songs ensure they will never part again. The popular subject of dragons receives a new, heartwarming treatment in this lovely book.

Thompson, Kay. *Eloise*. Illustrated by Hilary Knight. 1955. Hardcover: Simon & Schuster. Ages 4–8.

Brilliantly funny pictures reflect the carefree life of Eloise, a girl who lives in New York's Plaza Hotel. Eloise turns the elegant hotel into her own playground, pouring water down mail chutes and dragging sticks along walls to irritate the other guests. A fold-out diagram shows her route as she commandeers the elevators for her own amusement. She casually orders room service for herself, her beloved nanny, her dog, Weenie, and her turtle, Skipperdee. Wearing sunglasses and slouching down in her chair, Eloise is utterly incorrigible. No one knows better how to drive adults crazy, yet her nanny never seems to mind and they have a cozy life together. This sophisticated book appeals to adults but also to children, who wish they could share Eloise's brash adventures.

Turkle, Brinton. *Do Not Open*. 1981. Hardcover: Dutton. Paperback: Puffin. Ages 3–7.

Children who enjoy being scared while assured of a happy ending will love this book. Miss Moody lives by the sea with her cat, Captain Kidd. The day after a big storm they go beachcombing to look for washed-up treasures such as old carpets and driftwood. When Miss Moody hears a cry from inside a glass bottle, she opens it up and a huge monster emerges. But the brave Miss Moody isn't frightened, which enrages the monster and makes it bigger. Thinking quickly, Miss Moody comes up with a way to trick the monster with the help of Captain Kidd. The richly colored illustrations create a fearsome monster and the stalwart beachcomber who defeats him.

Turner, Ann. *Through Moon and Stars and Night Skies*. Illustrated by James Graham Hale. 1990. Hardcover: Harper. Paperback: Harper. Ages 3–8.

In this gentle story about adoption, a little boy talks to his mother about the trip he took by plane from another country to meet his new parents. The soft watercolor pictures show him in an Asian country, being driven on a motorcycle past rice paddies. He carried with him photographs of his "new poppa and momma," their red dog, their white house, and his bed with a quilt on it. He talks about his fear of the night and the plane, and how he held the photographs in his hand. When he arrives in the United States, one by one he sees the sights in the photographs—his smiling parents, the house, the dog, and finally the quilt as he is tucked in for his first night. A poetic story about a loving family.

Van Allsburg, Chris. *The Garden of Abdul Gasazi*. **1979. Hardcover: Houghton. Ages 4–9.**

Superb black-and-white drawings illustrate this strange story of a boy and a dog. When Alan Mitz takes Miss Hester's dog, Fritz, for an afternoon walk, he runs into unexpected trouble. Mischievous Fritz gets away and dashes into the garden of Abdul Gasazi, a retired magician, whose sign reads: "Absolutely, Positively No Dogs Allowed in this Garden." After searching for Fritz with no luck, Alan bravely goes to the magician's huge mansion, where Gasazi the Great invites him in. Alan comes to believe that the magician has changed Fritz into a duck, and at the story's end, readers will remain uncertain if magic occurred or not. Gasazi, wearing his fez and blowing smoke rings, presents a deliciously mysterious figure in the large, effective pictures of this Caldecott Honor Book.

Van Allsburg, Chris. *The Polar Express*. **1985. Hardcover: Houghton. Ages 3–9.**

A sense of magic pervades this story and its magnificent illustrations. One Christmas Eve, a boy hears a train outside his house and, going to investigate, boards the Polar Express on its way to the North Pole. Hauntingly beautiful paintings show the train winding across a mountain, past wolves, and over an ice cap to Santa's city. Of the many children on the train, the narrator is chosen to receive the first gift of Christmas from Santa Claus and asks for one of Santa's silver sleigh bells. Although he believes he has lost the bell on his trip back, it appears as a gift under the Christmas tree— but only children or those who truly believe can hear its lovely sound. A Caldecott Medal winner, this is a modern masterpiece.

Vaughan, Marcia, and Patricia Mullins. *The Sea-Breeze Hotel.* **1992. Hardcover: Harper. Paperback: Harper. Ages 3–8.**

The Sea-Breeze Hotel, perched on Blow-Me-Down Bay, does not do much business because of the strong winds. Sam, the grandson of the hotel's handyman, Henry, is worried that the hotel will close, so he makes a kite to cheer up the owner and take advantage of the wind. Henry and the housekeeper join in the fun, making their own kites, and soon the four of them are out flying kites, each one different and beautiful. The kites attract visitors and word spreads, until the hotel has all the business it needs. Drawings and torn tissue paper collage that incorporates feathers and string make lovely buoyant pictures that perfectly suit the text. Likely to inspire some kite-making.

Viorst, Judith. *The Tenth Good Thing About Barney.* **Illustrated by Erik Blegvad. 1971. Hardcover: Atheneum. Paperback: Simon & Schuster. Ages 3–7.**

This thoughtful book will help children whose pet has died but will also interest children who are curious about death. The story opens with a boy talking about his cat, Barney, who died the previous Friday: "I was very sad. I cried, and I didn't watch television." His mother suggests that the boy think of ten good things about Barney to tell at the cat's funeral. He thinks of nine. But he cannot think of a tenth until after the funeral when he and his father are planting flowers together, and they talk about how Barney will change and become part of the ground that nourishes flowers. With quiet understanding and love, the boys' parents help him through his sadness without denying it. Illustrated in black-and-white, this small book is a gem.

Waber, Bernard. *Ira Sleeps Over.* **1972. Hardcover: Houghton. Paperback: Scholastic. Ages 4–8.**

This classic story addresses a universal theme with terrific pictures and a text that reads aloud beautifully. It opens: "I was invited to sleep at Reggie's house. Was I happy! I had never slept at a friend's house before." But his older sister gets Ira worried when she asks if he's taking his teddy bear Tah Tah, saying that Reggie will laugh at him if he does. It's a dilemma, since Ira has never slept without Tah Tah before. He consults with his caring parents, who assure him Reggie won't laugh. Ira vacillates on the question, finally deciding not to bring the teddy bear—only to find out that Reggie sleeps with his bear Foo Foo. Luckily, Ira can go home to fetch his own teddy bear. A wonderful, reassuring story. Followed by *Ira Says Goodbye*.

Waddell, Martin. *Can't You Sleep, Little Bear?* **Illustrated by Barbara Firth. 1992. Hardcover: Candlewick. Paperback: Candlewick. Ages 2–6.**

This is a warm story about a little bear and his loving father. One evening in a homey cave, Big Bear tucks Little Bear in, then starts to read a book by the fire. But Little Bear is scared of the dark, so Big Bear gets him a little lantern. The next request brings a bigger lantern, and then the Biggest Lantern of Them All. Restless, Little Bear claims to be scared of the dark outdoors. But when Big Bear patiently takes him outside, they find a huge yellow moon and twinkly stars, and Little Bear finally falls asleep. The soft watercolors, full of rounded shapes, reflect the loving way that Big Bear treats his child's nighttime fears and wiggles. The first in a short series.

Waddell, Martin. *Farmer Duck.* **Illustrated by Helen Oxenbury. 1992. Hardcover: Candlewick. Paperback: Candlewick. Ages 3–7.**

Fun for adults as well as children, this tongue-in-cheek story tells of a duck who works for a lazy farmer. The farmer, who stays in bed all day, yells out periodically, "How goes the work?," to which the duck replies, "Quack." The other farm animals, who appreciate the duck's hard work on their behalf, finally unite to chase the farmer away. Hilarious pictures of a duck sawing and ironing, hoeing and washing dishes, contrast with the scenes of the overweight farmer in bed eating bonbons. Children will join in with the duck's "Quack"s and cheer at the end when the animals triumph. Priceless.

Walsh, Ellen Stoll. *Mouse Paint.* **1989. Hardcover: Harcourt. Paperback: Harcourt. Ages 2–6.**

This simple, clever book is about three white mice who find three jars of paint—red, yellow, and blue—and climb in. When each different-colored mouse drips paint on white paper, the puddles provide an enjoyable lesson in mixing colors. The red mouse jumps in the yellow puddle, where "His red feet stirred the yellow puddle until . . ."—on the next page—the puddle has turned orange. They try all the combinations of the three colors, and are delighted with the results. The exquisite book design and illustrations combined with the well-written text make this an outstanding picture book. Also look for *Mouse Count*, a similar story about counting.

Wells, Rosemary. *Max's Dragon Shirt.* **1991. Hardcover: Dial. Paperback: Penguin. Ages 2–7.**

The disheveled bunny Max loves his ragged old pants and would like a Dragon Shirt to go with them. But when his older sister, Ruby, takes him to a big department store, it is to buy new pants. She gets distracted by some dresses, and while she tries them on Max snoozes. When he wakes up, she is gone. So Max goes looking for her and finds a Dragon Shirt on his way. Meanwhile, Ruby goes looking for him. She finds Max eating ice cream with a store guard, having dripped so much ice cream on his shirt that they must buy it, leaving no money for new pants. Irresistible pictures of plump rabbits fill the pages of this satisfying story. One in a delightful series.

Westcott, Nadine Bernard, adapter. *The Lady with the Alligator Purse*. 1988. Hardcover: Little, Brown. Paperback: Little, Brown. Ages 2–7.

"In comes the doctor, in comes the nurse, in comes the lady with the alligator purse"—so sounds the refrain of this old jump-rope rhyme, brought to life in whimsical illustrations. Tiny Tim has swallowed a lot of soap, to his mother's distress, so she calls for help. When the three answer her call, the lady with the alligator purse prescribes a remedy that children appreciate: pizza. The whole family gathers around a recovered Tiny Tim to enjoy the pizza. The many funny aspects of the pictures complement the lighthearted rhyme, which children soon chant on their own. A lark to read aloud.

Wiesner, David. *Tuesday*. 1991. Hardcover: Clarion. Paperback: Clarion. Ages 3–8.

This nearly wordless book depicts one wild night when frogs rise into the air on their lily pads and fly. Plump and green, they fly over the pond, watched by an openmouthed turtle and fish. Hundreds of frogs soar higher than telephone wires, diving at birds and grinning. They swoop low, straight into a clothesline, and several end up with capes made from laundry. Others float into a sleeping woman's living room and watch her television, with one of them operating the remote control with its tongue. Their beguiling adventure continues until dawn, when the magic ends, catching them by surprise and leaving lily pads all over the town's streets. Winner of the Caldecott Medal and a surefire hit.

Willhoite, Michael. *Daddy's Roommate*. 1990. Hardcover: Alyson Publications. Paperback: Alyson Publications. Ages 3–8.

The boy in this brief story spends weekends with his divorced father, who is gay and lives with his partner. As his mother explains it to the boy, "Being gay is just one more kind of love. And love is the best kind of happiness." The scenes of their weekends together make it clear that both men love the boy and want what is best for him. They read to him, tell him jokes, play ball, and explore nature. For outings, they all go to ball games, the zoo, and the beach. Large, colorful pictures, although not outstanding, portray the pleasant, low-key weekend visits. Noteworthy for its warm spirit and its depiction of a family arrangement rarely shown in children's books.

Williams, Vera B., and Jennifer Williams. *Stringbean's Trip to the Shining Sea*. 1988. Hardcover: Greenwillow. Ages 4–8.

Cesar Coe, known as Stringbean, and his much older brother, Fred, are driving from Kansas to the Pacific Ocean in a truck they call Harry-the-Chariot. Each page shows a postcard that Stringbean sends home to his parents and grandfather, telling them about the trip. The brothers camp near a circus, find a clown's shoe, and visit a ghost town. Their trip and their personalities come across in the imaginative postcards, which children will enjoy imitating on paper. The brothers don't always get along, but they make the trip work and their love for each other is clear. Read this before you go on a trip, or just for its fun and originality.

Winthrop, Elizabeth. *Lizzie and Harold.* **Illustrated by Martha Weston. 1986. Hardcover: Lothrop. Ages 4–7.**

Harold lives next door to Lizzie, who is looking for a best friend. He would be pleased to fill the role, but Lizzie is convinced that it needs to be a girl. She tries a few unsuccessful approaches: imitating a girl at school who isn't interested, then posting a notice advertising for a six-year-old girl. But when she realizes that Harold might find someone else as his best friend, Lizzie recognizes that he has been right all along. At the end, they walk away together hand in hand. The thoughtful Harold and exuberant Lizzie make a great pair in this story that defies stereotypes. Children will also enjoy the instructions for cat's cradle that appear in the cheerful pictures.

Wood, Audrey. *King Bidgood's in the Bathtub.* **Illustrated by Don Wood. 1985. Hardcover: Harcourt. Ages 2–7.**

King Bidgood plans to spend the day in his bathtub, no matter what anyone says. For each court member who thinks of a reason he should get out, the king has a better answer. One suggests it's time to fish, but upon entering the king's chambers sees the bathtub wreathed with water plants and filled with fish. Another who says it's time to lunch finds the tub bedecked with an astonishing array of food and the bearded king as happy as can be. Superb illustrations create magical effects, with the bathtub transformed in delightfully detailed scenes. In the end, a young page outwits the king. The kind of book children want to read again and again, this is a Caldecott Honor Book.

Wood, Audrey. *The Napping House.* Illustrated by Don Wood. 1984. Hardcover: Harcourt. Ages 2–7.

"There is a house, a napping house, where everyone is sleeping" begins this popular picture book. In a bouncing cumulative verse, different people and creatures pile up onto a bed and continue sleeping—a granny, a child, a dog, a cat, and a mouse. But just when children have joined in the refrain and think they know what's next, a "wakeful flea" upsets the routine. Wildly frantic pictures show all of them tossed into the air as they wake up. This unbeatable combination of catchy rhythm and terrific pictures is not to be missed.

Yashima, Taro. *Crow Boy.* 1955. Hardcover: Viking. Ages 4–8.

In this moving story, children in a Japanese village school spend six years ignoring their classmate Chibi, a small boy from the mountainside. Avoiding the children who tease him, Chibi spends his time closely observing the natural world. Beautifully wrought colored-pencil drawings underscore his isolation. But in his final year at school, a new teacher befriends the boy and the other children begin to look at Chibi in a new way. Their appreciation comes to a climax at the school talent show, when Chibi imitates crow calls in a hauntingly realistic manner. Not bitter, Chibi welcomes his new name of "Crow Boy" and his new status in the village. This Caldecott Honor Book is an evocative story with a timeless theme.

Yolen, Jane. *Owl Moon.* Illustrated by John Schoenherr. 1987. Hardcover: Philomel. Ages 4–8.

Exceptional pen-and-watercolor illustrations capture the magic of going out on a winter night to look for owls. A father and child, bundled against the cold, venture out from their farmhouse across snowy fields to the woods. The child narrator doesn't complain about the cold because "If you go owling you have to be quiet and make your own heat." In a snowy clearing, the father calls out like an owl and their patience is rewarded. The last picture shows the father carrying the child home to the lighted farmhouse, "under a shining Owl Moon." This poetic combination of words and watercolors will cast a spell on readers that lasts even when the story is finished. Winner of the Caldecott Medal.

Yorinks, Arthur. *Louis the Fish*. Illustrated by Richard Egielski. 1980. Hardcover: FSG. Paperback: FSG. Ages 3–8.

Nobody has made quirkier books than the team of Yorinks and Egielski. In this characteristically original work, an ordinary-looking man named Louis wakes up one morning as a fish: "Silvery scales. Big lips. A tail. A salmon." As the son of a butcher, Louis had received a gift-wrapped salami for one birthday, turkey for another, and came to hate meat. He obediently became a butcher, but his real love was fish. The brief story follows his life until the happy, fishy ending. With funny pictures of human-sized fish and cuts of meat, this unlikely book will satisfy children who thrive on the absurd.

Young, Ed. *Seven Blind Mice*. 1992. Hardcover: Philomel. Ages 3–7.

Exquisite illustrations and a simple text reinforce concepts about color, number, and days of the week in this brilliant book. Seven blind mice are curious about the new Something that has come to their pond. Each day, a mouse of a different color sets forth to determine what It is. Each one touches one part of the Something, but misinterprets what he feels. One mouse, for example, reports that the ear is a fan. The seventh and cleverest mouse puts all the clues together and, after she has made her excursion, reveals what the Something is—a solution that many listeners will also have figured out. Set against a black background, the collage artwork uses hand-made papers to create a stunningly beautiful book. A Caldecott Honor Book.

Zamorano, Ana. *Let's Eat*. Illustrated by Julie Vivas. 1996. Hardcover: Scholastic. Ages 3–7.

In Antonio's family, he is the smallest and "Mamá is the biggest," because she is about to have a baby. Mamá loves to gather the family together for a boisterous midday meal, shown in lovely watercolors. Every day one week, a different family member is too busy to eat lunch. The wide format repeatedly shows a round table, with most of the family talking and eating, and one person missing. On Saturday, Mamá is missing, because she has had a baby girl and is in the hospital, but a final, lovely picture shows the family with the new baby, all at the table together. The graceful, cadenced text, with occasional Spanish phrases, combines perfectly with the superb watercolors.

Zion, Gene. *Harry the Dirty Dog*. Illustrated by Margaret Bloy Graham. 1956. Hardcover: Harper. Paperback: Harper. Ages 2–6.

This old favorite continues to delight young listeners with its appealing story and wonderful illustrations. Harry, a white dog with black spots, likes everything—except getting a bath. One day he buries the scrubbing brush and runs away, getting dirtier and dirtier as he plays. When he returns home, the family doesn't recognize him, because he has turned into a black dog with white spots. Only by digging up the brush and begging for a bath does Harry solve his problem. Children respond sympathetically to Harry's dilemma and enjoy his outing as much as he does. The first in a series.

Zolotow, Charlotte. *William's Doll*. Illustrated by William Pène Du Bois. 1972. Hardcover: Harper. Ages 2–7.

This modern classic gives voice to a feeling boys have that is often ignored. William would like to have a doll: "He wanted to hug it and cradle it in his arms. . . ." His older brother makes fun of him when he sees William pretending to care for a baby doll, while their father hopes to dispel his son's interest in dolls with a basketball and an electric train, both of which William likes. But he still wants a doll, and when his grandmother visits, she understands and buys him one. Upset, his father exclaims, "He's a boy," but the grandmother explains that William needs the doll so that, when he's a father, he will know how to take care of his baby. In a small format, with apt illustrations, this is a wise, warmhearted book that imparts an important message.

2

Folktales

The magic of folklore, which has lasted for hundreds of years, relies on the power of stories to sound a chord with listeners. In choosing these books, I have included some traditional European stories as well as tales from other continents. Some are scary, some are funny, and some, enchanting. Often the protagonist is small or young but nevertheless prevails over larger, older characters—one of the reasons these tales appeal to children. I've included a few "fractured fairy tales" that parody well-known stories, with funny plot twists that many children enjoy.

The books in this section are for a wide range of ages; as with picture-story books, the age range given indicates listening level, not reading level. Many of the folktales work well for reading aloud because of their exciting plots and well-honed language. Outstanding artists often turn their talents to folktales, so many of the books listed have excellent illustrations. Most can be read alone by strong independent readers, although the vocabulary tends to be too difficult for beginners.

The first section lists illustrated versions of single tales, which resemble the picture-story books in the previous chapter. Most are thirty-two pages and can be read in one sitting. The second, shorter section is composed of collections of folktales, books with fifteen or more stories gathered together. These will interest older, independent readers as well as provide hours of reading aloud to younger children.

Single Tales

Briggs, Raymond. *Jim and the Beanstalk*. 1970. Paperback: Putnam. Ages 4–9.

In this funny retelling of "Jack and the Beanstalk," a boy named Jim climbs a beanstalk above his industrial town and finds a giant who used to love "fried boy" but no longer has teeth to chew with. Nor can he see to read his poetry books. When Jim suggests eyeglasses, the giant, who has never heard of them, is thrilled. Jim scoots back to the ground and buys a huge pair of glasses. Next Jim fetches some false teeth and finally a red wig for the bald giant, who loves his new appearance and rewards Jim handsomely. Wonderfully funny pictures show Jim marching through town with the gigantic glasses, teeth, and wig, and the huge gold coins the giant sends for payment. A clever version of an old favorite.

de Paola, Tomie. *Fin M'Coul: The Giant of Knockmany Hill*. 1981. Hardcover: Holiday House. Paperback: Holiday House. Ages 3–7.

Fin M'Coul and his enemy Cucullin are the two largest giants in Ireland, so huge they barely fit on the pages of this book. When Cucullin comes looking to fight Fin, Fin's smart, gigantic wife, Oonagh, comes up with a scheme to save her husband. The huge Fin dresses up as a baby and takes his place in a cradle, while Oonagh bakes loaves of bread with iron pans hidden in most of them. Once Cucullin arrives, she feeds Fin the loaves without the iron pans, fooling Cucullin into eating the rest, which destroy his teeth. This is only the first of three tricks that send Cucullin on his way and leave Fin safe at home. Tidy, humorous pictures with attractive borders enhance the tale.

Emberley, Michael. *Ruby*. 1990. Paperback: Little, Brown. Ages 5–9.

In this irreverent retelling of "Little Red Riding Hood," the main character is a snappy little mouse named Ruby. She reluctantly agrees to take some cheese pies to Granny, who lives on the other side of Boston, and sets off through the city streets. Humorous details crowd the pictures, such as the No Parking sign that reads: "Don't Even Think About It." When Ruby encounters a nasty reptile who tries to steal her pies, she snarls, "Buzz off, barf breath." And when a well-dressed cat helps her and then wants to know where she's going, Ruby is suspicious enough not to give him the full truth. While some adults may not care for the wisecracking mouse, most children will find this urban tale very funny indeed.

Galdone, Paul. *The Three Billy Goats Gruff*. 1973. Paperback: Clarion. Ages 3–7.

After decades of telling, this simple story still works its magic for children. Three goats who want to go up to the meadow to make themselves fat must cross a bridge over a troll, "who was as mean as he was ugly." They "trip, trap, trip, trap" over the bridge, a sound that gets louder with each billy goat who goes across. The biggest Billy Goat Gruff takes on the troll, tosses him into the river, and then goes on up the hillside, where the three brothers get so fat they can hardly move. Excellent for reading aloud, the story is complemented by large illustrations with close-ups of the long-haired, slightly comical troll and the hungry goats. A surefire hit with the younger crowd.

Gershator, Phillis, reteller. *Tukama Tootles the Flute: A Tale from the Antilles.* **Illustrated by Synthia Saint James. 1994. Hardcover: Orchard. Ages 4–8.**

Striking graphics in bold colors illustrate this traditional story from the island of St. Thomas. A naughty boy repeatedly ignores his grandmother's need for his help, and runs off to climb among the rocks and play his flute. He likes to do as he pleases, even when it worries his grandmother, who warns him, "Don't you know a two-headed giant runnin' about here, lookin' for wild children to eat?" Sure enough, when he stays out too late one day, a huge two-headed giant takes him home to fatten him up. Children will enjoy how the boy outwits the giant's wife with his music and escapes. Jaunty song lyrics and outstanding illustrations make this an unusually enjoyable folktale.

Gerson, Mary-Joan, reteller. *People of Corn: A Mayan Story.* **Illustrated by Carla Golembe. 1995. Hardcover: Little, Brown. Ages 7–11.**

An author's note at the beginning of this book gives information about the ancient Mayan culture in which this creation tale was told. The story itself harks back to the beginning of the world, when all was dark and silent. Two exotically colored gods, Plumed Serpent and Heart of Sky, create life, drawing maps and pictures across the sky until the earth is made, full of wonderful plants and animals. The gods want to be thanked for their work, but the animals cannot talk or sing songs of praise. So, after one failed plan, the gods mold humans out of corn, creating new creatures who dance and give their thanks. Richly textured paintings with a striking palette enhance this creation tale.

Goble, Paul, reteller. *Iktomi and the Boulder: A Plains Indian Story*. 1988. Hardcover: Orchard. Paperback: Orchard. Ages 4–9.

In this amusing tale, the trickster Iktomi dresses up in his fancy clothes to go visit friends in the next village. But as he walks along, the sun rises higher and Iktomi gets so hot that he stops in the shade of a huge boulder, where he leaves his blanket. Singing praises of his own generosity, he drapes the blanket on the boulder as a gift. But farther on, it looks like rain, so Iktomi returns and takes back the blanket to protect his clothes. To his shock, the boulder starts following him and pins him to the ground, so that Iktomi must use all his ingenuity to escape. Elegant pictures filled with humorous comments from Iktomi complement the well-honed text. A pleasure to share or read alone, this is one of several books about the Sioux trickster.

Hamanaka, Sheila, reteller. *Screen of Frogs: An Old Tale*. 1993. Hardcover: Orchard. Ages 4–9.

A subtle message about ecology comes across in this witty Japanese folktale about a lazy man and some grateful frogs. Koji is a wealthy, lazy boy who becomes a wealthy, lazy man, content to watch others work while he lounges around. But he has to sell his land to maintain his leisure, and finally has only a large house, a mountain, and a lake left. He plans to sell it until a giant frog startles him in his sleep and explains that woodcutters will buy the land and destroy life for the bees, birds, frogs, and other animals. Koji heeds the frog's words and receives a magical gift in return. Expansive, often comic, acrylic and collage artwork adds to this folktale's charm.

Han, Suzanne Crowder. *The Rabbit's Escape.* **Illustrated by Yumi Heo. 1995. Hardcover: Henry Holt. Ages 4–9.**

Outstanding pictures enhance this Korean folktale about a turtle and a rabbit, with the text in both English and Korean. The original art style creates an intriguing undersea world where the Dragon King of the East Sea lives. When the king becomes sick, a turtle offers to fetch the only cure for him, a rabbit's liver. The turtle makes his way to land where he flatters a rabbit into accompanying him back to the undersea kingdom. Thanks to quick thinking, the rabbit convinces the Dragon King that he doesn't have his liver with him "at the moment." In the end, everything works out well for the clever rabbit, the faithful turtle, and the king. With its large format and fresh artwork, this folktale is a treat.

Hong, Lily Toy, reteller. *Two of Everything.* **1993. Hardcover: Albert Whitman. Ages 4–8.**

Rounded, tidy pictures illustrate this humorous Chinese folktale. Told in simple language, the story introduces a poor couple, Mr. and Mrs. Haktak, who dig up a large brass pot in their garden. By chance, Mr. Haktak tosses his purse into the pot before he carries it into the house, and lo and behold, when Mrs. Haktak takes it out, there are two purses. They duplicate the purse many times to be able to buy anything they want, but they never expect Mrs. Haktak to fall into the pot by accident and duplicate herself! In the chaos that follows, Mr. Haktak falls in as well. What will they do now? The funny story line makes this a big hit with children.

Hooks, William H. *The Three Little Pigs and the Fox.* **Illustrated by S. D. Schindler. 1989. Paperback: Aladdin. Ages 5–9.**

Set in the Great Smoky Mountains, this variant of "The

Three Little Pigs" captures the flavor of the region in its colorful language. In a twist on the original, a smart young piglet named Hamlet saves her two lovable but dim older brothers from a "mean, tricky old drooly-mouth fox." When the first brother gets too huge to stay home, his mother sends him out into the world, where the fox immediately captures him and saves him for a future meal. The second brother suffers the same fate, having ignored his mother's advice to build a strong house. But clever Hamlet builds a strong house and rescues her brothers, then sends the fox downriver in a butter churn. The pigs go home safe and sound to visit their mother. A pleasure to read aloud, this snappy tale has high child appeal.

Isaacs, Anne. *Swamp Angel*. Illustrated by Paul O. Zelinsky. 1994. Hardcover: Dutton. Paperback: Penguin. Ages 4–9.

This original tall tale introduces the larger-than-life frontierswoman Angelica Longrider, known as Swamp Angel. After relating her remarkable childhood deeds, the story turns to Swamp Angel's fight with a gigantic bear who has defeated many men. The two of them, both so big that they seem to stretch beyond the book itself, wrestle from dawn to night. Beautiful paintings in a folk-art style accent the outlandish nature of this tall tale heroine and her deed. Ultimately she wins the fight, and leaves the overcrowded Tennessee frontier, dragging an enormous bearskin behind her. A Caldecott Honor Book, this is a fresh addition to American folk yarns.

Lester, Julius. *John Henry*. Illustrated by Jerry Pinkney. 1994. Hardcover: Dial. Ages 6–10.

Two masters of their arts have joined talents to produce a superb retelling of the John Henry legend. Scholar and former folksinger Lester writes beautifully, incorporating oral tradition and humorous modern references into the story of a black hero. Starting with the birth of John Henry, when he grew taller than the house on his first day of life, the tall tale describes a few examples of his prowess before it reaches the well-known story about John Henry and his race with a steam drill to dig a tunnel through a mountain, a race John Henry wins but which kills him. "He had hammered so hard and so fast and so long that his big heart had burst." Pinkney's incomparable watercolors clothe the legend in magic, creating a larger-than-life hero who stands out against a subdued landscape. This Caldecott Honor Book is a pleasure in every way.

Manna, Anthony L., and Christodoula Mitakidou. *Mr. Semolina-Semolinus: A Greek Folktale*. Illustrated by Giselle Potter. 1997. Hardcover: Atheneum. Ages 4–8.

When a princess named Areti cannot find a suitor she likes, she bakes herself a man, who becomes known as Mr. Semolina-Semolinus. The fact that "He was five times beautiful and ten times kind" becomes known around the world, prompting a faraway queen to come and kidnap him. Areti travels far and wide to find her creation, seeking help from the sun, moon, and stars, and their mothers. She wears out three pairs of iron shoes before she rescues her beloved. In the end, the princess and Mr. Semolina-Semolinus sail home, "where they lived blissfully but no better." Lyrical writing that preserves the sounds of oral tradition combined with original, stylized illustrations add up to a charming folktale.

Martinez, Alejandro Cruz. *The Woman Who Outshone the Sun: The Legend of Lucia Zenteno*. Translated by Rosalma Zubizarreta. Illustrated by Fernando Olivera. 1991. Hardcover: Children's Book Press. Ages 4–8.

This legend from the Zapotec Indians of Oaxaca, Mexico,

with its message about tolerating differences, tells of a woman named Lucia Zenteno, who was both wonderful and strange. Because she understood the ways of nature, when she bathed in a nearby river it rose and flowed through her long black hair. But fear of the unusual made some of the villagers cruel to Lucia. Driven out, she went to live in a cave with the river, which wouldn't leave her hair. Soon the villagers found life without their river impossible. Regretting their unkindness, they asked Lucia's forgiveness, which she granted. The surreal paintings, replete with mystical images and shimmering colors, set the mood for the story, which is given in Spanish and English.

McDermott, Gerald. *Raven: A Trickster Tale from the Pacific Northwest*. 1993. Hardcover: Harcourt. Ages 5–8.

As this folktale opens, brightly colored Raven is posed against the misty grays of a country where people are living in darkness and cold. Raven resolves to get them light, and flies to the shining house of the Sky Chief. In his usual clever way, Raven carries out a plan to be born to the Sky Chief's daughter. Doted on by the Sky Chief, Raven cries until he gets the sun, then flies off to give his gift to the world, turning from child back to raven as he soars away. Drawing on the stylized art of totem poles, McDermott creates a memorable Raven in the outstanding illustrations of this Caldecott Honor Book.

Mollel, Tololwa M. *The Orphan Boy: A Maasai Story*. Illustrated by Paul Morin. 1990. Hardcover: Clarion. Paperback: Houghton. Ages 5–9.

Richly textured pictures add depth and mystery to this story of a boy and an old man. One night, the old man notices that one of the stars in his beloved night sky is missing, and the next day a boy appears out of nowhere. Saying his name is

Kileken and that he is an orphan, the boy stays with the old man, doing all the hard work and keeping the cattle fat even during drought. Although the man comes to love the boy, his curiosity gets the better of him and he spies on the boy one night, an action he comes to regret. An evocative folktale with a universal theme, this stands out because of its unusual, exquisite artwork.

Rogasky, Barbara, reteller. *The Water of Life: A Tale from the Brothers Grimm.* **Illustrated by Trina Schart Hyman. 1986. Hardcover: Holiday House. Paperback: Holiday House. Ages 6–10.**

Enchanting illustrations create a magical setting for this Grimms fairy tale about a king who has three sons, two who are greedy and one who is kind. The king is ill and may die soon. When his sons hear about the Water of Life, which could save him, the oldest son offers to seek it. Motivated by greed instead of love, he sets off, foolishly scorns a dwarf on the way, and ends up trapped in a ravine. The second son has the same fate, but the third treats the dwarf with respect and so learns the secret of the Water. His quest suffers setbacks and his father doubts his love, but ultimately the third son's kindness is rewarded. A traditional tale that extols virtue.

Sabuda, Robert, reteller. *Arthur and the Sword.* **1995. Hardcover: Atheneum. Paperback: Simon & Schuster. Ages 6–9.**

Artwork that resembles stained-glass windows enhances this retelling of how Arthur became king of England. "Long ago in the time of great darkness, a time without a king, there lived a fair boy called Arthur," it begins. A sword has mysteriously appeared buried in a stone, with an inscription explaining that only the "rightwise born king" of England will be able to remove it. No knight can pull it out, but one day young Arthur needs a sword and takes it, without knowing the significance of his deed. The magician Merlin confirms that Arthur is the new king who will raise "the country out of darkness." The formal language and glowing illustrations suit this fine old tale and may prompt readers to seek out longer books about Arthur and his knights.

San Souci, Robert D. *The Faithful Friend*. Illustrated by Brian Pinkney. 1995. Hardcover: Simon & Schuster. Ages 6–10.

Swirling pictures develop this West Indian folktale about friendship and magic. Clement, who is white, and Hippolyte, who is black, are close friends who have been raised together on a plantation. When Clement falls in love with Pauline, the niece of a *quimboiseur*—a wizard—Hippolyte goes with him to visit her. When they arrive, her uncle objects to the match, but Pauline leaves with the young men. On their way back, Hippolyte overhears three female zombies planning black magic against Clement, and he vows to save his friend, a promise that brings about a dramatic climax. Children will be captivated by the blend of black magic and striking pictures in this Caldecott Honor Book.

San Souci, Robert D. *Pedro and the Monkey*. Illustrated by Michael Hays. 1996. Hardcover: Morrow. Ages 4–8.

In this version of "Puss in Boots" from the Philippines, a poor young man named Pedro is rewarded for helping a monkey. Even though the creature has been stealing his crops, the kind Pedro lets him go. When the monkey promises to help Pedro prosper, Pedro trusts him enough to give the monkey his only three coins. The monkey cleverly uses the money to trick a wealthy neighbor, after which Pedro and the monkey defeat a fearsome giant. Large acrylic paintings on linen add to the sense of place and bring the characters, especially the monkey, to life.

San Souci, Robert D. *The Samurai's Daughter.* **Illustrated by Stephen T. Johnson. 1992. Hardcover: Dial. Paperback: Penguin. Ages 5–10.**

A samurai's daughter, who lives in medieval Japan, is the heroine of this exciting folktale. As her father's only child, Tokoyo has learned the fighting arts of the samurai, and can shoot and ride skillfully. She also dives with local women who gather abalone and oysters from the ocean. When her father is unjustly arrested and imprisoned on an island, Tokoyo sets out to rescue him, using all her skills. After a hazardous journey, she reaches the island, where she dives to destroy a hideous sea serpent, a deed that saves her father. Expansive illustrations establish the setting and bring Tokoyo's courageous quest to life in powerful images.

Sanfield, Steve. *Bit by Bit.* **Illustrated by Susan Gaber. 1995. Hardcover: Philomel. Ages 4–8.**

A storyteller invites children into the pages of a book, shown in the illustrations, that contains a story about a poor tailor named Zundel. Zundel saves his money and makes himself a beautiful coat, which he wears until "bit by bit he w-o-r-e it out." But he sees that there is still enough cloth to make a jacket, and when that wears out, to make a vest. He is sad every time the garment wears out, but he keeps making smaller and smaller things, all the way down to a button. After the button wears out, the storyteller sees that there is still enough cloth "to make a story." Lovely illustrations extend the story far beyond the text, adding Zundel's wedding, his wife, and their new baby who grows to boyhood as the story goes on. Wonderful for reading aloud and a pleasure to look at.

Scieszka, Jon, and Lane Smith. *The Stinky Cheese Man & Other Fairly Stupid Tales.* **1992. Hardcover: Viking. Ages 5–10.**

The surgeon general's warning early in this book that states "these tales are fairly stupid and probably dangerous to your health" is only one way this book turns tradition on its head. Even before the title page, labeled "Title Page" in huge letters, the little red hen begins her story. The book proceeds with the tale of Chicken Licken in which the Table of Contents falls instead of the sky, followed by "The Princess and the Bowling Bowl" and "Little Red Riding Running Shorts," among others. The imaginative collages and the brilliantly playful book design suit the spirit of the fractured fairy tales. Full of broad humor, this Caldecott Honor Book will have children howling with laughter.

Stamm, Claus. *Three Strong Women: A Tall Tale from Japan.* **Illustrated by Jean and Mou-sien Tseng. 1990. Hardcover: Viking. Paperback: Puffin. Ages 4–9.**

A famous wrestler who meets a country lass one day in rural Japan cannot resist tickling her, not knowing that he has more than met his match. She giggles, but when she won't let go of his arm, he realizes that she is stronger than he. She takes him home to meet her mother and her tiny grandmother, who can both outwrestle him. The three strong women train the wrestler until he meets their standards, having him wrestle the grandmother so he won't get hurt. When he can finally pin her, though not the other two, he is ready to wrestle before the emperor and win. Engaging watercolors paint a lovely landscape of the Japanese countryside in this highly recommended tall tale.

Stevens, Janet. *Tops & Bottoms*. **1995. Hardcover: Harcourt. Ages 4–9.**
Children will pore over these wonderfully detailed pictures and laugh out loud when they see where the funny tale is headed. Rabbit, who needs food for his family, dreams up a way to trick Bear, who has land but is lazy. Rabbit offers to farm Bear's land and lets Bear decide if he wants the tops or the bottoms of the harvest. When Bear chooses the tops, Rabbit plants carrots, radishes, and beets. Angry, Bear insists on a second planting and chooses the bottoms, only to be tricked again. The third time, Bear chooses tops and bottoms, convinced he cannot lose, but wily Rabbit wins again. The pictures of Bear draped over a chair asleep, and Rabbit in his house made from a tennis shoe, are priceless. This Caldecott Honor Book delights a wide range of ages.

Trivias, Eugene. *The Three Little Wolves and the Big Bad Pig*. **Illustrated by Helen Oxenbury. 1993. Hardcover: McElderry. Paperback: Simon & Schuster. Ages 6–10.**
"Once upon a time, there were three cuddly little wolves with soft fur and fluffy tails who lived with their mother"—so begins this outrageous parody of "The Three Little Pigs." The mother sends the wolves into the world, warning them against the "big bad pig." The three build themselves a secure brick house, which the belligerent pig smashes with a sledgehammer. "The pig wasn't called big and bad for nothing." The pig uses a pneumatic drill on the concrete house they build, and sets off dynamite under the one with barbed wire, armor plates, and reinforced steel chains. But, surprisingly, when the beauty-loving wolves build a house of flowers, they win over

the pig. An absurd tale, charmingly illustrated, this may have some parents shaking their heads and most children laughing out loud.

Wahl, Jan. *Little Eight John.* **Illustrated by Wil Clay. 1992. Hardcover: Lodestar. Paperback: Dutton. Ages 4–8.**

Transcribed from an old African-American man in North Carolina, this folktale, used "to keep the young ones in line," tells of a contrary boy named Little Eight John, who was "mean as mean there was." Whenever his mother warns him not to do something because it will bring bad luck on the family, Little Eight John does it on purpose and laughs when bad luck follows. Dramatic acrylic paintings show him hiding and chuckling as he watches the effects of his disobedience. But when one of his contrary actions brings Old Raw Head Bloody Bones into their kitchen to work magic on the boy, Little Eight John learns his lesson and mends his ways. A moral tale told in an amusing way.

Wisniewski, David. *Golem.* **1996. Hardcover: Clarion. Ages 7–11.**

Stunning cut-paper illustrations heighten the drama of this old Jewish legend about Golem, a monster made out of clay who helped save the Jewish people. Set in 1580, a time when Jews were persecuted and confined to a ghetto in Prague, the chief rabbi has a dream telling him to create Golem to defend against the many attackers. The huge creature, given life through secret spells, does his job well, but also shows a poignant love for the world around him and a fear of being dissolved once the Jews are saved, which is indeed what happens. The solemn story, best suited to older children, comes to life in the vivid, intricate pictures that won the Caldecott Medal.

Wolf, Gita, adapter. *The Very Hungry Lion: A Folktale.* **Illustrated by Indrapramit Roy. 1996. Hardcover: Annick. Ages 4–8.**

Notable for its eye-catching artwork, this folktale is illustrated using a technique adapted from the Warli tradition of folk painting in India, in which white pigment figures decorate the mud walls of houses. The story concerns a hungry lion who, thinking he can avoid the work of hunting, is tricked first by a sparrow's suggestion that she should be eaten only with rice cakes. The sparrow sends the lion off to get the ingredients. On his way back, he is fooled by a lamb with a similar ruse, and then by a deer. Bewildered, the lion concludes he had better go on a real hunt the next day. Touches of humor, a jaunty text, and striking folk art combine to make a charming whole.

Yep, Laurence. *The Man Who Tricked a Ghost.* **Illustrated by Isadore Seltzer. 1993. Hardcover: Bridgewater. Paperback: Bridgewater. Ages 5–9.**

Boldly colored paintings create a wonderfully monstrous ghost in this retelling of a Chinese folktale. When a fearless man named Sung leaves a friend's house late one night to walk home, he meets the ghost of a fierce warrior. The ghost confides that he is on his way to frighten a fearless man named Sung, and goes on to boast about the many people he has scared. Thinking quickly, Sung claims to be a ghost, too—a new ghost who doesn't know much. Sung eggs the ghost on to become scarier and scarier, then asks what ghosts themselves are afraid of. The answer gives Sung a solution to his problem, and he emerges safe and richer than before. The large-scale, stylized illustrations add to the fun of this ghost story.

Zelinsky, Paul O., reteller. *Rumpelstiltskin*. 1986. Hardcover: Dutton. Ages 3–7.

With his pointy-toed shoes, his wide black hat, and his impudent air, this Rumpelstiltskin outshines all other versions. The miller's daughter, bewildered at being expected to spin straw into gold, is a soft-faced foil to Rumpelstiltskin's witty figure. Simple, well-chosen language retells the familiar story, and the pictures do all the rest, portraying the imp's pleasure when he thinks the miller's daughter, now the queen, cannot guess his name. He flies ecstatically around a fire on a spoon, crowing, "I brew my beer, I bake my loaves. And soon the queen's own son I'll claim." But, overheard by the queen's faithful servant, Rumpelstiltskin is thwarted, responds by jumping up and down in fury, and flies away on his spoon. In this Caldecott Honor Book, glorious oil paintings echo a medieval art style and create a memorable, magical little man.

Collections

Bierhorst, John, editor. *The Dancing Fox: Arctic Folktales.*
Illustrated by Mary K. Okheena. 1997. Hardcover: Morrow.
Ages 5–10.

In this fine collection, a careful introduction lays the
groundwork for understanding these eighteen Arctic tales.
Bierhorst discusses the place of storytelling in the Inuit culture, now and in the past, and explains details about Inuit life,
such as types of boats and houses mentioned in the stories.
Each tale is drawn from Inuit oral tradition, as recorded by
explorers and folklorists, and retains the rhythm of stories told
aloud. They are supernatural tales of talking animals, giants,
medicine men and women, and long, magical journeys. Full of
danger and suspense, the stories typically end on a happy note.
Prints by an Inuit artist add a fitting accompaniment to each
story and make an unusually elegant dust jacket.

de Paola, Tomie. *Tomie de Paola's Favorite Nursery Tales.*
1986. Hardcover: Putnam. Ages 3–9.

The renowned illustrator Tomie de Paola has thoughtfully
assembled and illustrated a collection of tales, fables, and a
few poems that every American child should know because
they are a part of our cultural heritage. He includes the stories
from which we derive such widely used metaphors as "sour
grapes," "the boy who cried wolf," and "the Emperor's new
clothes." His versions of "The Three Little Pigs," "The Three
Bears," "The Little Red Hen," and "The Three Billy-Goats
Gruff" preserve the traditional rhythms and refrains that make
folktales so appealing to children. A handful of well-known

children's poems such as "The Owl and the Pussycat" provide a change of pace from the stories. De Paola's characteristic illustrations add color and humor as they frame the pages in a tidy, appealing way. This excellent basic collection, which avoids the scary details found in some Grimm stories, is suitable to read aloud to young children and for older children to enjoy on their own.

Hamilton, Virginia. *In the Beginning: Creation Stories from Around the World.* **Illustrated by Barry Moser. 1988. Hardcover: Harcourt. Paperback: Harcourt. Ages 8–14.**

In this splendid book, creation myths from cultures around the world are retold in beautifully honed language. Well-known stories from the Bible and Greek mythology stand side by side with less familiar myths from Australian aborigines, Native Americans, and African and Asian cultures. Dramatic full-page oil paintings enhance the tales, as does the unusually elegant book design. With her characteristic care, Hamilton adds notes that explain the sources of the twenty-five myths. Excellent for reading aloud, these myths also lend themselves to discussions. This Newbery Honor Book is highly recommended.

Hamilton, Virginia. *The People Could Fly: American Black Folktales.* **Illustrated by Leo and Diane Dillon. 1985. Hardcover: Knopf. Paperback: Knopf. Ages 7–12.**

This outstanding folktale collection assembles twenty-four tales from the tradition of American black folklore, accompanied by graceful black-and-white illustrations. Informative notes after each story and an extensive bibliography add to the book's high quality. Seven animal tales, such as "He Lion, Bruh Bear, and Bruh Rabbit," tell of small animals tricking bigger ones, while a slave character called John the Conqueror outwits a slave owner in several other tales. The magical, scary, funny, and moving stories read aloud beautifully and will keep listeners entranced.

Hodges, Margaret, and Margery Evernden. *Of Swords and Sorcerers: The Adventures of King Arthur and His Knights.* **Illustrated by David Frampton. 1993. Hardcover: Macmillan. Ages 6–12.**

This elegant volume gracefully retells timeless stories about King Arthur and his Knights of the Round Table. The tales begin with the childhood of Merlin and the fierce fight between two dragons, then turn to Arthur's childhood. The birth of the Round Table, Arthur's marriage to Guinevere, and the coming of Lancelot are followed by stories about individual knights and the search for the Holy Grail. After that quest is accomplished, the Round Table loses its meaning and Arthur's story ends in battle and sadness. In this version, Guinevere does not betray Arthur, although other women have either negative or minimal roles. Couched in suitably formal language, with striking woodcut illustrations, these legends will entrance readers looking for tales of chivalry, fighting, and magic.

Phelps, Ethel Johnston. *Tatterhood and Other Tales.* **Illustrated by Pamela Baldwin Ford. 1978. Paperback: Feminist Press. Ages 6–13.**

Here are twenty-five entertaining folktales, from different countries, with heroines who are strong, brave, and smart. For example, in "Kupti and Imani," a king's daughter has such good financial sense that she builds up her own business until she is as rich as her father. In others, an Incan heroine braves monsters to fetch water from a magic lake, and a shrewd Chinese woman becomes head of her husband's family and makes their fortune. Sisters rescue brothers and wives rescue husbands, reversing the usual fairy-tale patterns. The tales are exciting, funny, and full of magic. Although the small print makes it accessible only to older independent readers, this is a fine collection for reading aloud.

Shannon, George. *Stories to Solve: Folktales from Around the World.* Illustrated by Peter Sis. 1985. Hardcover: Greenwillow. Paperback: Beech Tree. Ages 9–12.

Few children can resist the lure of "mini-mysteries" or "stories with a hole." In this enjoyable volume, each of the fourteen short stories gives the reader a puzzle to solve, with the solution on the following page. For example, in the Ethiopian tale "The Cleverest Son," a father announces he will leave his farm to the one of his three sons who takes the coin his father gives and buys something that will fill a whole room. The first son buys straw and the second buys feathers, but the third buys two small things that fill the room completely. Most children love stretching their minds on such puzzles. Well documented, with delightful illustrations by Peter Sis, this is a crowd pleaser. Also enjoy *More Stories to Solve, Still More Stories to Solve,* and *True Lies.*

3

Books for Beginning Readers

Learning to read is an exciting, almost magical process, during which it's crucial to keep children supplied with books they are eager to read, because it's easy to get discouraged if progress is slow. I have divided the books for beginning independent readers into four categories, starting with "Easy Readers," which are specifically geared toward the early stages of reading. They use a controlled vocabulary with many words that children can sound out. They also have illustrations on almost every page that closely follow the story, providing clues to words the reader doesn't know.

As they progress, children are often eager to jump into "chapter books," but are not yet ready for long pages of unbroken text. "Short Novels," the second category, contains books known to educators as transitional, since they move children from the first stages of reading to longer novels. These slim chapter books have large print, an open design, and frequent illustrations. In the past, it has been difficult to find books at this level, since most children's novels are geared toward more advanced readers, but publishers have begun to offer more simple novels, often in series. Children at the upper end of this reading stage should also check Chapter 4, "Books for Middle Readers," which lists other possibilities for this group.

The third category, "Biographies," introduces important and exciting people. Most of these books also have large print and lots of pictures. They cover a wide spectrum of people: rulers, aviators, scientists, artists, and more. Some of the subjects are famous; others are little-known historical figures. Children who prefer "true" stories will especially enjoy these books, which combine facts with well-chosen anecdotes.

The final category, "Nonfiction," is divided into sections: History; Nature and Science; Trucks, Planes, and Other Technology; Hobbies and Sports; and Poetry. A number of these selections are easy to read, while others are slightly more challenging. All are illustrated and geared toward keeping readers excited about books. Because much more nonfiction than I've listed is available, especially at libraries, use this list as a jumping-off point to find more books on topics that grab your child's attention. There are many more crafts books, sports books, poetry collections, nature books, and science experiment guides to be explored and enjoyed. Note that the age ranges for biographies and nonfiction cover both interest and reading levels. For example, "5–10" indicates that five- to seven-year-olds will enjoy listening, while children approximately eight to ten will be able to read the book independently.

It is important not to limit your choices to this chapter alone. All children at this stage should also be listening to books read aloud, including picture-story books and folktales, most of which are still too difficult for them to read by themselves. Also check the "Books for Middle Readers" for longer books to read aloud, such as the fantasy books about animals, popular with all ages.

Easy Readers

Bang, Molly Garrett. *Tye May and the Magic Brush.* **1981. Paperback: Mulberry. Ages 4–8.**

When the orphan Tye May finds herself unwelcome in a boys' painting class, she teaches herself to draw using sticks and reeds. One night in a dream, a mysterious woman brings her a magic brush, and the girl realizes when she awakes that everything she paints with the brush comes to life. She generously paints tools and other useful items for her poor neighbors, but soon trouble sets in. A wicked landlord locks her up to make her paint what he wants, but Tye May draws a way out and a net to trap her pursuers. She goes on to outwit a greedy emperor with her magic brush. Delicate black-and-white pictures with touches of red echo the Chinese origins of this engaging story.

Brenner, Barbara. *Wagon Wheels.* **Illustrated by Don Bolognese. 1978. Hardcover: Harper. Paperback: Harper. Ages 3–8.**

This intriguing tale is based on a true story about a black father and his three sons who traveled by wagon to Kansas in the 1870s, where they survived the winter in a dugout house with help from Osage Indians. Convinced he will do better farther west, the father leaves the sons by themselves while he seeks better land. Eleven-year-old Johnny takes care of his younger brothers and, when they get a letter from their father, leads them 150 miles to their new home. Informative black-and-white illustrations complement the text. A fascinating introduction for beginning readers to the role of blacks in the West.

Buck, Nola. *Sid and Sam.* **Illustrated by G. Brian Karas. 1996. Hardcover: Harper. Paperback: Harper. Ages 4–8.**

Very simple vocabulary makes this upbeat book excellent for beginning readers. Sam enjoys his friend Sid, a loud, exuberant girl who wears a baseball cap, cowboy boots, and binoculars. Sometimes, though, he finds her overwhelming. She likes to sing fast, loud, and long, even when he suggests, "Sing slower, Sid" and "Sing softer, Sid." Sitting, waiting for her to stop singing, the mild Sam comes up with a clever plan. He calls out, "That song is so long," and Sid echoes back, "So long?" Now Sam has an opening to say good-bye, "So long," and "See you soon." Full of alliteration and wordplay, with whimsical illustrations, this is a treat.

Byars, Betsy. *My Brother, Ant.* **Illustrated by Marc Simont. 1996. Hardcover: Viking. Ages 3–8.**

In four short chapters, a boy describes living with his younger brother, Anthony, known as Ant. First the brother has to scare away a monster that's under Ant's bed. Then they have an argument over a picture of a spider Ant says he didn't draw on his brother's homework. In the third chapter, the brother tells the story of the three little pigs—or is it figs? And finally he writes a surprising letter for Ant to an unlikely recipient. Simont's characteristically delightful pictures add to the fun of these stories about two brothers who like each other.

Coerr, Eleanor. *The Big Balloon Race.* Illustrated by Carolyn Croll. 1981. Hardcover: Harper. Paperback: Harper. Ages 4–8.

An exhilarating hot-air balloon race in the 1880s is the subject of this historical fiction for beginning readers. A girl named Ariel, whose father makes hot-air balloons and whose mother, Carlotta the Great, races them, falls asleep by accident in the gondola of her mother's balloon just before a race begins. When she awakes, they are already in the air and cannot go back. Ariel's extra weight diminishes their chance of winning, but they do their best. Just before the end of the race, Ariel has a chance to help out and, to their surprise, she and her mother win. Cheerful, tidy pictures capture the thrill of the contest.

Coerr, Eleanor. *Chang's Paper Pony.* Illustrated by Deborah Kogan Ray. 1988. Hardcover: Harper. Paperback: Harper. Ages 4–8.

Five short chapters relate the story of a Chinese immigrant boy named Chang who lives in California during the Gold Rush. He helps his grandfather, a hotel cook, studies with a Chinese teacher, and struggles with racial prejudice from miners and other children. Most of all, Chang longs to have his own pony, not just the painting of a pony on the hotel wall. A sympathetic miner takes him out to pan gold, with disappointing results. Instead, Chang finds his gold in an unexpected way. Based on historical facts, with attractive soft-edged illustrations, this is a charming introduction to a slice of American history.

Hazen, Barbara Shook. *Digby.* Illustrated by Barbara J. Phillips-Duke. 1997. Hardcover: Harper. Ages 5–8.

In this inviting book, a young boy comes to terms with the

fact that his dog, Digby, is getting old. He wants to play ball, but, his older sister tells him, "Digby is too old to play catch with you." She reminisces about when she was young and Digby could play, but then adds that the dog can do other things better now: "She is better at understanding." As a consolation, the sister offers to take her brother out and teach him to catch. In the brightly colored pictures, the children are dressed in fashionably oversized clothes, with bulky sneakers. A congenial portrait of a tolerant older sister, a younger brother, and the old dog they love.

Hoban, Lillian. *Arthur's Pen Pal*. 1976. Hardcover: Harper. Paperback: Harper. Ages 4–8.

Like many older brothers, the chimpanzee Arthur sometimes gets tired of his younger sister, Violet. He envies his new pen pal Sandy, who has only an older brother. He knows Sandy plays the drums and is learning karate, which sound great to Arthur. One evening when the baby-sitter keeps finding fault with Arthur, and praising Violet, Arthur complains, "Little sisters are no fun. . . . It must be nice to have a little brother like Sandy." So he is surprised when he receives a photograph from his pen pal that shows *her* throwing her older brother with a karate move. The news makes Arthur reassess his feelings about his own sister. One in a series of entertaining easy readers about Arthur and his escapades.

Lobel, Arnold. *Days with Frog and Toad*. 1979. Hardcover: Harper. Paperback: Harper, Scholastic. Ages 3–8.

Everyone should get to know Frog and Toad. These five stories about their friendship, beautifully illustrated in greens and browns, are humorous and wise. Told in short, simple words and sentences, they show problems and situations familiar to everyone. In the first story, Toad procrastinates about everything until he realizes that, if he does it now, he can be lazy later. The friends fly a kite, persisting until they succeed, and enjoy "having the shivers" together with a scary tale. The final story shows Frog's quiet joy in being alone sometimes. Among the best books in children's literature, this and *Frog and Toad Are Friends*, *Frog and Toad Together*, and *Frog and Toad All Year* are must-reads.

Lobel, Arnold. *Uncle Elephant*. 1981. Hardcover: Harper. Ages 3–8.

In nine very short chapters a young elephant and his old, previously unknown, uncle become friends after the youngster's parents are lost at sea. After a train journey, Uncle Elephant makes his nephew feel at home in the uncle's cozy house and introduces him to his beloved garden. The kind uncle tells his nephew stories, writes a song for him, and tries to keep up his spirits. In the joyful end, the parents return, and the young elephant and his uncle rejoice in their new friendship. Lobel's priceless pictures and his wonderful way with simple words are at work again in this charming beginning reader.

Maccarone, Grace. *Soccer Game!* Illustrated by Meredith Johnson. 1994. Paperback: Scholastic. Ages 3–7.

This upbeat story follows a soccer game between two coed teams, showing boys and girls exerting themselves and having a good time. To add to the fun, each team has a dog as a player, one in red and one in blue to match the team colors. The extremely brief text, made up of simple sentences such as "We pass" and "We run," is accessible to the very beginning reader. Good sportsmanship prevails in this cheerful easy reader, certain to appeal to soccer fans.

Marshall, James. *Fox Be Nimble.* **1990. Hardcover: Dial. Paperback: Puffin. Ages 4–8.**

In the first of three stories about the rambunctious Fox, he fantasizes about being a rock star, but instead finds himself baby-sitting bear children in his neighborhood. When he can't control the wild children, he sends them outside, then sees them float away holding on to balloons. His search for them makes him unexpectedly famous. In "Fox the Brave," Fox fusses about a fall he has taken until his brave younger sister falls harder but doesn't complain. Finally, "Fox on Parade" gives the likable fox a chance to show off in a good cause. Just the sort of reading material that will keep beginners excited about books.

Mills, Claudia. *Gus and Grandpa.* **Illustrated by Catherine Stock. 1997. Hardcover: FSG. Ages 6–9.**

Gus loves Grandpa's house where he can mess around in the yard with Grandpa's dog, Skipper. One day Gus creates a mess while feeding Skipper. When Grandpa has Gus sweep it up, the boy decides, "Sweeping was fun. Maybe he would become a famous sweeper." In the next chapter, Grandpa and Gus enjoy a shopping trip, even though they almost lose Grandpa's car. And in the final chapter, they bake a wonderful cake together for their birthdays, which are two days apart. Energetic watercolors convey love and humor in this portrait of a caring grandfather and grandson.

Mozelle, Shirley. *Zack's Alligator.* **Illustrated by James Watts. 1989. Hardcover: Harper. Paperback: Harper. Ages 4–8.**

Who wouldn't want an alligator the size of a key chain that expands when wet? Zack is thrilled when his uncle in Florida sends him an alligator, Bridget, who sparkles with fun and lively ideas. She fiercely wrestles with the garden hose, under the impression that it's a snake, then bites the tire of a mail truck. At the playground, she tries every piece of equipment, even the merry-go-round. By the story's end, Zack knows that his only quiet moments will be when Bridget returns to her key-chain size for a while. Droll pictures develop the alligator's active personality. In the sequel, *Zack's Alligator Goes to School*, Bridget stirs things up in the classroom.

Pomerantz, Charlotte. *The Outside Dog*. Illustrated by Jennifer Plecas. 1993. Hardcover: Harper. Paperback: Harper. Ages 4–8.

Readers will relate to Marisol's longtime wish to have a dog. When a stray keeps coming back to the small home she shares with her grandfather in Puerto Rico, Marisol gets her hopes up. Her grandfather insists that they cannot keep the dog, but Marisol's persistence slowly pays off. First Grandfather lets her feed the dog, which she calls Pancho, then he lets her buy Pancho a flea collar. When Pancho disappears for a few days, Grandfather is as worried as Marisol and just as happy when the dog—now a part of the family—returns. Charming, childlike pictures create a rural setting, and the inclusion of Spanish words, defined before the story begins, adds a nice touch.

Porte, Barbara Ann. *Harry's Dog*. Illustrated by Yossi Abolafia. 1984. Hardcover: Greenwillow. Ages 4–8.

Harry has a new dog, but he also has a problem. He hasn't told his father, who is badly allergic to dogs, about Girl, as he has named her. But his father realizes that Harry is hiding something in his room, sees the dog, and asks for an explanation. "So I tell him my story" about a spaceship landing on their lawn, but then Harry admits that an acquaintance who was moving gave Harry the dog and drove off. Just when it looks like Girl must go, Harry's aunt Rose offers to keep Girl at her nearby house where Harry can take care of her. The warm family relationships and happy solution to the problem will appeal to beginning readers. One in a series.

Rylant, Cynthia. *Henry and Mudge: The First Book of Their Adventures*. Illustrated by Suçie Stevenson. 1987. Hardcover: Bradbury. Paperback: Aladdin. Ages 3–8.
In seven short chapters with pictures on every page, Henry gets his dog, Mudge, learns to love him, and then almost loses him. The simple text, which is lyrical and funny, speaks directly to children. Before Mudge came, Henry worried on his walk to school about "tornadoes, ghosts, biting dogs, and bullies." Once he has the huge Mudge with him, Henry thinks about "vanilla ice cream, rain, rocks, and good dreams." Cheerful, humorous pictures show the friendship of this sympathetic pair. The first in a wonderful series.

Rylant, Cynthia. *Mr. Putter and Tabby Pour the Tea*. Illustrated by Arthur Howard. 1994. Hardcover: Harcourt. Paperback: Harcourt. Ages 4–8.
In this gentle story, an older man named Mr. Putter lives alone and wishes he had some company. He would like to share his pleasant quiet life—with its English muffins, cups of tea, and store of wonderful stories—with someone. "Mr. Putter wanted a cat," but all he can find at the pet store are kittens. So he goes to the pound and finds a yellow cat that resembles him: old, a bit deaf, with creaking bones. Mr. Putter and Tabby, as he names her, go home, where they enjoy daily life and the change of seasons together. Congenial pictures

show Mr. Putter and Tabby, and the pleasure they take together in the garden and the kitchen. The first in a cozy series.

Schwartz, Alvin, reteller. *In a Dark, Dark Room and Other Scary Stories.* **Illustrated by Dirk Zimmer. 1984. Hardcover: Harper. Paperback: Harper. Ages 4–8.**

Beginning readers who like to be scared will like this unusual collection of seven tales. One is a widely known story about a girl who always wears a ribbon around her neck and won't say why. When she is on her deathbed, she allows her husband to remove the ribbon—and her head falls off! Another familiar ghostly legend concerns a man who gives a boy a ride home one night, and loans him a sweater. When the driver stops by the next day to get his sweater, he learns that the boy died a year earlier, and he finds his sweater on the boy's gravestone. The angular, homespun illustrations amplify the scariness of some stories and add humor to others in this popular easy reader.

Seuss, Dr. *The Cat in the Hat.* **1957. Hardcover: Random House. Ages 3–8.**

On a dreary day, the narrator and his sister, Sally, are home alone until the arrival of the rambunctious Cat in the Hat, who knows "some good games" they could play. Although their rule-abiding pet fish objects to the visitor, the Cat in the Hat starts a few silly games, then brings in two mischievous creatures, Thing One and Thing Two, who make a mess of the house. When the fish spies the children's mother returning, the Cat in the Hat cleans up the house pronto and leaves with a tip of his hat. Seuss's whimsical illustrations in this modern classic instill a wonderful personality in the Cat in the Hat, while the rhyming text of mostly one-syllable words is geared to young readers. Followed by *The Cat in the Hat Comes Back*.

Sharmat, Marjorie Weinman. *Nate the Great*. Illustrated by Marc Simont. 1972. Paperback: Dell. Ages 3–8.

Nate the Great has the narrative style of a hard-boiled detective, with short sentences and a tough manner. But he also likes pancakes, and leaves a note for his mother letting her know he is wearing his rubber boots. His current case concerns his friend Annie, who is missing a picture of her dog, Fang. Nate starts by investigating Fang: "He sniffed me. I sniffed him back." His next lead takes him to a strange girl named Rosamond, whose lost cat Nate finds. Back at Annie's, Nate uses his knowledge of colors to solve the mystery. Then he settles down to a second breakfast of pancakes, with the observation "I, Nate the Great, like happy endings." With memorable illustrations that add to the fun, this is the first in a popular series.

Short Novels

Adler, David A. *Cam Jansen and the Mystery at the Haunted House.* Illustrated by Susanna Natti. 1992. Paperback: Puffin. Ages 6–9.

This is one of many mysteries starring Cam Jansen, a fifth-grade detective with a photographic memory. She can look at anything, say, "Click," and implant the details in her memory, a handy talent when detecting. Cam and her friend Eric get caught up in a mystery at an amusement park when Cam's aunt and several others have their wallets stolen. Recalling details she has seen during the day, Cam comes up with suspects and eventually solves the crime. The amusement park with its haunted house and colorful characters provides a good setting for this quick-paced mystery. Large print, short chapters, and frequent black-and-white illustrations make this an excellent series for readers new to chapter books.

Blume, Judy. *Freckle Juice.* Illustrated by Sonia O. Lisker. 1971. Hardcover: Simon & Schuster. Paperback: Dell. Ages 6–9.

"Andrew Marcus wanted freckles" is how this humorous story about a second-grade boy begins. Every day in school, Andrew admires Nicky Lane's freckles, sometimes so intently that he doesn't hear his teacher. When he asks Nicky how he got freckles, another student offers to sell Andrew a recipe for freckle juice, for fifty cents. Andrew buys it, and concocts the mixture of grape juice, vinegar, mustard, and more, but all it does is make him sick. Determined to arrive at school with freckles, Andrew resorts to a blue Magic Marker, the only one he could find. Thanks to his understanding teacher, he comes to realize that he looks fine without freckles—and that Nicky Lane would like to get rid of his. An entertaining introduction for younger readers to a popular author.

Brown, Jeff. *Flat Stanley*. Illustrated by Tomi Ungerer. 1964. Hardcover: Harper. Paperback: Harper, Scholastic. Ages 6–9.

This story, with its tongue-in-cheek humor, opens with Arthur Lambchop fetching his parents one morning to see an astounding sight: His older brother, Stanley, has been flattened by a bulletin board. It doesn't hurt, and the doctor has no advice, so Stanley makes the best of his new, half-inch-thick self. He enjoys sliding under doors and being mailed to California in a huge envelope. Best of all, he disguises himself as a museum painting and captures two art thieves. When Stanley gets tired of being different, a clever idea from Arthur restores him to his old self. Although there are no chapter divisions, the frequent, funny pictures help make this accessible to transitional readers. Followed by *Stanley and the Magic Lamp* and *Invisible Stanley*.

Bulla, Clyde Robert. *The Chalk Box Kid*. 1987. Paperback: Random House. Ages 6–9.

Gregory is having a hard time because his father has lost his job and the family has to move on Gregory's birthday. Then, just when it looks as if he will have his own room, his unemployed uncle moves into it with him. And when everyone else at his new school, where he has not made friends, gets seeds to plant a home garden, Gregory doesn't take any because his new house has no yard. An artist at heart, Gregory, using chalk, draws an elaborate garden on the walls of a nearby burned-out building for his own pleasure, but when his classmates learn of it, the results help turn his life around. A touching story about loneliness and art.

Cameron, Ann. *The Stories Julian Tells*. Illustrated by Ann Strugnell. 1981. Hardcover: Pantheon. Paperback: Knopf. Ages 6–10.

This outstanding book centers around an African-American boy named Julian, his younger brother, Huey, and their parents. In the first of five stories, Julian's boisterous father makes a special lemon pudding for his wife that tastes "like a whole raft of lemons, like a night on the sea." But the boys cannot resist eating it before their mother gets home. Their punishment? A "beating" in which Huey beats egg yolks and a "whipping" in which Julian whips egg whites to make a new pudding. The other stories concern a garden they plant, Julian's loose tooth, a fig tree, and Julian's friendship with a girl. The book's gentle humor, lyrical writing, and graceful illustrations raise it above most books for this reading level. The first in a series.

Christopher, Matt. *The Dog That Stole Football Plays*. Illustrated by Bill Ogden. 1980. Paperback: Little, Brown. Ages 6–9.

This slight story features Harry, a dog who can communicate with his owner, Mike, and read his mind. The amazing Harry can also do handstands, roll over, and wiggle his ears. When Mike takes Harry to his football game, the dog listens in on the other team's plays and tells Mike what they're planning. Mike's team wins that game and several more, thanks to the dog's information. But just when Mike starts to worry about the fairness of the scheme, Harry misses a big game and Mike has to compete on his own. Although not divided into chapters, this short book's subject matter and many sketches will recommend it to younger readers who like sports.

Cleary, Beverly. *The Mouse and the Motorcycle.* **Illustrated by Louis Darling. 1965. Hardcover: Morrow. Paperback: Avon Camelot. Ages 7–10.**

Ralph the mouse cannot believe his luck when he gets to ride a motorcycle. One day a boy named Keith and his parents check into the old hotel where Ralph lives. Keith has a collection of toy vehicles, including the motorcycle that Ralph can't resist trying. Ralph and the motorcycle end up in a wastebasket, where Keith finds them, which begins their friendship, for "two creatures who shared a love for motorcycles naturally spoke the same language." The motorcycle leads to exciting adventures for Ralph, who races it up and down the hall, almost gets sucked into a vacuum, and risks his life to find an aspirin when Keith gets sick. Except for its dated stereotypes of women, this popular novel has a timeless quality and a keen understanding of what children like. Followed by *Runaway Ralph* and *Ralph S. Mouse*.

Cleary, Beverly. *Ramona the Pest.* **Illustrated by Louis Darling. 1968. Hardcover: Morrow. Paperback: Avon. Ages 7–10.**

The feisty Ramona Quimby has kept children reading and laughing for three decades. Her realistic problems and mistakes appeal to a wide range of readers, who sympathize with her situation as a younger sister who wants to grow up fast. Often stubborn, she sometimes loses her temper, but other times sings out her happiness and twirls with joy. Ramona wants to be good and please her kindergarten teacher, but she can't always resist the temptation to do forbidden things like pull a schoolmate's bouncy curls. Though somewhat dated in its view of women, this remains a popular read-aloud for younger children and beginning chapter book for independent readers. One in a wonderful series.

Duffey, Betsy. *The Gadget War*. Illustrated by Janet Wilson. 1991. Hardcover: Viking. Paperback: Puffin. Ages 7–10.

Eight-year-old Kelly Sparks, who plans to be a "Gadget Whiz" when she grows up, has already come up with forty-three inventions, for which she followed a careful process. Even for something as outrageous as her new food-fight catapult, she makes notes in her Inventor's Log. After designing it, she tests it in her kitchen, where, for the sake of science, she gets food all over the walls. When the new boy who joins her class also claims to be an inventor, a rivalry springs up and they try to out-invent each other. But when Kelly's food catapult launches an orange right at the school principal, both inventors get into trouble. As the book ends, their rivalry is turning into friendship. A breezy story that makes inventing look like fun.

Erickson, Russell E. *A Toad for Tuesday*. Illustrated by Lawrence Di Fiori. 1974. Hardcover: Lothrop. Paperback: Morrow. Ages 6–9.

What a cozy life the toad Warton leads with his brother, Morton. Morton loves to cook, and Warton keeps their home shiny clean. But, restless, Warton embarks on an adventure into the wintry landscape to take some beetle brittle to Aunt Toolia. He fashions a pair of skis, bundles up, and skims across the snow. He rescues a mouse, then is captured by an owl who plans to eat the toad in five days, on a Tuesday. Warton, trapped in the owl's high home, passes the time by making the dreary room as cozy as possible, and tries to befriend the owl. Will the owl's heart soften by Tuesday? Or can Warton escape through his own ingenuity? An entertaining story with wonderful illustrations and a heartwarming end. The first in a series.

Gannett, Ruth Stiles. *My Father's Dragon.* **Illustrated by Ruth Chrisman Gannett. 1948. Hardcover: Random House. Paperback: Knopf. Ages 6–9.**

Rounded black-and-white illustrations, well integrated into the text, are the highlight of this magical adventure in which a boy named Elmer Elevator journeys to the Wild Island, where he has close escapes from a lion, a rhino, a tiger, and other animals. Luckily, he has packed his knapsack with everything he needs to distract the animals. The rhino, whose tusks have yellowed, is delighted with a toothbrush, while the crocodiles enjoy lollipops. In the end, Elmer rescues the flying dragon he came for, who had been tied up by the animals. Unfortunately, except for the cat, females have weak roles, and Elmer's mother whips him for feeding a stray cat. A Newbery Honor Book with an imaginative plot and charming pictures. Followed by *Elmer and the Dragon* and *The Dragons of Blueland.*

Giff, Patricia Reilly. *The Beast in Ms. Rooney's Room.* **Illustrated by Blanche Sims. 1984. Paperback: Dell. Ages 6–9.**

Richard Best, who calls himself "Beast," has to repeat second grade because he has trouble reading. At first he doesn't want to be friends with his new, "baby" classmates, but he slowly changes his mind. He and the other three students in his special reading group persuade their classmates to try for the school banner given weekly to the best class. Despite a few setbacks, such as the time Richard flies paper airplanes out the window, the class succeeds in its goal. Readers who like books about real children will enjoy this long series about the kids of Polk Street School.

Heide, Florence Parry. *The Shrinking of Treehorn.* **Illustrated by Edward Gorey. 1971. Hardcover: Holiday House. Paperback: Holiday House. Ages 5–8.**

This small book hinges on the idea that adults don't pay close enough attention to children's concerns. One day, Treehorn notices that he is shorter than usual and can't reach his closet shelf anymore. He announces this amazing news to his mother, who barely listens. When she does notice and comments on it, Treehorn's father insists, "Nobody shrinks." And Treehorn's teacher comments, "I'll let it go for today, but see that it's taken care of before tomorrow. We don't shrink in this class." After pages of funny dialogue, Treehorn discovers why he is shrinking and solves that problem, only to develop a strange new symptom. Droll pictures by Edward Gorey are the perfect match for this irresistible tale. Followed by *Treehorn's Wish.*

Hooks, William H. *The Girl Who Could Fly.* **Illustrated by Kees de Kiefte. 1995. Hardcover: Macmillan. Ages 7–10.**

Ten-year-old Adam Lee knows there is something strange about the new girl in his building, Tomasina Jones. She can stop balls in midair, and makes maps of oceans with waves that really move. So Adam is not shocked to learn she can fly. He realizes that her magical powers could win his baseball team a championship, but she agrees only to coach them, for the sake of fairness. Disguised as a boy named Tom, she whips the team into shape and they beat their archrivals. But after the winning game, Tomasina has places to go that are not on the planet Earth. A lighthearted story of a friendly alien who makes a great baseball coach.

Howe, James. *Pinky and Rex.* **Illustrated by Melissa Sweet. 1990. Hardcover: Atheneum. Paperback: Avon. Ages 6–9.**

Five chapters introduce two best friends, a boy named Pinky and a girl named Rex. In the simple plot, the two, Pinky's younger sister, Amanda, and Pinky's father go to a local museum, where Pinky and Rex want to save the best— the dinosaur room—for last. Despite Amanda's loud protests, they get their way. But when all three want the same stuffed dinosaur at the gift shop, Amanda has a chance to get her way, too. Howe, who based the friendship on his own childhood, breaks stereotypes in a way that rings true as he develops the characters. An unusually attractive design and attractive color illustrations characterize this book and its many sequels.

Hurwitz, Joanna. *The Adventures of Ali Baba Bernstein.* **Illustrated by Gail Owens. 1985. Hardcover: Morrow. Paperback: Avon. Ages 7–10.**

As one of four Davids in his third-grade class, David Bernstein wants a more unusual name, which he finds while reading *The Arabian Nights*. Although he has a hard time convincing his parents and teacher to call him "Ali Baba," he persists. Oddly enough, as soon as he changes his name he finds a trunk in the apartment basement that appears to be full of jewels. One adventure follows another, concerning lost jewels, frogs, snails, and warts. In the final chapter, David concocts an original plan for his birthday party and realizes that his name offers more possibilities than he knew. Large print and amusing pictures add to the appeal of this book, the first in a series. Also try Hurwitz's series about Aldo Sossi, starting with *Much Ado about Aldo*.

Jukes, Mavis. *Like Jake and Me*. Illustrated by Lloyd Bloom. 1984. Paperback: Knopf. Ages 5–10.

Alex admires his strong, cowboylike stepfather, Jake, and wishes he could be more like him. Instead, Alex feels young, clumsy, and weak. So it is especially encouraging to learn that Jake is afraid of something Alex isn't afraid of: spiders. When a hairy wolf spider crawls onto Jake, it is up to Alex to calm Jake down and help him find the creature. In the end, Jake dances Alex around in an affectionate scene, with Alex's pregnant, pleased mother looking on. This is an outstanding story about a boy and his stepfather, beautifully written with warmth and humor, and aptly illustrated. A Newbery Honor Book.

Landon, Lucinda. *Meg Mackintosh and the Case of the Missing Babe Ruth Baseball*. 1986. Paperback: Secret Passage Press. Ages 7–10.

Aspiring detectives will get right into the spirit of this clever book as they search for clues in the black-and-white pictures on every page. When Meg's grandfather was a boy, his cousin planted the clues leading to a hidden baseball signed by Babe Ruth, but the grandfather never found it. Now detective Meg Mackintosh is hot on the trail, and hopes to beat her older brother, Pete, to the baseball. The clues, which aren't easy, include one in code, and others that require a knowledge of nursery rhymes. With large print, many pictures, and challenging clues, this is one in a very popular series.

Mahy, Margaret. *The Good Fortunes Gang.* **Illustrated by Marian Young. 1993. Hardcover: Delacorte. Ages 8–10.**

Ten-year-old Pete Fortune is worried about his family's move from Australia to New Zealand to live near his father's many relatives. What if the four cousins around his age don't like him? At first, his fears seem to have good cause, when the gangleader Tracey insists that Pete pass some tests. To Tracey's chagrin, Pete succeeds with the first test, singing old family songs. The next part is worse: spending the night in the family cemetery. Pete, who sometimes suffers from nightmares, gets up his nerve and has a wilder time than he expects. The first in a series of short novels about the Fortune cousins and their escapades.

Marshall, James. *Rats on the Roof and Other Stories.* **1991. Hardcover: Dial. Ages 3–8.**

This is the kind of simple chapter book that makes children want to keep reading. Comic pictures of animals in unlikely clothes and cozy homes add to the appeal of the seven stories about talking animals and their funny problems. In the title story, a dog couple has been kept awake at night by rats dancing on the roof, so they decide to get a cat. The dapper cat who answers their ad explains all his needs and promises to add grace and elegance to their home, but loses his cool when the dogs mention rats. Luckily, the uproar he creates drives the rats away. In other stories, small creatures defeat larger ones, such as birds who outwit a dinosaur, and mice who scare away a hungry cat. A surefire winner. Also enjoy *Rats on the Range and Other Stories.*

Osborne, Mary Pope. *Dinosaurs Before Dark*. 1992. Hardcover: Random House. Paperback: Random House. Ages 6–9.

When Jack's younger sister, Annie, climbs up to a mysterious new tree house, he objects but follows her. The tree house is filled with books, which is exciting to Jack, who loves to read, and he starts to browse through them. Looking at a dinosaur illustration, he says, "I wish I could see a pteranodon for real," and suddenly he does. The tree house spins around wildly and they land in the time of dinosaurs. The venturesome Annie makes friends with the pteranodon and a triceratops, but when tyrannosaurus rex comes along, they know they have to escape. Working together, the brother and sister figure out how to get home, but plan to go on more adventures. The first in the "Magic Tree House" series, this features short chapters, many illustrations, and an appealing theme.

Peterson, John. *The Littles*. Illustrated by Roberta Carter. 1967. Paperback: Scholastic. Ages 7–10.

The Littles, a family of tiny people with mouselike tails, live in the walls of the Biggs' house. They eat the Biggs' leftover dinner scraps, and in return keep the house's pipes and wires in good shape. All is well until the Biggs go away and rent their house to the Newcombs, who care nothing about cleaning or good cooking. In the ensuing mess, mice and then a cat arrive on the scene, and threaten the Littles. Young Lucy Little attacks a mouse to save her father, while her older brother, Tom, comes up with a plan to deal with the cat. While not in a league with Stuart Little (p. 225) or the King-Smith books (p. 222), this first book and its many sequels continue to be popular among younger readers.

Pinkwater, Daniel. *Wingman*. 1975. Paperback: Bantam. Ages 7–10.

As the only Chinese-American student in his New York City school, Donald Chen is lonely. When his insensitive teacher singles him out as poor, he quits going to school and spends his days on the George Washington Bridge, where he reads comic books, daydreams, and meets the magical Wingman, a flying hero clad in armor and feathers. Caught by a truant officer, Donald returns to school, where a new teacher encourages his love of drawing, and his comic books lead to new friends. Pinkwater's bold illustrations in comic-book style add the perfect touch. Anyone who has felt like an outsider will find this story comforting as well as entertaining.

Sachar, Louis. *Marvin Redpost: Kidnapped at Birth?* Illustrated by Neal Hughes. 1992. Hardcover: Random House. Paperback: Random House. Ages 6–10.

Could nine-year-old Marvin Redpost be a prince? When he learns that the king of Shampoon is looking for his blue-eyed, red-haired, nine-year-old son who was kidnapped at birth, Marvin believes that he must be the kidnapped prince, because the rest of his family has brown hair and brown eyes, while Marvin has red hair and blue eyes. His friends love the idea, and speculate that his parents could be kidnappers, a possibility that Marvin doesn't like. As he pursues the issue, Marvin realizes that he doesn't want to leave his family, even for a royal palace. An exaggerated story with a likable main character. The first in a series.

Schlein, Miriam. *The Year of the Panda*. Illustrated by Kam Mak. 1990. Hardcover: Thomas Y. Crowell. Ages 7–10.

Lu Yi, a Chinese farm boy, finds a baby panda near his mountainside home, just below the pandas' territory. When he finds it, Lu Yi knows he cannot keep it, but for a short time he enjoys nurturing the cuddly creature. Lu Yi receives a reward and gets to fly with Su Lin, as he has named the panda, to a rescue center. There the boy meets an American panda expert and learns more about the animals from her. When the time comes to say good-bye to Su Lin, Lu Yi knows he will come back someday to visit and learn more. This warm, simple story will appeal to all children who love animals or like reading about other countries.

Scieszka, Jon. *Knights of the Kitchen Table*. Illustrated by Lane Smith. 1991. Hardcover: Viking. Paperback: Puffin. Ages 7–11.

This lively book combines elements to attract even reluctant readers: adventure, magic, slapstick humor, and zany illustrations. The narrator, Joe, is celebrating his birthday with his pals Fred and Sam when Fred opens a book from Joe's magician uncle. When he wishes they could see knights, the three are suddenly transported back to the time of King Arthur, where a huge Black Knight is about to attack them. By luck, they defeat him, then face a challenge at King Arthur's court to fight a giant and dragon. Sam comes up with a clever solution, after which they stumble into a way to get home. Funny dialogue, with "gross" descriptions of the giant, will have readers laughing their way through this first entry in "The Time Warp Trio" series, which includes *The Not-So-Jolly Roger*, *The Good, the Bad, and the Goofy*, and others.

Sherman, Charlotte Watson. *Eli and the Swamp Man*. Illustrated by James Ransome. 1996. Hardcover: Harper. Ages 7–9.

Eli misses his father, who left after his parents' divorce three years earlier, and he won't accept his stepfather, Ari.

Now Ari wants to take Eli, his older sister, and their mother to New Orleans for Mardi Gras. Instead, Eli secretly decides to bicycle from Seattle to Alaska to see his father. Early in his journey, Eli has to pass through a swamp, where the Swamp Man lives. Scared, Eli crashes his bike before the Swamp Man even appears, and when he does, Eli learns that people are not always what they seem. By the end of his time with the wise Swamp Man, the boy decides to give his family another try. A sympathetic portrayal of an African-American boy struggling with family changes.

Skurzynski, Gloria. *The Minstrel in the Tower*. Illustrated by Julek Heller. 1988. Hardcover: Random House. Ages 7–10.

Set in France, this historical adventure concerns Roger, an eleven-year-old boy, and his younger sister, Alice. Their father never returned from the Crusades and their mother appears to be dying. She feverishly tells them to seek out an uncle they know nothing about and ask him to come quickly to her side. During the three-day journey, Roger sings for their meals while Alice climbs trees to fetch fruit and scout the land ahead. Stopping to look at a deserted tower, the two are captured by some ruffians and must devise a way to escape. Their persistence and courage lead to a happy ending. Occasional black-and-white pictures show the medieval setting of this adventure.

Smith, Doris Buchanan. *A Taste of Blackberries*. Illustrated by Charles Robinson. 1973. Paperback: Scholastic. Ages 8–11.

Jamie has been the narrator's best friend forever. He can be annoying, the way he exaggerates everything, but he's usually a great companion. So the day Jamie gets stung by a bee and makes a big fuss, the narrator isn't worried—until the ambulance comes. Even then, the boy telling the story is completely unprepared when his mother tells him that Jamie has died from an allergic reaction. Slowly, with the help of his loving parents, he comes to terms with the death, without forgetting his friendship and how much they shared. A thoughtful, gentle novel about death that will interest curious readers and comfort those who have experienced the death of a friend.

Stolz, Mary. *Go Fish*. Illustrated by Pat Cummings. 1991. Hardcover: Harper. Ages 5–9.
The graceful way that illustrations are integrated into the text makes this book a visual standout. The story about a boy and his grandfather, told in six chapters, also rises above other transitional novels in its writing and mood. Thomas lives with his grandfather in Florida, where they read, fish, cook, play cards, and talk together. After a day of slow but satisfying fishing, Grandfather tells Thomas a story about their Yoruba ancestors, and Thomas thinks about the time to come when he will be a grandfather, telling stories to his grandchildren. A sense of love and understanding pervades the book, but it also has jokes and fishing lore to balance the quieter moments. Highly recommended. Preceded by the picture book *Storm in the Night* and followed by the more advanced novel, *Stealing Home*.

Waggoner, Karen. *Partners*. Illustrated by Cat Bowman Smith. 1995. Hardcover: Simon & Schuster. Ages 6–9.
Jamie loves his new mice, which he bought with his older brother, Gordon. He names them and gives them treats, and they become his friends. Gordon seems to look on the mice as something that will make them money, although Jamie isn't

sure how. When he realizes that Gordon plans to feed the mice's babies to snakes, Jamie has to think fast to change his brother's mind. Surprisingly, his new friendship with a girl at school and the math problem they have to devise together lead to a happy ending for Jamie and the mice. The siblings, including a teenage sister, disagree and even bicker, but it's clear that they care about each other in ways that matter. Light entertainment with a likable young hero and a plug for math.

Walter, Mildred Pitts. *Justin and the Best Biscuits in the World.* **Illustrated by Catherine Stock. 1986. Hardcover: Lothrop. Paperback: Knopf. Ages 7–10.**

Justin would rather be playing basketball than doing his chores, which he isn't good at, as his older sister, Evelyn, constantly reminds him. Whenever he makes his bed, it looks lumpy. When he washes dishes, soapsuds get everywhere. But a trip to his grandfather's ranch turns Justin's view of housework around. His cowboy grandfather cooks and cleans, and takes time to show Justin how to do things right and to bake great biscuits. He also tells Justin stories about black pioneers and cowboys, and takes him to a rodeo. Back home, Justin shows off his new skills by making dinner for his mother and sisters. Although longer than most books in this category, large print and pencil sketches help make this fine story accessible to younger readers.

Biographies

Adler, David. *Lou Gehrig: The Luckiest Man.* Illustrated by Terry Widener. 1997. Hardcover: Harcourt. Ages 5–8.

Yankee baseball legend Lou Gehrig never missed a game in fourteen years as first baseman. And before that, he never missed a day of grade school. Although his German immigrant mother wanted him to stay in school, he left college in 1925 to play for the New York Yankees. Rounded, dramatic paintings with an old-fashioned air show Gehrig on the field with his fellow Yankees, including Babe Ruth. When he was thirty-five, Gehrig learned he had a disease called amyotrophic lateral sclerosis, which killed him two years later. But in the intervening two years, his fellow players and Yankee fans expressed their love and admiration for Gehrig, who spoke about how lucky he felt, even with his "bad break." Well written, with striking illustrations, this is a moving tribute to a man and a sport.

Blos, Joan W. *Nellie Bly's Monkey: His Remarkable Story in His Own Words.* Illustrated by Catherine Stock. 1996. Hardcover: Morrow. Ages 5–9.

In this fictionalized biography, a monkey narrates the story of his journey with journalist and adventurer Nellie Bly, who traveled around the world in seventy-two days. In 1899, Bly left New York City and headed east. She acquired the monkey in Singapore, naming him McGinty, and they traveled together by ship and train through Asia, then across the United States. Each double-page spread features a watercolor-and-ink illustration of their escapades. Greeted everywhere by huge crowds, the journalist and her pet finally made it to New York City, where Bly went back to her job as a writer and McGinty found a home at the New York Menagerie. A note at the end, labeled "For Those Who Wish to Know More," gives details about Bly. An exciting glimpse of the world at the turn of the century.

Coles, Robert. *The Story of Ruby Bridges.* **Illustrated by George Ford. 1995. Hardcover: Scholastic. Ages 5–9.**

Six-year-old Ruby Bridges showed extraordinary courage as the first African American to integrate a New Orleans elementary school, in 1960. Guarded by armed federal marshals, she walked with dignity past hate-filled crowds on her way to the first-grade classroom. There she and her teacher worked alone, because white parents refused to send their children to an integrated school. Ruby drew strength from her religious beliefs; the final scene shows her praying to God to forgive the angry mob. An afterword relates that white children eventually returned to the classroom, and by second grade, Ruby no longer had to face the mobs. Large illustrations enhance this inspiring, powerful introduction to the struggle for civil rights.

Cooper, Floyd. *Mandela: From the Life of the South African Statesman.* **1996. Hardcover: Philomel. Ages 6–10.**

This fully illustrated biography conveys Nelson Mandela's life from childhood through his election as president of South Africa, emphasizing his commitment to standing up for what he believes. Soft evocative paintings show him moving from his small village to a larger one and finally to a city where he continued his education. Details about his adult life include information about his family and his increasingly important work as a political leader, which led to his lengthy imprisonment but ultimately resulted in great gains for his people. The illustrations outshine the text in this story about a great modern statesman.

Downing, Julie. *Mozart Tonight*. 1991. Hardcover: Bradbury. Paperback: Simon & Schuster. Ages 6–9.

This book, beautifully illustrated with watercolors, provides a good introduction to the renowned composer. Told largely in Mozart's voice, the narrative describes his early talent and the concert tours he took as a child to perform with his sister. Using dialogue to make the scenes more immediate, the story moves on to his clashes with patrons, his money problems, and his joy in composing. It culminates in the successful debut of *Don Giovanni*, and closes with a picture of Mozart taking his bow before a cheering audience. An author's note adds information about this elegant picture-book biography.

Fradin, Dennis Brindell. *Hiawatha, Messenger of Peace*. 1992. Hardcover: McElderry/Macmillan. Ages 7–10.

Hiawatha was a leader who strove to unite the five tribes of the Iroquois. The incorrect version of Hiawatha's life popularized by Longfellow is widely known. This short biography, illustrated with photographs, prints, and paintings, draws from oral tradition and historical fact to offer a more accurate version. When Hiawatha's wife and daughter were killed by a man named Ododarhoh, Hiawatha broke tradition by not avenging their deaths. Instead he became a hermit, then joined forces with a member of the Huron tribe known as the Peacemaker. The two introduced the concept of a federation of tribes, with representatives and a constitution, ideas that influenced the formation of the U.S. government. A useful introduction to an influential Native American.

Fritz, Jean. *What's the Big Idea, Ben Franklin?* **Illustrated by Margot Tomes. 1976. Hardcover: Putnam. Paperback: Putnam. Ages 7–10.**

Detail after interesting detail about Benjamin Franklin, his life and his accomplishments, fills this short biography. When he served as a diplomat in France, the French "hung his picture over their mantels and wore his picture in their rings," he was so popular. The lively accumulation of details and facts provides a strong introduction to the life of a man who excelled as statesman, inventor, scientist, and more. Expressive illustrations with a suitable homespun flavor add information and humor.

Giblin, James Cross. *Thomas Jefferson: A Picture Book Biography.* **Illustrated by Michael Dooling. 1994. Hardcover: Scholastic. Ages 7–10.**

Dramatic oil paintings cover each double-page spread of this picture-book biography about Thomas Jefferson. Anecdotes and interesting details are woven into the factual chronology that includes the main points of his career and personal life. For example, in describing Jefferson's presidency, the biographer explains his role in purchasing the Louisiana Territory, but also mentions the pet mockingbird he let fly in his study. Jefferson's ambiguity about slavery is discussed briefly, but this account concentrates mainly on his extensive public accomplishments. The large paintings, with a range of moods, give depth to his character and a flavor of the times.

Golenbock, Peter. *Teammates.* **Illustrated by Paul Bacon. 1990. Hardcover: Harcourt. Paperback: Harcourt. Ages 5–9.**

This short informational picture book introduces Jackie Robinson and sets his history-making career in the context of segregated America. A photograph shows a smiling Jackie Robinson with Dodgers manager Branch Rickey, who hired Robinson as the first black in the major leagues, but a painting of Robinson in the dugout, where no teammate would sit near him, brings home some of the pain he suffered. He was helped in his struggle by Pee Wee Reese, the Dodger shortstop who refused to sign a petition to throw Robinson off the team. Instead, at a game where the crowd was taunting Robinson, Reese expressed his support by putting his arm around Robinson's shoulder. A look for young children at segregation and the courage it took to overcome it.

Horenstein, Henry. *My Mom's a Vet*. 1994. Hardcover: Candlewick. Paperback: Candlewick. Ages 5–10.

The veterinarian in this lively photo-essay treats large farm animals such as horses and cows. Clear color photographs show the vet and her daughter, Darcie, who accompanies her mother on her rounds for a week. Darcie holds the tail while her mother and a farmer help a cow deliver her first calf, and watches her mother X-ray a horse's ankle. The photos show the graphic details when the vet dehorns a goat using a hot iron, and when she performs surgery on a cow with a twisted stomach. Children who dream of becoming a vet will get a realistic glimpse of the work, with its ups and downs, while anyone who likes animals will also enjoy this week with a farm vet.

Kunhardt, Edith. *Honest Abe*. Illustrated by Malcah Zeldis. 1993. Hardcover: Greenwillow. Ages 5–9.

In bright yellows, reds, and blues, large paintings on every page dominate this short biography of Abraham Lincoln, sixteenth president of the United States. The folk-art style, with its stiff, out-of-proportion figures and whimsical use of color, has a homespun feel suited to its subject. Children will enjoy the blue horse with a red mane that Lincoln rides on his rounds as a lawyer, and the many other strangely colored animals. The simple text supplies facts about Lincoln from his childhood to his funeral, with an emphasis on his younger years. The words of the Gettysburg Address and a timeline of Lincoln's life appear on the last two pages. A memorable biography for younger children.

Lomas Garza, Carmen, as told to Harriet Rohmer. *Family Pictures/Cuadros de Familia.* **Translated by Rosalma Zubizarreta. 1990. Hardcover: Children's Book Press. Paperback: Children's Book Press. Ages 7–9.**

Lomas Garza recaptures her Texas childhood in vivid folk-art paintings, accompanied by descriptions in both English and Spanish. Each double-page spread features a detailed painting full of people, bright colors, and intriguing activities, many with a Mexican flavor. One picture shows her many friends and relatives outdoors, watching the painter as a blindfolded child hitting a piñata. In another scene the family has gone to Padre Island in the Gulf of Mexico, where they encounter a fisherman and the huge, bloody shark he has caught. The striking mixed-media paintings transport the reader into the past, to an evocative time and place.

Miller, Robert H. *The Story of "Stagecoach" Mary Fields.* **Illustrated by Cheryl Hanna. 1995. Hardcover: Silver Press. Paperback: Silver Press. Ages 4–8.**

"Stagecoach" Mary Fields, the second woman to deliver the U.S. mail, did her job driving a stagecoach, with her six-shooter ready to protect the mail and herself from bandits. She sometimes fought off wolves on her route, but more often faced blowing snow and treacherous roads. Born a slave in

Tennessee around 1812, Fields moved to Montana sometime after the Civil War, where she spent eight years delivering the mail, then opened up her own laundry. Large colored-pencil drawings on each page portray this unusual woman in action.

Patterson, Francine. *Koko's Story*. Photographs by Dr. Ronald H. Cohn. 1987. Paperback: Scholastic. Ages 7–10.
Who would think that a gorilla could learn sign language? In 1972, Dr. Francine Patterson began to work with a one-year-old female gorilla named Koko to teach her American Sign Language (ASL). Anecdotes and color photographs convey how Koko learned to sign, and show the reader how she can tell jokes and even lie in sign language. The photographs illustrate a typical day in Koko's life: playing with her pet kittens, interacting with Patterson, and brushing her teeth. This fascinating account may inspire young readers to consider a career in studying animals. Another book about these two is *Koko's Kitten*.

Pinkney, Andrea Davis. *Alvin Ailey*. Illustrated by Brian Pinkney. 1993. Hardcover: Hyperion. Ages 6–9.
Flowing paintings convey the spirit of modern dance in this short, highly illustrated biography of dancer and choreographer Alvin Ailey. With a good sense of what interests children, the biography describes significant incidents from Ailey's younger years, and concludes in 1960 with his groundbreaking dances "Blues Suite" and "Revelations." The text stresses how Ailey drew from his own background and African-American tradition to create a new approach to modern dance. An afterword gives more information about his life, success, and influence. An excellent combination of picture and text, this biography evokes an excitement about dance and one of its great artists.

Pinkney, Andrea D. *Bill Pickett: Rodeo-Ridin' Cowboy.* **Illustrated by Brian Pinkney. 1996. Ages 5–9.**

This picture-book biography tells the remarkable story of an African-American cowboy who became famous for his rodeo skills. Bill Pickett, son of a former slave, grew up in Texas in the late 1800s and was fascinated with cowboys. As a boy, he came up with the idea of "bulldogging" cattle by biting their upper lips to subdue them. At fifteen, he left home and fulfilled his dream of becoming a cowboy. His increasing skill with cattle and his famous "bulldogging" earned him a place in the rodeo circuit; he later joined a show that took him as a star attraction to Europe, Canada, and South America. The energetic artwork suits this action-packed story.

Pinkney, Andrea Davis. *Dear Benjamin Banneker.* **Illustrated by Brian Pinkney. 1994. Hardcover: Harcourt. Ages 5–9.**

Evocative pictures and a well-written narrative describe this impressive man, considered by some to be America's first black scientist. Born in 1731, Banneker was raised on his parents' tobacco farm in Maryland and as an adult worked for years as a tobacco farmer. He learned mathematics and astronomy on his own, and dedicated himself to writing an almanac, a reference book popular in colonial times. Banneker wanted to prove that a black man could write an accurate almanac, and he was highly successful in his venture. Banneker also wrote a letter, which is quoted, to Secretary of State Thomas Jefferson to protest slavery and received a respectful response. A good introduction to an important historical figure.

Provensen, Alice, and Martin Provensen. *The Glorious Flight: Across the Channel with Louis Blériot.* 1983. Hardcover: Viking. Paperback: Puffin. Ages 5–9.

Witty paintings detail the story of Louis Blériot, the first person to fly across the English Channel. The text, which reads like a story, opens with the Frenchman and his family on an outing in their car. When the future aviator sees an airship in the sky, he resolves to build his own flying machine, which is shown on its first unsuccessful flight over a river. One machine after another is built and tested, until Blériot enters the big contest to cross the Channel in 1909. His glorious flight takes him through fog from France to the cliffs of Dover. The outstanding illustrations with their folk-art style enrich this story about early aviation. Winner of the Caldecott Medal.

Say, Allen. *El Chino.* 1990. Hardcover: Houghton. Paperback: Houghton. Ages 6–10.

This exquisitely illustrated biography resembles a photograph album, with watercolors framed on the pages like family pictures. The story of Billy Wong, the first Chinese bullfighter, starts with a picture of his parents, who emigrated from China to the United States, where "you can be anything you want to be." Billy doesn't have the height to be a basketball player, which is his dream, so he becomes an engineer. But on a vacation to Spain, he finds a new dream: to be a bullfighter. He succeeds, sacrificing everything to become "El Chino," the Spaniards' name for him that means "The Chinese." Stunning pictures enhance the concise text in this inspiring picturebook biography.

Scioscia, Mary. *Bicycle Rider.* Illustrated by Ed Young. 1983. Paperback: Harper. Ages 7–9.

An African-American man named Marshall Taylor, who

grew up in Indianapolis, was the fastest bicycle rider in the world around the turn of the century. In five short chapters, this fictionalized biography describes his first two bicycle races. When young Marshall stops in front of a bicycle shop to show his brother bicycle tricks like pedaling with his hands, he impresses the shop owner enough to land a job. Marshall goes to bicycle races one Saturday with the owner, who decides at the last minute that Marshall should race, representing the store. Thrilled, Marshall rides in the one-mile race and comes in seventh. He enters the ten-mile race and, to his own astonishment, wins. Well written, with lots of dialogue, this tribute to a remarkable athlete is accompanied by evocative pencil illustrations.

Sis, Peter. *Starry Messenger*. 1996. Hardcover: FSG. Ages 7–12.

Creative, original illustrations characterize this slim picture-book biography of Galileo, which briefly describes his work and the challenges he faced. The intricate, large-format pictures fill most of the page and are accompanied by a paragraph of text in large type and quotes from Galileo in tight, artistically arranged handwriting. The overall impression is of a book made long ago, with maps that even show sea monsters. Young readers will be able to read the larger typeface and absorb the enchantment of the pictures, while older readers will find the handwritten parts accessible. In either case, this is a magical introduction to one of the world's great thinkers. A Caldecott Honor Book.

Spivak, Dawnine. *Grass Sandals: The Travels of Basho*. Illustrated by Demi. 1997. Hardcover: Atheneum. Ages 5–8.

Matsuo Basho, one of Japan's most honored poets, traveled around seventeenth-century Japan, noting his observations in prose and in the poetry form haiku. This attractive book combines the story of his travels with delicate illustrations, examples of his haiku, and Japanese brushstroke characters that relate to the text. The book conveys Basho's appreciation of nature and the delight he took in small things such as morning glories and dyed-blue shoelaces. It presents a life of simplicity that is rich in meaning and friendship. A graceful portrait of an inspiring man.

Stevenson, James. *When I Was Nine*. 1986. Hardcover: Greenwillow. Ages 5–9.

James Stevenson, who is a genius with watercolors and a talented writer, uses both skills to describe the year he was nine, choosing incidents and objects that will capture a child's interest. The time is the late thirties, so he listens to the radio instead of watching television, and his father has boots and a bugle from serving in World War I. But many other details are timeless: climbing trees, fighting with his older brother, and sliding down a waterfall. Warmth and humor fill the pictures and writing, which are simple but remarkably effective. Don't miss this wonderful picture-book autobiography and its several sequels.

Towle, Wendy. *The Real McCoy: The Life of an African-American Inventor*. Illustrated by Wil Clay. 1993. Paperback: Scholastic. Ages 6–10.

Elijah McCoy patented more than fifty inventions in his lifetime, including a train oil cup referred to as "the real McCoy." Born in Canada in 1844, McCoy was supported in his mechanical interests by his parents, former slaves, who sent him to Scotland to study engineering. When he finished his training and moved to the United States, he could find work only as a fireman and oilman for a railroad. This led to his invention of an oil cup, which improved train efficiency and became a standard device. He designed, among other things, a portable ironing board, a lawn sprinkler, and a lubricator for new locomotives. He was influential in his Detroit community, and variations on his inventions are used today. Richly colored illustrations enhance the story about this talented inventor.

Venezia, Mike. *Paul Klee.* **1991. Hardcover: Children's Press. Paperback: Children's Press. Ages 6–9.**

This slim volume uses large print, color reproductions of paintings, and humorous cartoons to introduce children to the life and work of Paul Klee. After a brief description of Klee's art, the text gives a few facts about his childhood and education. His work is placed in the context of the time and of some of his fellow artists. Large and small reproductions show the range of his styles, while commentary in the text helps readers appreciate the pictures. One in an appealing series called Getting to Know the World's Greatest Artists, which combines information and humor to introduce important painters.

Wallner, Alexandra. *Beatrix Potter.* **1995. Hardcover: Holiday House. Ages 5–9.**

Children who know Peter Rabbit and Squirrel Nutkin will enjoy reading about their creator, Beatrix Potter, who grew up in Victorian England. Isolated by her strict upbringing, Potter filled her life with art and animals, and turned her energies to writing and illustrating small books for children. She had her first book, *The Tale of Peter Rabbit*, printed herself when publishers turned it down. Thanks to the financial success of her books, she fulfilled her dream of buying a farm and stocking it with many animals. Ornate illustrations complement the short text and supply details about Potter and her animals.

Wisniewski, David. *Sundiata: Lion King of Mali.* 1992. Hardcover: Clarion. Ages 6–10.

Extraordinary cut-paper artwork dominates this picture-book biography about the legendary leader Sundiata. Well-honed writing tells the story, passed down through oral tradition, of Sundiata, the son and chosen heir of a powerful king of Mali. Born to a hunchbacked mother who was said to possess the spirit of a buffalo, Sundiata overcame his inability to talk and walk. Forced into exile when his father died, he traveled extensively until he was ready to gather an army and claim his kingdom. A note gives more details about Mali and Sundiata, and information about the illustrations. Readers will be drawn to this story of courage by the glorious cover illustration of Sundiata on his charging horse.

Nonfiction

History

Guiberson, Brenda Z. *Lighthouses: Watchers at Sea.* **1995. Hardcover: Henry Holt. Ages 7–10.**

Black-and-white photographs, drawings, diagrams, anecdotes, and facts are brought together in this entertaining history of lighthouses. Navigation was a tricky business in the past, particularly during storms and at night. Lighthouses saved thousands of lives, while lighthouse keepers sometimes lost their own lives rescuing others. One of the five chapters looks at the enemies of lighthouses, including thieves who thrived on shipwrecks, and wartime enemies who benefited from darkened lighthouses. The final chapter explains that many lighthouses and all but one lighthouse keeper have been replaced by advances in technology. A fascinating history, made accessible to younger readers by its large print and many illustrations.

Kroll, Steven. *Pony Express!* **Illustrated by Dan Andreasen. 1996. Hardcover: Scholastic. Ages 6–9.**

For an enterprise that lasted only eighteen months, the Pony Express has made a strong impact on the imagination of Americans. This large, heavily illustrated book tells the story of the first Pony Express riders, who headed east from California and west from Missouri in April 1860. Each passed the mail to the next rider in the chain. Despite the hardships detailed in the text and pictures, the mail got through in ten days, a tribute to excellent planning and stalwart riders.

Appendices tell more about the Pony Express and the U.S. mail. The lively paintings, surrounded by a wood-grain border, show rider after rider on his way across the country.

Maestro, Betsy, and Giulio Maestro. *The Discovery of the Americas.* **1991. Hardcover: Lothrop. Ages 7–10.**

This slim book offers a balanced history of the peoples and explorers who came to the Americas before and after Columbus. It begins with the last Ice Age, when a migration started across a landmass that connected Asia and North America. The concise text discusses the civilizations that developed in the Americas, then turns to European explorers, including Leif Eriksson, Columbus, Cabot, Balboa, and Magellan. The authors note that explorers often mistreated native people, bringing hardship, disease, and death. Sweeping illustrations show the Americas and the relevant ocean voyages. Maps and appendices add to the information. An excellent beginning history of the Americas.

Waters, Kate. *Samuel Eaton's Day: A Day in the Life of a Pilgrim Boy.* **Photographs by Russ Kendall. 1993. Hardcover: Scholastic. Paperback: Scholastic. Ages 7–10.**

For those who have a hard time picturing colonial America, a visit to the "living history museum" at Plimouth Plantation in Massachusetts can bring the past to life. This photo-essay follows a boy through his day at the Plantation as if it were a day in July of 1627. He plays the role of a real boy, Samuel Eaton, who sailed on the *Mayflower*, and lived with his father, stepmother, and little half-sister. Color photographs show Samuel getting dressed in his seventeenth-century garb, fetching water, checking his snares, gathering firewood, and helping with the harvest. By the day's end, he is tired but proud of his work. A vivid introduction to colonial life.

Nature and Science

Ardley, Neil. *The Science Book of Electricity.* **1991. Hardcover: Harcourt. Ages 6–10.**

In this well-designed book, thirteen experiments are explained in numbered steps, with excellent photographs of each step. A red warning sign notes the few tasks that require adult supervision, such as pushing a nail through cardboard. The materials needed, many of them household items, are shown at the outset of each experiment in labeled photographs. The experiments range from rubbing a balloon on a sweater to explore static electricity to making a simple electric circuit using a battery, which leads to more complicated projects. An excellent hands-on introduction to simple principles of electricity. Other books in the series focus on magnets, water, and how things grow.

Cole, Joanna. *The Magic School Bus at the Waterworks.* **Illustrated by Bruce Degen. 1986. Hardcover: Scholastic. Paperback: Scholastic. Ages 3–8.**

Ms. Frizzle, "the strangest teacher in school," gets readers enthusiastic about science through her magical outings. Her students, who have put in a month of research, embark on a most unusual field trip in an old bus driven by Ms. Friz. Soon the children find themselves clad in scuba gear on a cloud where they shrink to a tiny size, fall as rain, swim to a reservoir, and start their journey through the city water-purification system. Each brightly illustrated page incorporates facts and splashes of humor. Notes at the end separate the real from the imaginary, "for students who do not like any kidding around when it comes to science facts." This outstanding, popular series explores other topics, including volcanoes, the human body, and the solar system.

Duke, Kate. *Archaeologists Dig for Clues*. 1997. Hardcover: Harper. Paperback: Harper. Ages 5–9.

Two boys and a girl accompany an archaeologist named Sophie to her local dig. At first the children are disappointed that the dig looks like a hole in the ground and that they won't be excavating anything exotic. But as the day goes on, they get drawn into the digging process, and the discovery of an Archaic awl, a needle without a hole used for sewing, thrills them. Upbeat pictures, diagrams, and sidebars deliver lots of interesting information. This is one of the high-quality Let's-Read-and-Find-Out Science series.

Jenkins, Steve. *Biggest, Strongest, Fastest*. 1995. Hardcover: Ticknor & Fields. Paperback: Houghton. Ages 3–8.

Striking collage illustrations are the highlight of this informational book. Each double-page spread shows a noteworthy animal, which is the strongest, smallest, longest, fastest, or another superlative. The animals are described in one short sentence using large typeface, such as "The Etruscan shrew, the world's smallest mammal, could sleep in a teaspoon." A few sentences in smaller print add information: "From the tip of its nose to the end of its tail, this shrew is only $2^1/_2$ inches long. It weighs about as much as a Ping-Pong ball." Apt comparisons such as these make the information easy for children to absorb, while the pictures will delight their eyes. Good for reading aloud to preschoolers, but also accessible to beginning readers, this is outstanding nonfiction.

Lavies, Bianca. *A Gathering of Garter Snakes*. 1993. Hardcover: Dutton. Ages 7–10.

Stunning photographs follow the life cycle of red-sided garter snakes in Manitoba, Canada, where thousands winter in limestone caverns and migrate ten miles in the spring. Piles of snakes swarm out of the cavern, then mate before continuing their journey. On their trip to local marshes, which takes them through a small town, they get into people's houses. An amusing photograph shows a woman chopping onions and smiling at a snake stretched out on her counter, while more graphic photos show a snake eating a frog still visible in its mouth and a snake giving birth, expelling a bloody sac along with the baby snakes. The large, well-focused photographs and the straightforward, informative text are a combination likely to appeal to many children.

Martin, James. *Chameleons: Dragons in the Trees*. Photographs by Art Wolfe. 1991. Hardcover: Crown. Ages 7–10.

No one could read this top-notch book and not become interested in chameleons. Vivid color photographs show different types of chameleons, their habits, habitats, and various features. A remarkable series of photographs illustrates how the chameleon uses its tongue, which can extend farther than the length of its entire body. Other shots demonstrate its ability to shift colors in order to communicate with other chameleons. The well-organized text uses crisp language and apt examples to make its information easy to understand. An exceptionally good introduction to an amazing creature. Look for other books by Martin such as *Tentacles: The Amazing World of Octopus, Squid, and Their Relatives* and *Hiding Out: Camouflage in the Wilderness*.

Simon, Seymour. *Our Solar System*. 1992. Hardcover: Morrow. Ages 8–12.

"Think of this: If Earth were the size of a basketball, the sun would be a giant globe as big as a basketball court." Such effective images are used to make scientific facts come alive for the reader in this basic book about our solar system. The well-written, informative text is complemented by excellent photographs from NASA. Readers will feel the excitement of space exploration as they learn about the sun, the planets, comets, and meteoroids. Many will want to read Simon's similarly excellent books about each planet, the sun, the moon, and the stars.

Trucks, Planes, and Other Technology

Gibbons, Gail. *How a House Is Built*. 1990. Hardcover: Holiday House. Ages 3–8.

How is a wood-frame house built? This simple text with its cheerful pictures follows the steps from an architect drawing plans through a family moving in. A double-page spread shows the dozens of people who will work on the house, such as heavy-equipment operators, well drillers, carpenters, plumbers, masons, and more—including a number of women. In the drawings, the names of machines, parts of the house, and materials are labeled, while some pages are split into panels to show several stages of an operation such as laying the foundation. Like Gibbons's many other books, this is easy to understand and full of information that interests younger children. Look for her books on airplanes, filling stations, and sunken treasures, among others.

Kuklin, Susan. *Fighting Fires*. 1993. Hardcover: Bradbury. Ages 3–8.

Colorful photographs introduce a company of firefighters and show them at work. Each member's job is pictured and explained, with new words highlighted and defined. Although the terms refer to "men" such as "roof man" by tradition, some of the firefighters in this company are women. Readers learn about the clothing the firefighters wear to protect themselves, and the different parts of fire trucks. A final page gives fire-prevention tips and advice on what to do in case of a fire. An attractive volume by a well-respected author/photographer, this is certain to appeal to many children.

Marston, Hope Irvin. *Big Rigs*. 1993 revised and updated. Hardcover: Cobblehill. Ages 3–8.

For the child who likes large vehicles, this book is a treat. Each page has a vivid photograph of a large truck known as a big rig. These eighteen-wheelers usually consist of a tractor, which holds the engine and the cab, and a trailer where the load is carried, although some have two or even three trailers. The photographs show many different types of big rigs, while the simple text supplies their nicknames, functions, and other information. A final series of photographs show specific companies' rigs and emblems, such as Freightliner, Oshkosh, and seven others. An appendix supplies CB terms that truckers use. Great fun for truck enthusiasts.

Pallotta, Jerry, and Fred Stillwell. *The Airplane Alphabet Book*. Illustrated by Rob Bolster. 1997. Hardcover: Charlesbridge. Ages 3–8.

Future fliers will gravitate toward this alphabet book that describes a variety of planes. From "A" for Aviation Trainer Six, or AT-6, to "Z" for Zero, the nickname for a Mitsubishi

A6M fighter plane, each page shows an aircraft and describes it in a short paragraph or two. They range historically from the Wright Flyer to the modern Ultralight, and in size from bombers to small personal planes like the Piper Cub. Since it is organized alphabetically, the book doesn't follow a historical sequence, and the brief information may raise questions that require further research. Nevertheless, this has high child appeal, especially for children who care more about information than stories.

Hobbies and Sports

Brooks, Bruce. NBA *by the Numbers*. Photographs from the National Basketball Association. 1997. Hardcover: Scholastic. Ages 5–10.

Excellent color photographs of current NBA players in action, with a few black-and-white shots of former players, will make this popular with pro basketball followers. Each double-page spread features a number, starting with "1 Alert Dribbler," which has a photo of Scottie Pippin and a paragraph of conversational text about the importance of dribbling. Two photographs show "Tricky Passers," three show "Smart Layups," and so on, to the final spread—of the NBA's fifty greatest players of all time. On most pages, the players aren't named in captions, but they are listed on the book's last page, for those who want to test their knowledge. A snappy celebration of a popular professional sport.

Hall, Katy, and Lisa Eisenberg. *Grizzly Riddles*. Illustrated by Nicole Rubel. 1989. Hardcover: Dial. Paperback: Puffin. Ages 5–8.

"Why do grizzlies have such sticky hair? They use honeycombs." So goes one of the characteristic riddles in this book designed for beginning readers. The accompanying picture, which provides clues to the riddle's answer, shows a bear using a honey-colored comb, with frowning bees flying around the bear's head. All the riddles have a similar format, with one joke and a silly but informative color illustration per page. The riddles rely on wordplay and standard joke formats, with many puns based on the word "bear." For children who enjoy stumping others with riddles, this will supply them with an easy-to-read repertoire. Look for similar books, such as *Fishy Riddles* and *Buggy Riddles*.

Katzen, Mollie, and Ann Henderson. *Pretend Soup and Other Real Recipes*. Illustrated by Mollie Katzen. 1994. Hardcover: Tricycle. Ages 3–9.

The author of the *Moosewood Cookbook* joined forces with a preschool teacher to produce this wonderful cookbook for children. Nineteen recipes range from quesadillas to blueberry pancakes, noodle pudding to chocolate-banana shakes. Each recipe has advice "To the Grown-ups," cooking hints, a list of tools, the directions, and a double-page spread that illustrates each step. Most require adult supervision, unless the child is old enough to use a knife and stove. The authors do a good job, too, of explaining how cooking benefits children by developing early math skills in measuring and counting, small motor skills, practice in following directions, and much more. Beautifully illustrated, this stands out among cookbooks for the younger set.

Petersen-Fleming, Judy, and Bill Fleming. *Kitten Training and Critters, Too!* Photographs by Darryl Bush. 1996. Hardcover: Tambourine. Ages 6–10.

This useful photo-essay offers simple ways to train kittens, while it shows professional animal trainers working with various animals. Each double-page spread has advice for young owners on the left-hand page and pictures of people training exotic animals on the right. The instructions, accompanied by clear photographs, tell the reader how to approach training and use specific commands such as "No" and "Come." On each page a short paragraph adds an interesting piece of information, such as "An alligator grows teeth continually throughout its life." Photographs show male and female kitten owners and animal trainers, and refer to the animals as male and female. A wonderful beginning guide to kitten training. See the authors' books on puppy training, and kitten and puppy care.

Rosenthal, Bert. *Soccer*. 1995 revised edition. Hardcover: Children's Press. Ages 5–8.

Large print, simple sentences, and lots of color photographs make this brief book on soccer good for young readers. Although it doesn't teach techniques, the short book provides a solid overview of how soccer is played, who plays it, and what the rules are. It describes the field, equipment, players' roles, officials, and fouls. Two pages list famous professional players, with photographs of a few, including Pelé. A glossary and index add to the book's usefulness. Children new to the sport will enjoy this entry in New True Books, a series geared to younger readers about many topics.

Sirett, Dawn. *My First Paint Book*. 1994. Hardcover: Dorling Kindersley. Ages 5–9.

This thin, oversized book features life-size photographs of the components for twelve art projects. It teaches readers to decorate gift bags and a stenciled box, paint T-shirts, make and paint papier-mâché pins, and more. Each activity starts with labeled pictures of the materials and a checklist of equipment, followed by step-by-step instructions illustrated in small boxed photographs. Although children will probably not produce results as polished as the ones shown, they will enjoy the process and be able to give the artwork as presents. Other books with the same eye-catching format include *My First Science Book*, *My First Nature Book*, and *My First Cook Book*.

Poetry

Kennedy, X. J., and Dorothy Kennedy, selectors. *Talking Like the Rain: A First Book of Poems.* **Illustrated by Jane Dyer. 1992. Hardcover: Little, Brown. Ages 3–9.**

This exceptional array of more than one hundred poems is perfect for reading aloud but also accessible to strong younger readers. Familiar words and short sentences characterize most of the poems, which are gracefully illustrated in watercolor on large, open pages. The categories range from "Play" and "Just for Fun" to "Wind and Weather" and "Day and Night." Readers will recognize older poets, including Robert Frost, Robert Louis Stevenson, and Christina Rossetti, as well as newer talents like Jack Prelutsky and Karla Kuskin. A pleasure to look at, with poems to read and reread.

Kuskin, Karla. *Soap Soup and Other Verses.* **1992. Hardcover: Harper. Paperback: Harper. Ages 5–8.**

Kuskin has fashioned appealing poetry out of simple words and everyday topics, with small colorful pictures integrated into each verse. Children muse about the weather—"In winter there is too much ice./In summer/ice is very nice"—and talk about their bodies—"My hair sits underneath/my hat./And that is why/my hair lies flat." Some of the short poems are funny; others are thoughtful. Without titles, each flows seamlessly into the next one, making it possible to read the entire short book at one sitting or read each page by itself. Deceptively simple, this is one of the few books of poetry specifically for beginning readers.

Prelutsky, Jack. *Tyrannosaurus Was a Beast.* Illustrated by Arnold Lobel. 1988. Hardcover: Greenwillow. Paperback: Morrow. Ages 3–9.

In this well-designed book, catchy poems about dinosaurs are illustrated with humorous pictures. Poems describe specific beasts from brachiosaurus to stegosaurus, iguanodon to seismosaurus, with the fourteen dinosaurs, their eras, sizes, and locations listed in the table of contents. The rhyming poems range from four lines to twenty, each with clever twists and rhythms. Of ankylosaurus, Prelutsky writes, "It was armored in front, it was armored behind,/there wasn't a thing on its minuscule mind." Lobel's dinosaurs, so big they break the picture's frames, will delight young readers as much as the poems will.

Singer, Marilyn. *Turtle in July.* Illustrated by Jerry Pinkney. 1989. Hardcover: Macmillan. Paperback: Simon & Schuster. Ages 7–10.

This unusually beautiful poetry book moves through the year from January to December, focusing on different animals each month. Radiant watercolors convey the seasons and expand the personalities of the animals. The bullhead, a curious-looking fish, appears throughout the book, offering an underwater perspective on the seasonal changes. Singer infuses the poems with sounds that catch the spirit of the animals and their actions, such as the excited bounces of the dog in "April is a dog's dream," which can be heard in the rhythm of the poem. This slim volume offers a rare melding of poetry and pictures, not to be missed.

Westcott, Nadine Bernard, selector and illustrator. *Never Take a Pig to Lunch and Other Poems About the Fun of Eating.* **1994. Hardcover: Orchard. Ages 6–10.**

This is a rollicking cornucopia of light verse about food, illustrated with sprightly watercolors. The sixty-plus poems fall into four large categories: Eating Silly Things, Eating Foods We Like, Eating Too Much, and Manners at the Table. Chosen for their humor and rhythm, the verses have high child appeal. For example, one parody begins, "Mary had a little lamb,/A lobster, and some prunes,/A glass of milk, a piece of pie,/And then some macaroons." Each page is jampacked with cartoonlike pictures of people, animals, and brightly colored food. Certain to have children giggling and repeating funny lines.

4

Books for Middle Readers

Many readers come into their own in these years, approximately from age nine to eleven. Because a lot of wonderful authors gear their writing to this age group, middle readers have a wide range of engaging books from which to choose. Certain children at this stage start reading voraciously and rely on adults for a constant stream of new books to read, a challenge even to the most knowledgeable parent. Other readers develop an interest in one series or in a genre such as fantasy or mystery, and want to read those books almost exclusively. It is also common for middle readers to return to old favorites, which they read again and again. Children who take up hobbies and sports should be encouraged to turn to books in that area of nonfiction for advice or to expand their knowledge.

I have divided the list into Fiction, Biographies, and Nonfiction. Within Fiction are Adventure and Survival Stories, Historical Fiction, Contemporary Life, Humorous Stories, Sports Fiction, Mysteries and Ghost Stories, and Fantasy and

Science Fiction. Biographies are divided into Leaders and Activists; Artists, Musicians, and Writers; Scientists and Inventors; Men and Women in History; Adventurers and Explorers; and Sports Stars. Nonfiction categories are History, Nature and Science, Technology, Hobbies and Sports, Poetry, and a section about strange phenomena called Fact or Fiction? Probably Fiction.

Again, do not limit yourself to this chapter. Be sure to check for more suggestions in the preceding and following chapters, depending on your child's reading level. Children this age still benefit from reading picture books and folktales, which offer lyrical language and excellent art. In fact, some picture-story books with serious themes are geared specifically toward this age group. *The Wall*, for example, is a picture-book about the Vietnam Memorial that interests middle readers and may spark thoughtful discussions. Also keep in mind the folktale collections, many of which suit middle readers for enjoying alone or sharing aloud.

If you find your son turning away from books instead of enjoying them more than ever, try some of the suggestions I've given at the back of this book for encouraging boys to read. While not every child will become a devoted reader, everyone should understand what riches books offer them.

Fiction

Adventure and Survival Stories

Aiken, Joan. *The Wolves of Willoughby Chase*. **Illustrated by Pat Marriott. 1962. Paperback: Dell. Ages 10–13.**

For those who like books filled with heroes and villains, this adventurous melodrama is perfect. A cruel governess and a heartless orphanage director try to make life miserable for Bonnie, a plucky rich girl deprived of her wealth, and Sophie, her kind, poor cousin. A bleak landscape of snow and snarling wolves provides the perfect backdrop when Bonnie's parents leave her and Sophie in the hands of the scheming Miss Slighcarp at a wretched orphanage. The girls escape with the help of Simon, an orphan who lives in a cave and raises geese, and head to London to seek justice. One suspenseful scene follows another, with emotions running high and danger everywhere. The first in a series, this is great fun.

DeFelice, Cynthia. *Weasel*. **1990. Hardcover: Simon & Schuster. Paperback: Avon. Ages 10–13.**

For eleven-year-old Nathan and his younger sister, Molly, who live on the Ohio frontier, the name Weasel conjured up a bogeyman, scary and not quite real. But when their father leaves to hunt and doesn't come home, Nathan ends up meeting the real Weasel, who is more frightening than he had imagined. A kind, sad man named Ezra fetches the motherless children from their cabin and takes them to his hut, where they find their father recovering from an injury. When Nathan returns home the next day to feed the family animals, he finds them dead of gunshot wounds. On his way back to Ezra's, Nathan is stalked like an animal by Weasel. How can he escape? And how can he come to terms with the existence of such an evil person in his world? A memorable historical thriller.

Fleischman, Sid. *The Whipping Boy*. Illustrated by Peter Sis. 1986. Hardcover: Greenwillow. Paperback: Troll. Ages 8–11.

Every time Prince Brat, as he's known, annoys his father or tutor, his whipping boy Jemmy gets whipped in the prince's stead because it's illegal to hurt royalty. So when the prince wants to run away one night and take Jemmy with him, Jemmy plans to give him the slip as soon as possible. But they get caught by Hold-Your-Nose-Billy and his sidekick Cutwater, cutthroats who plan to ask for ransom. The boys escape, thanks to Jemmy, with the ruffians hot on their trail. For the first time, Prince Brat tastes freedom and starts to think about friendship, while Jemmy considers the disadvantages of being royalty. A satisfying ending tops this colorful, action-filled tale. Winner of the Newbery Medal.

George, Jean Craighead. *My Side of the Mountain*. 1988. Hardcover: Dutton. Paperback: Dutton. Ages 9–14.

Teenager Sam Gribley runs away from New York City to his family's land in the Catskill Mountains, where he teaches himself to live off the land with nothing but an ax and a flint and steel. His story, a first-person narrative interspersed with diary entries, will make readers want to try this adventure themselves. Although he makes many mistakes, he also experiences the magic of being alone in the wilderness, watching the seasons change. He befriends a raccoon and weasel, and trains a baby falcon, whom he names Frightful, to catch small game for him. Sketches show what he's learned—plants that are good for eating, for example, and how to devise a snare for game. An absorbing survival story with a timeless quality. A Newbery Honor Book. Followed by *On the Far Side of the Mountain*.

George, Jean Craighead. *The Talking Earth*. 1983. Hardcover: Harper. Paperback: Harper. Ages 10–13.

Thirteen-year-old Seminole tribe member Billie Wind knows her tribe's customs but doubts their importance. Wanting to know more, she goes to spend a night in the Everglades as a rite of passage, but a storm and a fire turn the single night into a long journey. She builds herself a dugout canoe and, with a young otter, meanders through the Everglades, joined by a panther cub and a turtle. She fishes, hunts, and harvests plants to survive and, as she studies the rich world around her, learns more about herself and her heritage. Her deep environmental concerns sometimes come across in a heavy-handed way, but the message is one that readers will appreciate. A hurricane provides a final, dangerous episode in her remarkable quest.

Graham, Harriet. *A Boy and His Bear*. 1996. Hardcover: McElderry. Ages 10–13.

Set in Elizabethan England, this adventure concerns the then-popular sport of baiting bears, setting dogs on them in a ring to amuse the public with a bloody fight. Dickon, who loves animals, is miserable as a new apprentice to a tanner, whose business is to preserve animal hides. When Dickon encounters a baby bear whose mother is going to be baited, his gentle touch with the animal convinces the Bear Garden owner that Dickon could teach the bear to dance. But the enterprise turns out to be dangerous. Dickon works out a plan to save himself from his job and the bear from its grim future, but everything goes wrong. Dickon, the bear, and his new friend Rosa have a long road ahead of them before all is well. A fast-moving story enriched by details about the time and place.

Mahy, Margaret. *Underrunners*. 1992. Hardcover: Viking. Paperback: Puffin. Ages 9–13.

Tris calls the network of tunnels and holes in the open land around his house in New Zealand "underrunners." He and his imaginary companion, intergalactic agent Selsey Firebone, face enemies in the underrunners, and plan escapes and hideaways. When Tris becomes friends with self-sufficient Winona from a nearby Children's Home, she joins the game, but suddenly her enemy is real and Tris is caught up in breathtaking danger. While facing the threat, he also confronts some of his own problems with his kind, surprisingly brave father and the mother who left them both. Mahy combines excellent writing with sympathetic characters and an exciting plot to produce another winner.

Myers, Edward. *Climb or Die*. 1994. Hardcover: Hyperion. Paperback: Hyperion. Ages 10–13.

Thirteen-year-old Jake and his sister, Danielle, who is one year older, know it is up to them to save their parents, after they're all in a car accident on a mountain road. Jake thinks he has seen a weather station on the top of the mountain, so the two set off uphill through the snow, relying on Jake's scientific skills and Danielle's wilderness training. With tools he brought from the car, Jake rigs up a compass and other tools needed for their survival. Danielle gives him a quick course in mountaineering, and he tests his strength as never before. Meanwhile, Danielle gains confidence in her ability to improvise with tools to create mountaineering aids. Faced with a perilous climb and repeated setbacks, they must pool their strengths and cooperate to survive and save their parents. This exciting story of physical challenges will keep readers in suspense until the very end.

Naylor, Phyllis Reynolds. *Shiloh.* **1991. Hardcover: Atheneum. Paperback: Bantam. Ages 8–12.**

When eleven-year-old Marty befriends his neighbor Judd Travers's dog, the boy realizes that Travers has been hurting the dog and denying it food. Marty's family is too poor to afford pets, but Marty cannot forget about the dog he calls Shiloh, so he builds a pen for the dog in the woods and sneaks food out to him. When Marty's parents learn about his dilemma with Shiloh, they sympathize but have no easy answers. Marty struggles with questions of law, ownership, and the treatment of animals in this compelling book, which offers a thoughtful variation on the time-honored topic of a boy and the dog he loves. Winner of the Newbery Medal. Followed by *Shiloh Season* and *Saving Shiloh.*

O'Dell, Scott. *Island of the Blue Dolphins.* **1960. Hardcover: Houghton. Paperback: Dell. Ages 9–13.**

Twelve-year-old Karana is accidentally left behind when her Indian tribe departs from an island off the coast of California in this riveting survival story. To survive alone, she remembers what she saw her elders do, and fashions spears and a bow and arrows to kill animals when she needs to. She also befriends a dog for companionship. Detailed descriptions of how she survives, makes shelters, hunts, and defends herself against the elements will draw readers deeply into her world.

A tsunami and an earthquake create drama, while her attempts to cross the water to the mainland to rejoin her tribe raise hopes. Based on fact, this beautifully written story won the Newbery Medal. The sequel, *Zia*, recounts the story of Karana's niece.

Talbert, Marc. A *Sunburned Prayer*. 1995. Hardcover: Simon & Schuster. Paperback: Aladdin. Ages 10–12.

When eleven-year-old Eloy resolves to walk the sixteen-mile pilgrimage to the New Mexican shrine of Santuario de Chimayo, he hopes it will keep his beloved grandmother from dying. He sneaks out of the house on Good Friday morning, without permission, and starts the arduous journey over hills to the highway, where he joins a stream of other pilgrims. Despite blisters, thirst, and the heat, Eloy slogs on, talking to himself and to God, worrying about his grandmother. When he finally reaches his destination, he finds a surprise that brings him both pain and pleasure. This perceptive novel weaves religious thoughts into the text just as they are woven into so many people's lives. A skillfully written story about a journey that changes a boy's life.

Historical Fiction

Avi. *The Barn*. 1994. Hardcover: Orchard. Paperback: Avon. Ages 9–13.

When his father falls ill in 1855, nine-year-old Ben leaves his boarding school in Portland, Oregon, and returns to the family farm thirty miles away. Since their mother is dead, Ben, thirteen-year-old Harrison, and fifteen-year-old Nettie must run the farm and take care of Father, as narrator Ben calls him. Father is so ill that he cannot walk or talk, he drools, and he "fouls himself." Ben takes on the depressing job of his care and resolves to build the barn his father has wanted, hoping to keep him alive. The three siblings pursue the arduous goal with all their strength, sustained by Ben's intensity and hope, and their stalwart love. This short novel draws a vivid picture of the past, yet links it to the present with emotions that the reader will understand.

Cross, Gillian. *The Great American Elephant Chase*. 1992. Hardcover: Holiday House. Ages 10–13.

Fifteen-year-old orphan Tad can't do anything right, according to the aunt with whom he lives. By mistake, he gets locked into a railroad car with a performing elephant named Khush and ends up far from home. His sure touch with the animal lands him a job, but then things go wrong again, and he finds himself fleeing from two enemies with the elephant and a girl named Cissie. Trying to keep the elephant a secret, Toby and Cissie head from Pennsylvania to the frontier country of Nebraska to find Cissie's friends. Cissie copes with a tragedy in her life, while Toby learns to appreciate his own strengths. With help from unlikely sources, a wild ride on an ark, and a heartwarming climax, this adventure across late-nineteenth-century America is terrific.

Curtis, Christopher Paul. *The Watsons Go to Birmingham—1963*. 1995. Hardcover: Delacorte. Paperback: Dell. Ages 10–13.

The mood of this fine novel changes when the Watsons, an African-American family, go from Michigan to Alabama near the story's end. Early on, a humorous tone prevails as ten-year-old Kenny describes his skirmishes with his irascible older brother, Byron, who teases Kenny mercilessly about his "lazy eye," and tricks him over and over again. Byron also gets into trouble when, admiring his good looks, he kisses the car's frozen rearview mirror and his lips stick to it. Hoping that time with his grandmother will straighten Byron out, his parents load up their car and drive into the worst trouble the family has ever known, in the turbulent South of 1963. This Newbery Honor Book draws a vivid picture of a time, place, and memorable family.

DeFelice, Cynthia. *The Apprenticeship of Lucas Whitaker*. 1996. Hardcover: FSG. Ages 10–13.

Lucas Whitaker is on his own at age twelve after tuberculosis, known as consumption, has taken his family. By luck, a kind, intelligent doctor in a small Connecticut town asks Lucas to be his apprentice. Lucas thrives as he learns about medicine from the doctor and a wise Pequot woman. But he is haunted by the thought that he could have saved his mother through a gruesome ritual that he hears about, which involves digging up bodies and taking out the hearts. Despite the doctor's skepticism, Lucas needs to learn for himself if this grim cure works. Based on historical research, this novel creates sympathetic characters and gives a mesmerizing glimpse of the past.

Hansen, Joyce. *The Captive*. 1994. Hardcover: Scholastic. Paperback: Scholastic. Ages 10–13.

As the son of a powerful Ashanti chief, Kofi has lived a sheltered existence, but slave traders put an end to his happiness. Kofi almost escapes the terrible fate before he finds himself on a ship to colonial America. Fortunately, two boys, one white and one black, befriend him on the ship and save him from the worst treatment. On reaching Boston, the three are sold to a farmer in Massachusetts—Tim as an indentured servant, Kofi and Joseph as slaves. Kofi contrasts the cold Puritan world with his warm Ashanti life, and longs for his home. Although he learns English, and the farmer's wife even teaches him to read and write, his spirit suffers. In the end, his friendships and a chance meeting with a remarkable free black man turn Kofi's fate around. Based on historical figures, this thought-provoking novel looks at slavery in the North through the eyes of a compelling young man.

Jensen, Dorothea. *The Riddle of Penncroft Farm.* **1989. Hardcover: Harcourt. Paperback: Harcourt. Ages 10–12.**

Lars resents moving from Minnesota to Pennsylvania to live on Penncroft Farm until he meets the ghost Geordie, who lived on the farm during the Revolutionary War. For the first time, history gains meaning for Lars as he listens to Geordie's stories about the war, during which Geordie's father was loyal to England while his brother, Will, joined the fight for independence. Meanwhile, Lars gets involved in a mystery about a missing will, which he must find to save his new home. Through his encounters with Geordie, his fondness for his old aunt, and his reluctant friendship with a girl nearby, Lars changes his views on people and history.

Krensky, Stephen. *The Printer's Apprentice.* **Illustrated by Madeline Sorel. 1995. Hardcover: Delacorte. Paperback: Dell. Ages 9–12.**

Set in New York City in the 1730s, this short historical novel incorporates real people such as the printer Peter Zenger and the lawyer Alexander Hamilton. The fictional main character is ten-year-old Gus Croft, a printer's apprentice who learns to think for himself as the story progresses. Although his employer deplores Peter Zenger's criticism of the British governor, Gus's friends and his independent mother agree with Zenger. When Gus is asked to help with the cause, which would put him in danger, he faces an important choice. Large print, a fast-paced plot, and some thought-provoking questions make this a good choice for reluctant older readers.

Llorente, Pilar Molina. *The Apprentice.* **Translated by Robin Longshaw. Illustrated by Juan Ramón Alonso. 1993. Hardcover: FSG. Paperback: FSG. Ages 10–13.**

Set in Florence during the Renaissance, this story of an apprentice gives a glimpse into the world of painters such as Michelangelo. Thirteen-year-old Arduino leaves his comfortable home to be apprenticed to the painter Cosimo. Homesick and miserable, he endures hardship because he truly loves art. Arduino discovers a former apprentice, Donato, who has been locked in an attic room by Cosimo. Unable to free Donato, whose artwork outshone his master's, Arduino sneaks up to talk with him about life and art. When a crisis strikes, Arduino must choose between jeopardizing his career and helping his friend. Sympathetic characters and a suspenseful plot keep readers involved in this winner of the Batchelder Award for the best translated children's book of 1993.

Lowry, Lois. *Number the Stars.* **1989. Hardcover: Houghton. Paperback: Dell. Ages 9–12.**

Set in Denmark during World War II, this moving story of friendship focuses on two girls, Annemarie Johansen and her Jewish friend Ellen Rosen. When Nazi occupation makes life increasingly dangerous for Ellen and her family, Annemarie's family risks their own safety to help their friends escape. In an early, frightening scene, Nazi soldiers push their way into the

Johansens' apartment where Ellen is spending the night, and the girls have a narrow escape. The action moves to the Danish coast, where Annemarie's strength is tested in another life-threatening encounter with Nazis. The extraordinary courage of the Danish people, both Jewish and Christian, comes vividly to life through the experiences of the girls and their families. Based on a true story, this gripping novel won the Newbery Medal.

Morpurgo, Michael. *Waiting for Anya*. 1991. Hardcover: Viking. Paperback: Puffin. Ages 10–14.

In this novel about World War II, a twelve-year-old boy in a small French village has an unexpected chance to prove his bravery. Jo, whose father is a German prisoner of war, is coping with school and tending the family sheep. He never expects to get involved with smuggling Jewish children over the mountains to Spain; in fact, he hasn't ever met a Jew before. But he gets drawn into helping and puts his life at risk when the Germans who occupy his village get suspicious. This compelling novel explores questions about morality and evil, along with the troubling issue of reluctant soldiers who carry out orders they know are wrong.

Paterson, Katherine. *Jip: His Story*. 1996. Hardcover: Lodestar. Ages 10–13.

Despite the many hardships in his eleven years, Jip has a talent for friendship with adults, children, and animals. At the nineteenth-century Vermont poor farm where he has always lived, Jip encourages slow-witted but strong Sheldon and befriends Put, a kind old man who has terrible fits. Things improve when a caring teacher enters Jip's life and helps him learn to read. Jip sometimes wonders about his parents—he fell off a wagon as a baby and ended up at the town poor farm—but his history rarely bothers him until a shifty stranger hints that Jip's father might be alive. Unexpected facts about his family, the help of new friends, and an old friend's generosity start Jip on a journey toward a new life. A beautifully written, suspenseful book about a warmhearted boy.

Reeder, Carolyn. *Shades of Gray*. 1989. Hardcover: Macmillan. Paperback: Avon. Ages 9–12.

The Civil War is over, and everyone in Will Page's immediate family is dead from fighting, disease, or heartbreak. Twelve-year-old Will goes to live with his mother's sister and her family, whom he hardly knows. A staunch Confederate, Will is furious with his uncle Jed for not fighting in the war, and unmoved by his explanation that he didn't believe in fighting to help rich people keep their slaves. As Will labors alongside his hardworking uncle, he revises his opinion of him. Meanwhile, Will becomes friends with his kind, outspoken cousin Meg. In the end, he must make a difficult choice about where his loyalties lie. An original, thought-provoking approach to the Civil War and its effect on the lives of ordinary people.

Robinet, Harriette Gillem. *Mississippi Chariot*. 1994. Hardcover: Atheneum. Paperback: Aladdin. Ages 9–12.

It's 1936 in Mississippi, where Shortning Bread Jackson is turning twelve. He vows to set his father, Rufus, free from a chain gang, where he is suffering for a crime he didn't commit. The brash Shortning Bread, whose real name is Abraham Lincoln Jackson, succeeds in an unlikely scheme for scaring the local sheriff, who knows Rufus Jackson is innocent. Shortning Bread also saves a white boy from drowning, an act that could cause trouble but instead brings him a reluctant white friend. That friendship furthers the plans to set Rufus free, but no friendship can save the family from the white sheriff's fury. So Shortning Bread's final plan, on which so much depends, involves the whole family's escaping to Chicago. A suspenseful adventure with moments of humor and a strong theme about racial bias.

White, Ruth. *Belle Prater's Boy.* **1996. Hardcover: FSG. Ages 10–13.**

In October 1953, Belle Prater disappeared. When her husband and her son Woodrow awoke, she was gone, but the only clothing missing was her nightgown. Woodrow goes to live with his grandparents in Coal Station, Virginia, next door to the book's narrator, his cousin Gypsy. The twelve-year-old cousins get to be best friends, sneaking out at night to wander around town or sit in their tree house. Gypsy has her own problems with a stepfather she dislikes and nightmares about her dead father. Thanks to caring relatives, the two survive their painful pasts and face the future, knowing at least that their friendship is certain. A lyrical novel full of humor and understanding, this is a Newbery Honor Book.

Contemporary Life

Brooks, Bruce. *Everywhere.* **1990. Hardcover: Harper. Paperback: Harper. Ages 9–12.**

The nine-year-old narrator, whose beloved grandfather has had a heart attack, feels confused and helpless. When a nurse comes to help out, she brings her nephew Dooley, who presents the narrator with a plan to save his grandfather. First they have to determine what kind of animal his grandfather looks like and find one, then perform a mysterious "soul switch" between the man and animal. As they set about their task, a tentative friendship develops between the two boys, quickly getting past the fact that the narrator is white and Dooley is black. Dooley, with his edge of bossiness, gives the narrator the distraction and reassurance he needs at a tough time. Written in crystal clear prose, with a keen ear for conversation and an understanding of emotions, this short novel lingers in the memory long after the book is closed.

Cleary, Beverly. *Dear Mr. Henshaw.* **Illustrated by Paul O. Zelinsky. 1983. Hardcover: Morrow. Paperback: Dell. Ages 8–12.**

Leigh Botts, a good-natured boy, is adjusting to his parents' divorce and to a new school. He rarely sees his father, a trucker, and while his likable mother acknowledges Leigh's problems, she is overwhelmed with work and school. At school, Leigh gets tired of having his lunch box raided, so he comes up with his own solution, a burglar alarm. It not only works, but it helps him make friends among his classmates, who admire its loudness. This engaging story is told through Leigh's letters to Mr. Henshaw, a children's book writer, and through the diary that Leigh starts. His letters combine serious themes with funny comments about his ups and downs. Notable for its clear, simple writing that reflects life as many children know it, this popular novel won the Newbery Medal.

Coman, Carolyn. *What Jamie Saw.* **1995. Hardcover: Front Street. Paperback: Puffin. Ages 10–13.**

This acutely perceptive novel opens with a heart-wrenching scene in which third-grader Jamie sees his stepfather throw Jamie's baby sister, Nin, across the room. His mother appears just in time to catch the baby, then gets Jamie out of the house. The skillful writing captures Jamie's confusion and fear in the days that follow. The fear makes Jamie and his mother act in strange ways, sometimes panicking, sometimes getting angry with each other. But his mother also remains strong for Jamie, even in her own confusion. With the help of a friend, they move into an isolated trailer house, where Jamie spends countless hours practicing magic tricks. A final confrontation with the stepfather, without violence, leaves Jamie and his mother exhausted but ready to face the future. A Newbery Honor Book, this powerful short novel will speak to children who have experienced fear, and especially those who have experienced violence.

Crew, Linda. *Nekomah Creek*. Illustrated by Charles Robinson. 1991. Hardcover: Delacorte. Paperback: Dell. Ages 8–11.

Fourth-grader Robby doesn't realize he has a problem until he is sent to a school counselor for reading on the playground. Although Robby truly enjoys his hectic house where his father stays home to look after the energetic two-year-old twins while his mother goes off to work, the counselor seems worried about it. Is there something wrong with a father who loves to cook? Is Robby jealous of the twins he thought he adored? When a fellow student is removed from her home by social workers, Robby really starts to worry. Meanwhile, he is teased by a macho boy and befriended by a new girl who also loves to read. Set in Oregon, this is a warm, funny story about coping with the problem of feeling different. Followed by *Nekomah Creek Christmas*.

Fenner, Carol. *Yolonda's Genius*. 1995. Hardcover: McElderry. Paperback: Aladdin. Ages 10–13.

Chicago street smarts come in handy even in a small

Michigan town. Yolonda, her younger brother, Andrew, and their mother have just moved to a safer but lonelier place. Even in this small town, though, drug-pushing bullies pick on Andrew and ruin his harmonica. Fifth-grader Yolonda, who is large and strong, defends her brother and vows to replace his harmonica. Certain that he is a musical genius, she uses her own genius for planning and persuasion to convince others of his talents, which gives Andrew a unique chance to prove himself. Yolonda plans to be a police officer like her dead father, perhaps the Chicago chief of police, a goal she may just reach. A strong read-aloud, this Newbery Honor Book is truly memorable.

Fine, Anne. *Step by Wicked Step*. 1996. Hardcover: Little, Brown. Paperback: Dell. Ages 9–12.

Three boys and two girls, who are schoolmates but not close friends, find a book labeled "Richard Clayton Hardwick. Read and weep." After they read Richard's story about running away from his harsh stepfather, each of them tells a story about difficult changes in their families. The stories illustrate difficulties that divorce can cause children who find themselves with two homes, or an absent father, or unwanted new siblings and stepparents. But in telling their stories, the children notice that other people in their lives, especially their new stepparents, are also facing problems. As one child says to another, "Everyone thinks that they're the only one," but they feel a bit less alone after listening to each other, and readers with similar family upheavals may feel the same.

Fitzhugh, Louise. *Harriet the Spy*. 1964. Hardcover: Harper. Paperback: Harper. Ages 10–13.

Harriet plans to be a writer when she grows up, while her best friend, Sport, wants to be a ball player. Harriet practices by writing all her observations in a notebook, recording what she sees her friends and neighbors doing, and what she thinks of them. Sport, whose father is a writer and whose mother has left, cleans the house, does the cooking, and pays the bills. Although they've been friends for years, when Harriet loses her notebook and the kids in her class find it, Sport is hurt and angry to hear what she wrote about him. Harriet finds herself isolated and lonely, especially after her beloved nanny, Ole Golly, leaves for a life of her own. But a clever solution saves the day. Nearly three hundred pages long, this modern classic is popular for its compelling story and its insights into children's feelings. Followed by *The Long Secret* and *Sport*.

Henkes, Kevin. *Words of Stone*. 1992. Hardcover: Greenwillow. Paperback: Puffin. Ages 10–12.

Blaze, whose mother died when he was five, has a lot of fears: big dogs, Ferris wheels, fire, sleeping in the dark. The summer when he is ten, a girl named Joselle, who comes to visit her grandmother near his house, introduces an exciting but troubling element into his life. Each chapter, titled "Blaze" or "Joselle," tells the story from that character's perspective. Hurt that her mother seemed so eager to send her away, Joselle sometimes takes her anger out on Blaze or her grandmother. But when she is feeling good, she exudes imagination and warmth, like no friend Blaze has had before. Exceptional writing develops these authentic characters and draws the reader into their lives.

Irwin, Hadley. *The Original Freddie Ackerman*. 1992. Hardcover: McElderry. Paperback: Simon & Schuster. Ages 10–13.

Twelve-year-old Trevor Freddie Ackerman, who likes rock music, malls, and video arcades, can't believe he has to spend the summer with his two great-aunts on a Maine island. His aunts have no television, and the island has nothing more exciting than a general store, a post office, and a library. Still, he finds it a welcome change that his aunts leave him to his own devices, and don't seem upset by his mishaps—even when he borrows his aunt's car and gets caught by the police. As the summer passes, he becomes friends with a local girl and gets involved in more than one mystery. Readers will identify with the imperfect Trevor and appreciate the great-aunts who accept him for who he is.

Kaye, Marilyn. *Real Heroes*. 1993. Paperback: Avon. Ages 9–12.

Sixth-grader Kevin admires his police officer father, Charlie, more than anyone in the world. When Kevin's mother left Charlie a few months earlier, Kevin chose not to go with her. Feeling that she betrayed Charlie, Kevin doesn't speak to her anymore. But when he and his father disagree about Mr. Logan, Kevin's P.E. teacher who is HIV-positive, Kevin starts to see how unreasonable his father can be. He defends his father's position to a friend whose older brother is gay, but feels uncomfortable knowing his father has sided with the bigoted Eric, another sixth-grader, whose sexism and homophobic comments Kevin dislikes. Kevin struggles with these issues and his new view of his father. The topic of gay teachers and AIDS is incorporated into this thoughtful story in a realistic, sympathetic manner.

Konigsburg, E. L. *The View from Saturday*. 1996. Hardcover: Simon & Schuster. Paperback: Atheneum. Ages 10–13.

Three boys and a girl tell the story of their eventful sixth-grade year, when they became friends and won a state Academic

Bowl. Noah accidentally serves as best man at the wedding of two old people—Nadia's grandfather and Ethan's grandmother. Nadia, whose parents are divorced, helps rescue baby turtles and take them to the Sargasso Sea. Ethan emerges from his quiet self when he is befriended by Julian, a newcomer to town, who draws the four together. The four distinct personalities express a range of feelings as they describe changes in their lives. Answers to the difficult Academic Bowl questions are at the back of the book, a nice touch. Winner of the Newbery Medal.

MacLachlan, Patricia. *Arthur, for the Very First Time*. 1980. Hardcover: Harper. Paperback: Scholastic. Ages 9–12.

When he goes to spend the summer with his great-aunt and great-uncle, ten-year-old Arthur is surprised to hear them speak French to their chicken Pauline, who sleeps in the house in a cradle. Aunt Elda also climbs high trees, and Uncle Wrisby sings to his pig. These eccentric relatives are just the relief Arthur needs from his tense, more conventional parents. It takes some adjusting for Arthur, but soon he is trying new things, exploring the countryside with his new outspoken friend Moira, and even coming to the rescue of an important pig. This funny, friendly, thoughtful book is highly recommended.

MacLachlan, Patricia. *Journey*. 1991. Hardcover: Delacorte. Paperback: Dell. Ages 8–12.

Perhaps Journey's mother chose his name to express her own restlessness. His father left long ago, and now, when Journey is eleven, his mother also takes off, leaving Journey and his older sister, Cat, with their grandparents. Journey is angry, but he doesn't want to blame his mother, so he takes it out on his patient grandfather. And he consoles himself with his new cat who wandered in one day on her own. Everyone in the family is coping with the hurt in a different way, until they can feel like a family again. In this short, beautifully written novel, MacLachlan breathes such life into her characters that they seem like real people: lovable, flawed, and wholly human.

Paterson, Katherine. *Bridge to Terabithia*. 1977. Hardcover: Harper. Paperback: Harper. Ages 10–13.

Jess Aarons's life is transformed when Leslie Burke moves to the farm next to his in rural Virginia. Even though she beats him and every other boy at running, they become friends. Leslie, who has grown up in Washington, D.C., with writer parents, is more literate and sophisticated than Jess, whose talent for art isn't valued by his parents. Leslie dreams up a kingdom in the woods, which they call Terabithia, where they can give their imaginations free rein. She introduces Jess to books and new ideas, and he feels lucky to be her friend. Leslie seems fearless next to Jess, who longs to be brave to impress his taciturn father. Only a tragedy almost too painful to bear brings Jess close to his father. Paterson has created believable, sympathetic characters who will win readers' hearts and change the way they look at the world. A Newbery Medal winner that no one should miss.

Paterson, Katherine. *Come Sing, Jimmy Jo*. 1985. Hardcover: Dutton. Paperback: Avon, Puffin. Ages 10–13.

What is it like suddenly to become a local celebrity? Eleven-year-old James has been happy living with his grandmother on their West Virginia farm while his parents, uncle, and grandpa are away performing country music. But he has the gift—as his grandma calls it—of a beautiful voice. So, despite his fear, he begins to sing with the family and becomes a success with the fans in the Virginia town they move to.

Homesick for his grandmother, angry at his mother and uncle, who are jealous of his success, and trailed by a man who claims to be his "real father," James has a lot of new problems. He depends on his loving, stable father, Jerry Lee, for comfort, but when Jerry Lee seems to choose James's mother over James himself, the boy doesn't know where to turn. This is a heartwarming but painful story by an outstanding writer about growing up and making choices.

Rylant, Cynthia. *Every Living Thing*. Illustrated by S. D. Schindler. 1985. Hardcover: Bradbury. Paperback: Aladdin. Ages 9–12.

Twelve stories explore the role that pets and wild animals play in the lives of children and adults. Dogs, cats, turtles, fish, a nest of robins, and even a hermit crab give characters the hope and love they need to get through hard times. Each story is short and beautifully written, with a mixture of happiness and sadness that will speak directly to readers. In the first story, for example, a boy who has always been "slower than the rest" finds a turtle for a pet, and is inspired to give a school report on preventing forest fires that entrances his fellow students. The response makes him feel fast, for the first time in a long time. Read aloud or alone, these thoughtful stories are certain to touch the reader.

Sachar, Louis. *There's a Boy in the Girls' Bathroom*. 1987. Hardcover: Knopf. Paperback: Knopf. Ages 9–12.

Bradley Chalkers, who repeated fourth grade, is the oldest and least popular student in his fifth-grade class. Although he doesn't understand why no one likes him, he is sure he'll never have a friend. When the new student Jeff seems friendly, Bradley is mean to him to avoid rejection later on. The new school counselor, who talks to Bradley and tries to help him overcome his many fears, convinces him he can do his homework if he tries, loans him a book he likes, and warms him with her friendliness. His anxieties about attending a birthday party for the first time in years provide a poignant turning point in Bradley's life, as he explains his fears to Jeff and gets the help he needs. Bradley will seem familiar to readers, as he resembles many children who disrupt classrooms and antagonize their fellow students. Although his turnaround is too quick to be wholly credible, it offers a welcome message of hope. The slapstick humor will make this insightful book appealing even to reluctant readers.

Humorous Stories

Byars, Betsy. *The Burning Questions of Bingo Brown*. 1988. Hardcover: Viking. Paperback: Puffin. Ages 9–13.

Bingo Brown is hilarious. In his sixth-grade class, he has to keep a journal, which he fills with questions that reveal his secret concerns, such as "Has there ever been a successful person with freckles?" After he has tried mousse on his hair and loves the effect, he asks, "Should I bring a bottle of mousse in my lunch box instead of a thermos?" Even his problems, such as suddenly falling in love with three girls at once, have their humorous sides. His new neighbor Billy, who dresses in military fatigues and acts tough, also seems like a problem until the two boys unite in their concern about a likable but troubled teacher. A wonderful novel, followed by several equally funny sequels.

Clements, Andrew. *Frindle*. Illustrated by Brian Selznick. 1996. Hardcover: Simon & Schuster. Ages 8–12.

Did you ever think about where words come from? When

fifth-grader Nick Allen tries to distract his teacher Mrs. Granger with a question about words, she assigns him an oral report on the dictionary. Intrigued by what he reads, Nick invents the word "frindle" to replace "pen." Pretty soon he has the whole school using "frindle." Mrs. Granger fights him every step of the way, or so he thinks. As the war over "frindle" attracts national media attention, and an entrepreneur gets involved, Nick's idea takes on a life of its own, and he must learn to deal with fame. The ending holds a surprise, a fitting conclusion to the humorous, thought-provoking story. Large print and short chapters make this approachable for younger readers and reluctant older readers.

Fleischman, Sid. *By the Great Horn Spoon!* Illustrated by Eric von Schmidt. 1963. Hardcover: Little, Brown. Paperback: Little, Brown. Ages 10–13.

This droll blend of history and humor opens with two stowaways popping up out of potato barrels in the hold of a ship. Twelve-year-old Jack and his family butler, Praiseworthy, plan to strike gold in California and save Jack's aunt from having to sell her home. After a wild ship ride through the straits of Magellan, the pair reach San Francisco, where they take off for the foothills to pan gold. They encounter several scoundrels, befriend rough-and-tumble miners, and become partners instead of master and servant. But once they make their fortune, how will it feel to return to stuffy Boston and their old lives? A rollicking Western tall tale.

Juster, Norton. *The Phantom Tollbooth.* Illustrated by Jules Feiffer. 1961. Hardcover: Knopf. Paperback: Knopf. Ages 10–13.

In this masterpiece of wordplay, a boy named Milo goes through a phantom tollbooth in his electric car to a strange land where he undertakes a dangerous mission. The land's geographical landmarks convey the flavor of this original fantasy: the city of Dictionopolis, the Forest of Sight, and the island of conclusions (to which many people jump). Accompanied by the dog, Tock, and the Humbug, a droll character who wants to be liked but lacks courage, Milo attempts to bring the Princesses Rhyme and Reason back from the Castle in the Air. Anyone who enjoys playing with words or numbers will love this clever novel, which is graced by whimsical illustrations.

Lowry, Lois. *All About Sam*. Illustrated by Diane deGroat. 1988. Hardcover: Houghton. Paperback: Dell. Ages 9–12.

Readers will laugh out loud at this novel that looks at the world from the point of view of a preschooler named Sam Krupnik. For instance, when his mother tells him that water drains "into the pipes," Sam goes to look at his father's collection of pipes—but doesn't find water. His mother then explains that water goes down special pipes, to the sea, and eventually turns into rain, so Sam flushes his sister's goldfish, Frank, down the toilet, expecting him to come down next time it rains. From his pet worm to the time he cuts his own hair into a punk hairdo, Sam's antics are realistic and amusing. Like Lowry's many outstanding books about Anastasia Krupnik, starting with *Anastasia Krupnik*, this is perfect for reading aloud or alone.

Lowry, Lois. *Switcharound*. 1988. Hardcover: Houghton. Paperback: Dell. Ages 9–12.

Neither computer genius J.P., who is thirteen, nor his eleven-year-old sister, Caroline, wants to leave New York to spend the summer in Des Moines, Iowa. But their father, whom they rarely see, is exercising his right to have them visit.

Instead of working on his electronics projects, J.P. gets stuck coaching his little half-brother's baseball team. Caroline, who loves paleontology and doesn't like babies, has to take care of her father and stepmother's twin baby girls. Resentful and bored, the siblings separately plot revenge and start to execute their schemes. Then, surprisingly, things improve, but it may be too late to undo their heartless revenge. A humorous story about real kids coping with the unfairness of life.

McKay, Hilary. *Dog Friday*. 1995. Hardcover: McElderry. Paperback: Aladdin. Ages 9–12.

Ten-year-old Robin Brogan, whose father died in a car accident two years earlier, lives with his outspoken mother in half of an old house that they run as a bed-and-breakfast, barely making ends meet. Their quiet life is disrupted first when Robin is injured by a dog and develops a fear of dogs, and then when the Robinson family, who are always in an uproar, moves into the other half of the house. The bed-and-breakfast business takes a downturn when the Robinson children hang a figure made of pork chop bones on the house's sign. But they make up for this by placing an odd yet appealing ad for the bed-and-breakfast in the local paper. Robin, with the help of his new friends, not only comes to like dogs but finds a stray, Dog Friday, which he hopes to keep. Laugh-out-loud situations combine with a warm sense of humanity in this outstanding British comedy. Followed by the also wonderful *The Amber Cat*.

Mowat, Farley. *Owls in the Family*. Illustrated by Robert Frankenberg. 1962. Paperback: Bantam. Ages 8–12.

The narrator, Billy, lives in Saskatoon and spends his free time on the prairie outside that Canadian city. One day he looks for owl's nests, hoping to get a baby owl as a pet, and after some catastrophes, ends up with Wol, a young great-horned owl. Wol, who lives in a large cage in Billy's yard, is so personable that eventually he's welcome in the house. The owl seems to think he is human, and keeps the family laughing with his escapades. A sunny atmosphere characterizes this story of a boyhood spent outdoors and in the company of well-loved pets. Based on Farley Mowat's childhood, this is beautifully written and great for reading aloud. Also try *The Dog Who Wouldn't Be*.

Park, Barbara. *Skinnybones*. 1982. Hardcover: Knopf. Paperback: Knopf. Ages 8–11.

Slapstick humor characterizes this popular novel about a boy named Alex who cracks jokes all the time. His teachers rarely appreciate the jokes, his classmates scream with laughter, and his parents tolerate it with good humor. One of Alex's problems, as he sees it, is being the smallest boy in his class and on his Little League team. Although he is terrible at baseball, he foolishly claims to be a good pitcher to make up for his size, and now the joke is on him. Luckily, another one of his jokes turns out so well that Alex comes out smiling. Chosen by children as an award winner in several states, this short novel has wide appeal. Followed by *Almost Starring Skinnybones*.

Robinson, Barbara. *The Best Christmas Pageant Ever*. Illustrated by Judith Gwyn Brown. 1972. Hardcover: Harper. Paperback: Harper. Ages 9–12.

Books don't get much funnier than this one, a story about a Christmas pageant that is infiltrated by the boldest, most incorrigible family in town. When the narrator's mother agrees to direct the church pageant, she expects to follow the traditional routine with no glitches. But for the first time ever, the dreaded Herdman children try out for it, and intimidate the other children into letting them have the best parts. One fiasco follows another as they put their own irreverent spin on the roles of Mary, Joseph, the Wise Men, and the Angel. Yet the Herdmans' fresh approach to the Christmas story turns the performance into something special. Read this aloud for its laughs and its surprisingly touching conclusion. Followed by *The Best School Year Ever.*

Rockwell, Thomas. *How to Eat Fried Worms.* Illustrated by Emily McCully. 1973. Hardcover: Watts. Paperback: Dell. Ages 8–11.

Would you eat a worm each day for fifteen days to win a fifty-dollar bet? In order to buy a mini-bike, Billy agrees to do it. Alan puts up his fifty dollars, believing Billy will never eat worms. But once Billy starts, coating his fried worms with ketchup, mustard, and more, Alan and his friend Joe do their best to deter him. They find the biggest worms they can and hint that worms cause serious medical problems. A fist-fight follows one of the sneakier tricks, but they are soon reconciled, and Billy continues his ordeal. Black-and-white sketches add to the boys' personalities and increase the humor. Brief chapters and the zany theme make this short novel a favorite even with reluctant older readers.

Soto, Gary. *The Pool Party.* Illustrated by Robert Casilla. 1993. Hardcover: Delacorte. Ages 8–12.

Ten-year-old Rudy Herrera comes from a tight-knit family in Fresno, California, that does yard work during the summer for wealthy people. Rudy knows how to have a good time whether he's working or hanging around with his pal Alex. When he gets invited to a pool party by a wealthy classmate whose yard the Herreras tend, he and Alex go looking for an inner tube. The huge inner tube leads them to several comical disasters as they ride it down a river and Rudy rolls inside it down a hill. Thanks to Rudy's good nature, even his disasters turn out fine. His family enjoys his high spirits, and he has a particularly good relationship with his understanding father. Laced with Spanish phrases, this story draws an engaging picture of a Hispanic boy and his family.

Sports Fiction

Avi. S.O.R. Losers. 1984. Paperback: Avon. Ages 8–12.
Because all students at South Orange River School have to play a team sport, Ed and his friends, who don't care about sports, end up on a soccer team together. Their kind coach, history teacher Mr. Lester, knows as little as the boys do about soccer, so they resign themselves to losing, often by a huge number of points. Meanwhile they enjoy each other's company and their varied interests in math, poetry, and rock and roll. But to the rest of the school, losing is shameful, so suddenly the team is under pressure to win at least one game, unlikely as it seems. How these witty friends deal with the pressure about their final game results in a wonderful, unexpected conclusion. A related book is *Romeo and Juliet—Together (and Alive!) at Last.*

Christopher, Matt. *Fighting Tackle*. 1995. Hardcover: Little, Brown. Paperback: Little, Brown. Ages 8–11.
Terry McFee cannot believe it when his football coach moves him from his favorite position of defensive safety to nose tackle. He has a hard time accepting that he is growing bulky and stronger, and losing his speed. Meanwhile, his younger brother, Nicky, who has Down's syndrome, is getting

faster all the time. They run together at the track, which leads to Nicky's plan to enter the Special Olympics. But as Terry broods on his problems, he starts to find his brother annoying and hurts his feelings. An emergency unites the two and shows Terry that they both have strengths of their own. Although his writing is somewhat simplistic, Christopher's books are popular with children who like sports fiction.

Dygard, Thomas J. *Game Plan*. 1993. Hardcover: Morrow. Paperback: Puffin. Ages 9–13.

The Barton High School Tigers have only one game left in the season when their coach gets hurt in a car accident. No other teacher at the small school can coach them, so the job falls to Senior "Beano" Hatton, the team manager for three years. A top student, Beano assumes he has the brains to come up with a good game plan, but can he get the team behind him in the coming week? Marty, the arrogant quarterback who wants to call his own plays, learns the hard way that Beano means business. The book's last third details the suspenseful game, in which Beano takes key risks as the Tigers face the equally strong Carterville Bobcats. A tightly written novel with realistic dialogue and lots of football action.

Gardiner, John Reynolds. *Stone Fox*. Illustrated by Marcia Sewall. 1980. Hardcover: Harper. Paperback: Harper. Ages 8–12.

In this short novel based on a legend, ten-year-old Willie is determined to save his grandfather's Wyoming farm. His grandfather has taken to his bed, not from sickness but from a grave worry that he won't tell Willie. Willie and his dog, Searchlight, manage to bring in the harvest before Willie learns the problem: They need five hundred dollars to pay back taxes. When he hears about a dog race with a five-hundred-dollar prize, Willie is sure that he and Searchlight can win, until the undefeated Arapaho Indian Stone Fox enters the race. Excitement, courage, and generosity mark the heart-wrenching climax that will leave many readers in tears.

Hughes, Dean. _The Trophy_. 1994. Hardcover: Knopf. Ages 9–12.

Fifth-grader Danny, who is short but quick, wants to do well during his first year on the basketball team. His sixth-grade friend Alan is willing to practice with him, but Danny still worries. He'd like to please his demanding, alcoholic father, who once won a basketball trophy. Danny's performance as a guard improves quickly, especially on defense, but when his father finally comes to a game, he humiliates his son by yelling at the coach. When Danny confides in a helpful adult about the problems with his father, things look as if they may start to improve, giving the story's ending a note of hope. Plenty of basketball action is woven into this realistic story about sons and fathers.

Korman, Gordon. _The Zucchini Warriors_. 1988. Paperback: Scholastic. Ages 9–12.

Gordon Korman, who wrote his first book about the boys at the boarding school Macdonald Hall when he was a seventh-grader, knows what kids enjoy. In this installment about the reckless Bruno and his more serious sidekick Boots, Bruno has his heart set on a new school recreation hall, complete with a large-screen television. A wealthy alumnus has agreed to donate a hall if the school's first football team is a winning one. Although the boys have little talent, they secretly recruit a skillful quarterback from a neighboring girls' school. Subplots about Manchurian hamsters and fried zucchini keep Bruno and Boots running around every minute. Zany and fast-moving, this is a comical novel with lots of football action. Also try *This Can't Be Happening at Macdonald Hall* and others in the series.

Myers, Walter Dean. *Me, Mop, and the Moondance Kid*. 1988. Paperback: Dell. Ages 9–12.

T.J. and his younger brother, Moondance, spent years in an orphanage before they were adopted. Now T.J.'s close friend Mop is hoping that the husband and wife who coach their softball team will adopt her. As T.J. chronicles the ups and downs of their softball season, he also describes adjusting to his new parents. Because his new father once played pro ball, T.J hopes to impress him by playing well but doesn't usually succeed. Hanging around with the scrappy Mop, T.J. gets into some exciting adventures on the ball field and off. Followed by *Mop, Moondance, and the Nagasaki Knights*.

Namioka, Lensey. *Yang the Youngest and His Terrible Ear*. Illustrated by Kees de Kiefte. 1992. Hardcover: Little, Brown. Paperback: Dell. Ages 8–11.

Baseball and music come together in this story about Yingtao, the youngest of the four Yang children and the only one who isn't musical. The Yang family has recently emigrated from China to Seattle, and Yingtao is adjusting to a new school and a new language. After school, he is supposed to practice the violin, even though he is terrible compared to his siblings. They are preparing for a recital to showcase their father's skill in teaching music, in hopes of bringing him more students, but Yingtao fears his bad performance will defeat the purpose. When he realizes his new friend Matthew has a talent for violin, the two cook up a scheme to make the recital a success. Meanwhile, thanks to Matthew, Yingtao discovers his own talent for baseball. This perceptive book weaves themes about bias and how parents limit their children into an enjoyable story. Followed by *Yang the Third and Her Impossible Family*.

Slote, Alfred. *Make-Believe Ball Player*. Illustrated by Tom Newsom. 1989. Hardcover: Lippincott. Ages 8–11.

Henry Smith loves sports, but he isn't good at them. So he spends his time playing make-believe baseball and football, throwing the ball, calling the plays, and giving voices to all the participants. When he gets pulled into a real game with his old baseball team, Henry gets so caught up in his fantasy that a fly ball hits him on the head. But because of the bump, Henry is home alone when something important happens and, to his surprise, he becomes a hero. He ends up on good terms with his old team, takes up a new hobby, and starts to appreciate his own strengths. Occasional black-and-white drawings add to this entertaining story.

Smith, Robert Kimmel. *Bobby Baseball*. Illustrated by Alan Tiegreen. 1989. Hardcover: Delacorte. Ages 9–12.

Ten-year-old Bobby "Baseball" Ellis, as he would like to be known, hopes to be a great pitcher and end up in the Baseball Hall of Fame. True, he doesn't have a strong arm, but he does throw strikes, so his Kids' Club coach, who is also his father, lets him try pitching as the season opens. Unfortunately, Bobby can't control his temper when his father lets another pitcher have a chance. He is also annoyed that two girls are on the team, although one shows a lot of promise. As the season progresses, Bobby learns that ambition isn't enough and that playing as a team matters more than each player's performance. He redeems himself after a burst of terrible temper, makes up with his father, and becomes friends with one of the girls. A lively read, not just for baseball fans.

Mysteries and Ghost Stories

Avi. *Something Upstairs.* **1988. Hardcover: Orchard. Paperback: Avon. Ages 9–12.**

When Kenny moves into an old house in Rhode Island, he finds a bloodstain on the floor of a small room next to his bedroom. The sound of a ghost pushing his way up through the bloodstain awakens him that night. The ghost, Caleb, who was a slave in 1800, needs Kenny's help to avenge his murder. Torn between fear and a desire to help, Kenny is transported back to Caleb's time on the night of his murder. The two boys get involved in the struggle between abolitionists and slave traders when they overhear the traders' plans, and Kenny encounters Caleb's killer. Can they prevent the slave traders from succeeding in their aims? Will Kenny save Caleb from being murdered? The suspenseful plot, filled with intriguing historical details, will keep readers turning the pages of this thriller.

Brittain, Bill. *Devil's Donkey.* **1981. Hardcover: Harper. Paperback: Harper. Ages 9–12.**

Dan'l Pitt is a congenial boy and his older cousin, Stew Meat, was glad to give him a home. Stew Meat only wishes Dan'l could respect the local superstitions in their small New England town, such as the ban against chopping the witches' Coven Tree. Only after Dan'l has taken his ax to the tree and a witch turns him into a donkey does he finally believe. But now it is too late—or is it? Each time Stew Meat, Dan'l, or their new friend Jenny seem to have broken the spell, something goes wrong again. It all comes down to a final, dangerous contest against the Devil himself. One in a short series.

Coville, Bruce. *My Teacher Is an Alien*. 1989. Paperback: Pocket. Ages 9–12.

The sixth-graders in Ms. Schwartz's classroom are disappointed that she isn't coming back for the last weeks of school, and that they are stuck with a boring substitute. But when Susan follows the sub home, hoping to get back a note he confiscated, she sneaks into his house and sees him peel off his face! He's an alien, who has plans to take five sixth-graders with him when he leaves the planet. Susan enlists the help of Peter, class brain and science fiction fan, but they don't know what to do. No adult is likely to believe them, and they know the alien teacher will be leaving Earth soon. Only by discovering the alien's weakness will they be able to save their classmates and themselves. This quick, entertaining read is the first in a popular series.

Fleischman, Sid. *Jim Ugly*. 1992. Hardcover: Greenwillow. Paperback: Dell. Ages 9–12.

It's 1894, and Jake Banneker's father, Sam, has been brought home in a pine box and buried in the local cemetery in Blowfly, Nevada—or so Jake is told. All that Jake, now an orphan, has as a remembrance is his father's dog, nicknamed Jim Ugly. Jake's older cousin, Aurora, believes that Sam left behind a bunch of diamonds, and so do the two strange characters who show up soon after the funeral. Suspicious about the death and diamonds, Jake and Jim Ugly head west to see if they can find Sam alive. Chased by a bounty hunter and befriended by a sharpshooting actress, Jake finds the answers to his questions, while he grows closer to the fierce but loyal Jim Ugly. A wild Western melodrama full of mystery, humor, and adventure.

Howe, Deborah, and James Howe. *Bunnicula: A Rabbit-Tale of Mystery.* Illustrated by Alan Daniel. 1979. Hardcover: Atheneum. Paperback: Avon. Ages 8–11.

"I come to writing purely by chance," the narrator, Harold, informs his readers. "My full-time occupation is dog." The mild Harold has recorded the story of what happened when his beloved owners, the Monroe family, bring home a bunny they found at a Dracula movie. Harold doesn't mind Bunnicula, as they name it, but his friend Chester, a well-read cat, is convinced that the bunny is a vampire. Amusing scenes follow in which the family finds white vegetables drained of their juices, and Chester tries to warn them by imitating a vampire. Harold's droll voice will have readers chuckling while Chester's serious concerns about the vampire keep the plot zipping along. The first in a popular series.

Lively, Penelope. *The Ghost of Thomas Kempe.* Illustrated by Antony Maitland. 1973. Hardcover: Dutton. Paperback: Puffin. Ages 10–13.

Rarely has anyone been haunted by such an ornery ghost as Thomas Kempe, a seventeenth-century sorcerer who wants James Harrison to be his apprentice. It all starts when James and his family move into an old English house where Kempe once lived. James's first clues are the strange words added to a blackboard his mother is using to sell apples: "Sorcerie, Astrologie, Geomancie, Alchemie, Recoverie of Goodes Loste, Physicke." James is blamed for those words and all of Kempe's increasingly destructive jokes. He finds unexpected help from a congenial handyman who knows exorcism and from the diary of a nineteenth-century woman who, with her nephew, also dealt with the strong-willed poltergeist. Except for the stereotyped characterization of James's sister, the writing is masterful, full of humor and lyricism. Don't miss this outstanding British ghost story.

Newman, Robert. *The Case of the Baker Street Irregular*. **1978. Hardcover: Peter Smith. Paperback: Macmillan. Ages 9–12.**

Andrew is penniless and all alone in the world. His aunt has died, he knows nothing about his parents, and now his tutor has been kidnapped from their London rooming house. When the kidnappers come after him, Andrew is saved by a streetwise girl nicknamed Screamer, her mother, and her brother, who works for Sherlock Holmes. While trying to solve his own mystery, Andrew gets involved in one of Holmes's mysteries concerning bomb threats and stolen paintings. In contrast to his quiet upbringing, he finds himself in the middle of danger and squalor. An exciting climax, in which Andrew and Screamer risk their lives, links the mysteries in an unexpected way. Mystery lovers will enjoy this quick-paced tale and its sequels.

Roberts, Willo Davis. *The Absolutely True Story . . . How I Visited Yellowstone Park with the Terrible Rupes*. **1994. Hardcover: Atheneum. Paperback: Aladdin. Ages 9–12.**

Had Lewis's parents known more about the Rupe family, they would never have let Lewis and his twin sister, Alison, go with them in a motor home to Yellowstone. Mr. Rupe knows less about driving than eleven-year-old Lewis does, while Mrs. Rupe smokes constantly and has stocked the refrigerator with candy bars. Lewis and Alison notice that the motor home is being followed by two men, who try to sneak in when it's empty. Meanwhile, one of the younger Rupe children has found some one-hundred-dollar bills but won't say where they came from. As the days pass, things get more dangerous until

Lewis and his sister draw on their courage and ingenuity to save themselves and the other kids. Winner of the Edgar Award from the Mystery Writers of America, this combines humor, adventure, and a good mystery.

Sobol, Donald J. *Encyclopedia Brown: Boy Detective.* **Illustrated by Leonard Shortall. 1963. Hardcover: Dutton. Paperback: Bantam. Ages 9–12.**

Each of the ten chapters in this popular book is a short mystery that the reader can try to solve along with Encyclopedia Brown, then check the answer in the back. Fifth-grader Leroy Brown, nicknamed Encyclopedia, is "like a complete library walking around in sneakers." Son of the town's chief of police, he cleverly helps his father catch criminals and sets up his own detective agency to solve mysteries for his friends. He puzzles out how a diamond necklace was stolen from right under his father's nose, and why a man must have robbed his own store. Many more books follow in this entertaining series of mini-mysteries.

Titus, Eve. *Basil of Baker Street.* **Illustrated by Paul Galdone. 1958. Paperback: Pocket. Ages 8–12.**

The mouse detective Basil and his faithful companion Dr. Dawson hit on the idea of settling their fellow mice in a community called Holmestead in the cellar at 221B Baker Street, where Sherlock Holmes lives. But almost immediately after everyone moves in, two young girl mice are kidnapped. A ransom note advises Basil to clear everyone out of Holmestead so that a gang run by the Terrible Three can take it over. Using Sherlock Holmes's methods of detecting clues and making deductions, Basil and Dr. Dawson journey to the seaside where they encounter danger and solve the mystery. Cozy illustrations add to the pleasure of this entertaining mouse mystery. The first in a series.

Winterfeld, Henry. *Detectives in Togas.* **1956. Paperback: Harcourt. Ages 10–13.**

Schoolmates in ancient Rome get caught up in political intrigue and mystery when one of their friends is sent to prison. Falsely accused of defacing a temple wall with the words "Caius is a dumbbell," Rufus is guilty only of having written that on a tablet. But the authorities believe he wrote on the temple, until Mucius and the other boys start investigating. First they free their teacher from a wardrobe where he was tied up by a burglar and consult with him, trying to learn the truth. A mysterious message from the imprisoned Rufus, "Tell my friends they must tear the sheep's clothing off the red wolf," finally becomes clear and they catch the villain—only to put themselves in grave danger. A quick-moving mystery, with fascinating details about ancient Rome.

Fantasy and Science Fiction

Alexander, Lloyd. *The Book of Three.* **1964. Hardcover: Holt. Paperback: Dell. Ages 9–13.**

Taran, the assistant pig-keeper to a kind enchanter, longs to be a hero. To him, courage consists of fighting and gaining glory, not tending to a quiet farm. When his chance for adventure comes, and he meets the famed warrior Gwydion, Taran disappoints himself by making mistakes. They need to warn the High King about enemy troops, but on the way an evil enchantress seizes them. Another, young enchantress Eilonwy, saves Taran and joins him to try to complete the mission. They face dangers and get magical help along the way to the exciting end. The first book in an outstanding fantasy series of which the fifth and final book, *The High King*, won the Newbery Medal.

Babbitt, Natalie. *The Search for Delicious*. 1969. Hardcover: FSG. Paperback: FSG. Ages 9–12.

In this lyrical fantasy, reaching a definition for the word "delicious" almost destroys a kingdom. When the king's minister, who is compiling a dictionary, defines delicious as "fried fish," everyone in the king's court disagrees and offers a different definition. So they send twelve-year-old Gaylen to take a survey throughout the kingdom and its four towns. Meanwhile, though, the king's enemy Hemlock is out stirring up discontent, and hostility awaits Gaylen in the towns. In the forests, he meets magical creatures, including the mermaid Ardis, dwarfs, and a nine-hundred-year-old wood dweller. Suspense builds as Hemlock carries out his evil plans and Gaylen must think of a way to save the kingdom. Wonderful for reading aloud.

Babbitt, Natalie. *Tuck Everlasting*. 1975. Hardcover: FSG. Paperback: FSG. Ages 9–12.

If you had the choice, would you live forever? This is a decision that ten-year-old Winnie Foster must make after she learns about a magic spring near her house. The worried Tuck family, who have drunk from the water themselves and will live forever, convince Winnie not to tell anyone about the water, which is not as wonderful as it seems. Winnie quickly grows fond of the helter-skelter Tuck family. But a greedy, mysterious man who followed Winnie and the Tucks confronts them, and disaster strikes. Suddenly it is up to Winnie, whose life has always been sedate and orderly, to defy her upbringing and help her new friends. No one should miss this beautifully written, magical story.

Cooper, Susan. *The Boggart*. 1993. Hardcover: McElderry. Paperback: Aladdin. Ages 9–13.

The boggart, a mischievous spirit from Celtic mythology,

disrupts the life of two siblings in Canada in this outstanding fantasy that combines computers and ancient magic. Ten-year-old Jess and his older sister, Emily, are thrilled when their family inherits a small Scottish castle. Although their parents decide to sell it, the family visits first and each child takes home a piece of furniture. Locked by mistake into Emily's desk is the invisible boggart. He means no harm when he starts playing sly tricks on the family, but the children get blamed for the trouble. They come to like the boggart but realize he is homesick and ill-suited to modern life. But before they can send him home, the spirit encounters modern technology in a way that jeopardizes his very existence. Can Jess and his computer buddies save the boggart? An original, engrossing fantasy. Followed by *The Boggart and the Monster*.

Dahl, Roald. *James and the Giant Peach*. Illustrated by Nancy Ekholm Burkert. 1961. Hardcover: Knopf. Paperback: Puffin. Ages 8–12.

Orphan James Henry Trotter, who is seven, lives unhappily with his nasty aunts Sponge and Spiker, despicable characters who soon get crushed by a giant peach. The peach, which grows larger than the tree itself, saves James, who crawls into it and finds himself among insects made human-size by magic. With them, he finds the love he has missed since his parents died. When the peach starts rolling away, he becomes leader of the expedition. After saving the peach from sharks, they take an extraordinary journey through the air. Readers will love the eccentric insects as much as James does in this magical tale.

Jacques, Brian. *Redwall*. Illustrated by Gary Chalk. 1986. Hardcover: Putnam. Paperback: Avon. Ages 9–13.

Redwall Abbey, set in the woods of Mossflower, is home to

a tight-knit group of mice, headed by a wise abbot. They tend their gardens and orchards, savor their homegrown food, and bask in their friendships. But into this sunny world comes the threat of Cluny the Scourge, a vicious bilge rat, and his gang of five hundred villains. His coming transforms the peaceful Redwall inhabitants into fighters, especially Matthias, a young mouse with the blood of warriors running in his veins. His mission is to recover a lost sword, the key to defeating the rats. Meanwhile, his comrades, male and female, defend the abbey. For readers who love to lose themselves in lengthy fantasies about honor and heroism, *Redwall* is pure pleasure. One in a long series.

Jones, Diana Wynne. *Witch Week*. 1982. Hardcover: Greenwillow. Paperback: Morrow. Ages 9–13.

Larwood House seems like a modern British school, but in this fictional England magic exists, performed by witches. Since witches come into their powers around adolescence, several students in the same class are only starting to realize what they can do: make themselves invisible, make wishes come true, and fly on broomsticks. Their new powers are exhilarating but dangerous. Parliament has passed a tough law to stamp out witches, and even though a witch underground helps some escape, others are burned. When a witch inquisitor comes to Larwood House, five of the young witches run away, with only a strange spell to bring them to safety. Will it work? Or have they put themselves in worse danger? A clever fantasy, with moments of absurd humor, this is highly recommended.

King-Smith, Dick. *Martin's Mice*. Illustrated by Jez Alborough. 1989. Hardcover: Crown. Paperback: Knopf. Ages 8–12.

Martin is nothing like his brother and sister, farm cats who love to eat mice. When he catches his first mouse, Drusilla, he keeps her as a pet, makes her a home in a bathtub, and supplies plenty of food and water. Drusilla has nine babies, and Martin is delighted. Drusilla, however, has had enough of being a prisoner, as she calls it, and runs away. When Martin is sold to a woman from the city and kept locked inside an apartment, he comes to appreciate Drusilla's point of view. But will he ever return to the farm and have a chance to tell her? One adventure follows another in the life of this tender-hearted cat. Good for reading aloud, the text is filled with subtle puns, and witty black-and-white pictures add to the fun.

Klause, Annette Curtis. *Alien Secrets.* **1993. Hardcover: Delacorte. Paperback: Dell. Ages 10–12.**

Science fiction mixes with a murder mystery in this exciting story that takes place on a spaceship to the planet Aurora. Puck, who witnesses what appears to be a murder before she boards the ship, soon realizes someone on board must be a criminal. The only person she trusts is an alien called Hush, who has been robbed of a precious artifact. Together they try to recover the sacred treasure and expose the criminals. Fighting danger at every turn and watching out for each other's safety cements their friendship, despite Puck's initial doubts about befriending an alien. Futuristic slang adds a note of humor to the taut adventure. The final, uplifting scene offers a message about understanding between different cultures. With so little science fiction published for children, this is a real find.

L'Engle, Madeleine. *A Wrinkle in Time.* **1962. Hardcover: FSG. Paperback: Dell, Scholastic. Ages 10–13.**

Professor Murry has disappeared, and his children are worried, especially Meg. She and her brilliant younger brother,

Charles Wallace, are the oddballs in the family, often teased by the kids at school. With the help of Meg's classmate Calvin, she and Charles Wallace try to find their father, a quest that takes them into another dimension and a fierce struggle with evil forces. Three strange women—Mrs. Who, Mrs. Which, and Mrs. Whatsit—lend magical help, but the children will succeed only by drawing on their strengths as they travel through time and space to the dangerous planet where Mr. Murry is imprisoned. Winner of the Newbery Medal, this absorbing fantasy is a favorite with many children. Followed by *A Wind in the Door*, *A Swiftly Tilting Planet*, and *Many Waters*.

Milne, A. A. *Winnie-the-Pooh*. Illustrated by Ernest H. Shepard. 1926. Hardcover: Dutton. Paperback: Puffin. Ages 9–12.

This animal fantasy classic, which is so beautifully written that families have read it aloud for decades, creates a memorable cast of talking animals and their wise human friend Christopher Robin. Pooh, the main character, is a lovable bear "of Very Little Brain" but a kind nature. Pooh, a bit stout, has a constant interest in food, or "a little something" as he calls it, which gets him into scrapes, like getting stuck in his friend Rabbit's doorway due to overeating. The world of Pooh and his many friends would be incomplete without Ernest Shepard's priceless illustrations, gracefully integrated into the text. (Anyone who settles for Disney pictures is making a big mistake.) The book's only drawback is the lack of female characters. Although adults often think of this classic as exclusively a book for the young, many independent readers enjoy reading the far-from-simple text themselves. One of the great joys of children's literature.

White, E. B. *Stuart Little*. Illustrated by Garth Williams. 1945. Hardcover: Harper. Paperback: Harper. Ages 8–11.

Stuart Little is born into a human family in New York City, but he looks very much like a mouse. In the first half of this charming fantasy, he has adventures around Manhattan, racing a model boat in a Central Park pond and getting lost in a garbage barge. He befriends a bird named Margalo, and when she leaves unexpectedly, Stuart decides to search for her and seek his fortune in the world. He sets out in a dashing little car on his travels through the countryside. In one outstanding scene, he acts as a substitute teacher, dismissing boring topics like arithmetic and spelling and instead discussing with the children what matters in the world. Humor alternates with lyrical writing, making this a pleasure to read aloud and as appealing to adults as it is to children. Garth Williams's illustrations suit the story perfectly. Every child should also know White's *Charlotte's Web*, a wonderful modern classic.

Wrede, Patricia C. *Dealing with Dragons*. 1990. Hardcover: Harcourt. Paperback: Scholastic. Ages 10–13.

Anyone who likes humor mixed with fantasy will love this clever story about a struggle between dragons and evil wizards. An adventurous princess named Cimorene finds castle life so boring that she runs off and gets a job as cook and librarian for Kazul, a dragon in the Enchanted Forest. When the King of the Dragons dies, and Kazul is laid low with poisoning, Cimorene suspects the Society of Wizards is responsible and, with help from some magical friends, she defends the Forest. Full of funny twists on fairy tales, this action-packed tale has an appealing cast of dragons, witches, magical cats, a stone prince, smart princesses, and ruthless wizards. The first of four Enchanted Forest Chronicles.

Biographies

Leaders and Activists

DeStefano, Susan. *Chico Mendes: Fight for the Forest.* Illustrated by Larry Raymond. 1992. Hardcover: Twenty-First Century Books. Ages 9–12.

This short biography, illustrated with black-and-white drawings, describes the life of Chico Mendes and his struggle to preserve the Brazilian rain forests. Mendes, the son of a poor laborer who tapped rubber trees for a living, joined his father at work when he was nine. Despite his lack of education, Mendes learned to read and became vitally interested in political issues. When he realized the danger that lumbering, farming, and ranching presented to the livelihood of rubber tappers and the life of the rain forest, he led his fellow workers in nonviolent protests. His progress and growing international stature put his life in danger, and he was murdered by a cattle rancher in 1988. While acknowledging the toll his work took on his family, this biography presents an admiring picture of a man dedicated to saving the earth's resources.

Freedman, Suzanne. *Ida B. Wells-Barnett and the Anti-Lynching Crusade.* 1994. Hardcover: Millbrook. Paperback: Millbrook. Ages 8–10.

The African-American journalist Ida Wells-Barnett was a figure of great courage. In 1892, when three black men were lynched in Memphis, she wrote a protest in the black newspaper *Free Speech.* As a result, her newspaper office was destroyed and her life threatened. She moved to New York, where she continued her crusade against the common practice of lynching. Her willingness to speak out despite personal danger was characteristic of Wells-Barnett. Born into slavery, she turned to education to get ahead, raised four children, and spoke out for women's rights as well as for rights for blacks. Amply illustrated with historical photographs and drawings, this is a well-written, absorbing biography of a remarkable leader.

Fritz, Jean. *Bully for You, Teddy Roosevelt!* Illustrated by Mike Wimmer. 1991. Hardcover: Putnam. Ages 10–13.

When Theodore Roosevelt was in his early twenties, a doctor advised him that he had a bad heart and should live a quiet life. Instead, Roosevelt vowed to live his life "full-tilt" until he was sixty and then worry about his heart. The writing combines intriguing details—Roosevelt once played ninety-one games of tennis in a day—with historical background, setting Roosevelt's accomplishments in the context of his time. For example, that his love of animals led him to shoot and stuff them may seem strange today but was standard for naturalists then. It is easier to appreciate Roosevelt's work establishing 150 national forests and five national parks. Almost larger than life, Roosevelt comes across in this lively biography as a vital force, with his faults duly noted but overshadowed by his contributions.

Fritz, Jean. *The Great Little Madison.* 1989. Hardcover: Putnam. Ages 10–13.

James Madison, fourth president of the United States and one of the authors of the Constitution, was a small man with a quiet voice. In her characteristic way, biographer Fritz seeks out fascinating details and anecdotes to add color to the historical information that forms the core of the biography. For example, Madison and Jefferson shared a great friendship and many interests, including science; when he was in France, Jefferson sent Madison "a portable magnifying glass that would fit into a cane." In following Madison through his childhood, his political offices, his role at the Constitutional Convention, and his presidency, the biography also supplies a history of the times. The biography provides a solid introduction to a distinguished American statesman.

Fritz, Jean. *You Want Women to Vote, Lizzie Stanton?* Illustrated by DyAnne DiSalvo-Ryan. 1995. Hardcover: Putnam. Ages 9–12.

As a girl in the 1820s, Elizabeth Cady jumped her fast horse over ditches and high fences, and excelled at Greek and math in a class where she was the only girl. But when she grew up, she found that she couldn't put her energy and talents to use in a career because she was a woman. She also learned that she couldn't vote, couldn't own property as a married woman, and couldn't ask for a divorce, although men could. Appalled at the unfairness of women's lives, Stanton helped organize the Seneca Falls Woman's Rights Convention, a key event in women's history that led in the long run to women securing their right to vote. The outspoken Stanton became a powerful orator in a time when women were discouraged from public speaking; her father threatened to cut her out of his will if she spoke publicly, but his disapproval didn't stop her. Fritz's biography, filled with interesting facts and anecdotes, captures the daring of this remarkable woman who broke conventions in order to obtain the rights that most men took for granted.

Haskins, Jim. *I Have a Dream: The Life and Words of Martin Luther King, Jr.* 1992. Hardcover: Millbrook. Paperback: Millbrook. Ages 10–13.

This excellent biography draws heavily from the writings and speeches of Dr. King and offers an array of black-and-white photographs. After a moving introduction by Rosa Parks, the chapters follow King's life and work chronologically. Since his life was so closely tied to the civil rights movement, the reader also gains an understanding of its history. Admiring in tone, the book emphasizes King's accomplishments and the traits that made him a great leader, and stresses his commitment to nonviolence. The large format, elegant design, and clear writing make it an effective summary of his life and work.

Osborne, Mary Pope. *George Washington: Leader of a New Nation.* 1991. Hardcover: Dial. Ages 9–13.

Washington's daring and his extraordinary sense of duty come across in this readable 117-page biography. In describing Washington as a person and a public figure, Osborne draws on prints, maps, reproductions of paintings, and excerpts from Washington's own writing. After touching briefly on his childhood, the biography covers his work as a land surveyor and his role in the French and Indian War. Washington's greatest wish was to lead a quiet life with his wife and stepchildren at their estate, Mount Vernon, but he was needed to lead the army during the Revolutionary War and then, as the most trusted man in the new country, to serve two terms as president. Washington's reluctance to pursue power helped ensure democracy, rather than the monarchy some of his contemporaries hoped for. A well-rounded portrait of Washington emerges in this appealing biography.

Artists, Musicians, and Writers

Beneduce, Ann Keay. *A Weekend with Winslow Homer.*
1993. Hardcover: Rizzoli. Ages 10–13.

This large attractive volume with many color and black-and-white reproductions is written as if the painter Winslow Homer himself were speaking to the reader. Reminiscing, Homer describes his carefree childhood in rural New England, which inspired some of his artwork. At eighteen, he was apprenticed to a printer to learn the art of illustration, and went on to become a popular newspaper and magazine illustrator. But his goal was to become a painter, so he gave up his secure job to paint, and success followed. The narration incorporates information about art techniques and the trends in art during his lifetime, along with ample facts about his career. An appendix lists many museums that display his paintings. One in a series, this is an engaging introduction to an important American artist.

Fleischman, Sid. *The Abracadabra Kid: A Writer's Life.*
1996. Hardcover: Greenwillow. Ages 10–13.

Award-winning children's book writer Sid Fleischman infuses this witty autobiography with the animation and sparkle of his fiction writing. Each of the forty-two short chapters begins with a quotation from a letter he has received from a reader, such as "I've loved your book *Jingo Django*. Have you read it?" His early interest in performing magic, which he turned into a brief career, prompted him to publish a book of tricks. He describes his navy service during World War II, his books for adults and screenplay writing for movies, and his move into children's book writing. Anecdotes and dialogue make the book read like a novel, while the black-and-white photographs add the flavor of a family photo album. An unusually entertaining autobiography.

Gherman, Beverly. *E. B. White: Some Writer!* 1992. Hardcover: Atheneum. Paperback: Morrow. Ages 10–13.
The title refers to one of the phrases—"Some Pig!"—that Charlotte the spider wove into her web in E. B. White's *Charlotte's Web*, one of the best-loved children's books ever written. Children who love White's books will enjoy reading this straightforward biography about his life and work. Particularly interesting are the details about his childhood and the cross-country driving trip he took in 1922 in a Model-T, a trip full of funny adventures that will remind the reader of *Stuart Little*. White's love of nature shines forth in the description of his childhood pets and his happy days as an adult on his Maine farm. His dedication to writing also comes across, with examples of several openings for *Charlotte's Web* that show how much he revised his books. A good eye for detail, clear writing, and the occasional photograph or cartoon make this an enjoyable biography.

Krull, Kathleen. *Lives of the Musicians: Good Times, Bad Times (And What the Neighbors Thought).* Illustrated by Kathryn Hewitt. 1993. Hardcover: Harcourt. Ages 9–14.
Learning about musicians is a pleasure with this witty volume. The stories about twenty famous musicians are packed full of intriguing personal details as well as basic information about professional accomplishments. For example, Johann Sebastian Bach had twenty children, including five boys named Johann and two girls named Johanna, four of whom became respected composers. Mozart liked to eat liver dumplings and sauerkraut; Beethoven liked macaroni and cheese, and ground his own strong coffee. Influential European

and American composers and performers are included, each pictured in a caricature. Specific pieces of music are mentioned, providing ways to learn more about the subjects. An ingenious way to introduce notable musicians.

Peet, Bill. *Bill Peet: An Autobiography.* **1989. Hardcover: Houghton. Paperback: Houghton. Ages 8–12.**

Every one of the nearly two hundred pages in this beautifully designed autobiography tells Peet's life story with crisp, often funny, black-and-white drawings and well-chosen words. Although he doesn't gloss over the problems in his childhood, Peet focuses on the pleasures of drawing, watching trains, visiting circuses, and spending time outdoors. Those familiar with his many picture books will see their origins in his childhood joys. After art school, he landed a job at the Disney Studios, where he helped animate such movies as *The Sword in the Stone* and *One Hundred and One Dalmations.* Finally Peet embarked on his career of writing and illustrating children's books, a childhood dream. This Caldecott Honor Book, with its original approach to autobiography, will captivate readers with its story and energetic drawings.

Stanley, Diane. *Leonardo da Vinci.* **1996. Hardcover: Morrow. Ages 9–12.**

Although this large, slim volume resembles a picture book, the subject and extensive text are most appropriate for older readers, who will also appreciate the illustrations. Da Vinci's extraordinary breadth of interests and talents reflects the excitement of the Renaissance. This fascinating biography describes his childhood and entry into the painters' guild, and the varying paths his life took, including painting, inventing, the study of anatomy and nature, and more. On each double-page spread, a page of text is illustrated with small drawings from his notebooks, while the opposing pages are filled with large paintings, some of which incorporate photographs of da Vinci's own paintings. The elegant combination of text and art is a fitting tribute to this man, whose farsighted brilliance will amaze readers.

Stanley, Diane, and Peter Vennema. *Bard of Avon: The Story of William Shakespeare.* **Illustrated by Diane Stanley. 1992. Hardcover: Morrow. Ages 9–12.**

This short, heavily illustrated biography provides a rich introduction to the life and work of Shakespeare. It draws on the assortment of facts found about the playwright in books and letters of his contemporaries, and a variety of other sources. The text carefully distinguishes between fact and speculation, a process described in an author's note. Well-chosen information about Elizabethan theater and daily life fills out the story. Intricately detailed full-page paintings add to the sense of time and place, with many scenes from Shakespeare's plays that give the flavor and range of his work. An exemplary illustrated biography.

Scientists and Inventors

Fisher, Leonard Everett. *Gutenberg.* **1993. Hardcover: Macmillan. Ages 8–10.**

With grave, dark pictures and straightforward text, this short biography introduces Johann Gutenberg, who pioneered modern printing. After briefly covering the history of printing and books, the biography concentrates on the ups and downs of Gutenberg's career. A jewel cutter, Gutenberg became fascinated with the possibility of printing words mechanically in an age when books were hand-printed. He experimented with making individual letters out of pieces of lead that could be moved around to make new words, a goal that nearly drove him into bankruptcy. His first large project was to print a book on grammar, and in 1454, he began printing a Bible of "stunning beauty." Despite many setbacks, Gutenberg survived in the printing business and changed the course of the world.

Goodall, Jane. *My Life with the Chimpanzees.* **1996 revised edition. Paperback: Pocket. Ages 9–11.**

Noted ethologist Jane Goodall lived so closely with chimpanzees in Tanzania that she knew each one and its habits. In a conversational tone, Goodall describes her childhood and education, tracing the roots of her interest in animals. She notes the dangers and pleasures of her research, in which she encountered buffalo, leopards, scorpions, and poisonous centipedes but persisted in observing the chimps. Animal lovers and budding scientists will especially appreciate the details Goodall includes about the chimps, their habits, and their family life. Small black-and-white photographs give a glimpse of this intrepid scientist and her African surroundings.

Parker, Steve. *Thomas Edison and Electricity.* **1995. Hardcover: Chelsea House. Ages 9–12.**

This short biography employs a variety of illustrations, including photographs and sidebars, to convey the details of Edison's life and work and the times in which he lived. The main text briefly describes Edison's childhood, then concentrates on his achievements as an inventor and businessman. Those who think of Edison only as the inventor of the lightbulb will be surprised to learn about the range of his activities, including the invention of a stock market ticker, the machine that produces the tape that is used in ticker tape parades. He patented his own form of the telephone and designed a type of phonograph player. The sidebars discuss related topics such as how patents work, how the vacuum in lightbulbs was created, and Michael Faraday, "the father of electricity." This heavily illustrated volume provides a good, if brief, introduction to an influential man.

Pringle, Laurence. *Jackal Woman: Exploring the World of Jackals.* **Photographs by Patricia D. Moehlman. 1993. Paperback: Simon & Schuster. Ages 8–11.**

Behavioral ecologist Dr. Patricia Moehlman, an expert on jackals, studies two species of this mammal in East Africa. She has spent much of the last twenty years in Tanzania, living alone in a tent and observing jackals from her jeep, where she takes notes on a laptop computer. This fine biography, illustrated with many color photographs, describes how Moehlman got into her field and what her work entails. The reader will also learn a lot about jackals: their habitat, behavior, family patterns, and more. Animal lovers and future scientists will find this a fascinating short study. Look for similar books by the same author, such as *Dolphin Man, Scorpion Man,* and others.

Streissguth, Tom. *Rocket Man: The Story of Robert Goddard.* **1995. Hardcover: Carolrhoda Books. Ages 9–13.**

Even though rockets are now a fact of life, this biography creates a feeling of suspense as Robert Goddard pursues his dream of building a rocket, a strange notion in 1899 when he began. An excellent math and science student, Goddard and his father read *Scientific American* and did experiments together. Goddard went on to study engineering and teach college, but his real interest was rocket design. The smoothly written text incorporates scientific information without losing the excitement of Goddard's experiments with fuels and explosives to launch missiles. Step-by-step, he improved his designs, overcoming temporary puzzles and funding problems. In 1926, he succeeded in launching a liquid-fueled rocket for the first time in history, an extraordinary feat. Science and history buffs will especially enjoy this biography of a space pioneer.

Men and Women in History

Douglass, Frederick. *Escape from Slavery: The Boyhood of Frederick Douglass in His Own Words.* **Edited by Michael McCurdy. Illustrated by Michael McCurdy. 1994. Hardcover: Knopf. Paperback: Knopf. Ages 9–13.**

Frederick Douglass, who never attended school, was a talented writer. This autobiography, excerpted and edited from his *Narrative of the Life of Frederick Douglass, An American Slave, Written by Himself*, is characterized by elegant, powerful prose. Douglass describes his early life as a slave in Maryland, separated from his mother, denied adequate food and clothing. When he was eight, he was sent to live in Baltimore, where, for a short period, he was taught to read. Books opened his eyes to life's possibilities and its injustice, and soon he longed to be free: "The silver trumpet of freedom had roused my soul to eternal wakefulness." After severe mistreatment, he eventually escaped to New Bedford, Massachusetts, where this volume ends. Strong black-and-white woodcuts illustrate this exciting, moving book, which is highly recommended.

Equiano, Olaudah. *The Kidnapped Prince: The Life of Olaudah Equiano.* **Adapted by Ann Cameron. 1995. Hardcover: Knopf. Ages 9–13.**

In 1755, Olaudah Equiano was kidnapped into slavery in

Benin, which thrust him into a life of hardship and adventure. After he finally gained his freedom, he wrote a best-selling book, published in England, about those adventures and the injustices he had suffered, and became a prominent spokesman for the abolition of slavery. In crisp prose, this fine adaptation of his autobiography describes his life in a prosperous Benin family, his travels in Africa as a slave, and his miserable trip to the West Indies. The reader will come to respect this intelligent, hardworking man who suffered immeasurably before he finally bought his own freedom. With many dramatic scenes, this narrative reads like a well-written adventure novel.

Freedman, Russell. *Out of Darkness: The Story of Louis Braille.* **Illustrated by Kate Kiesler. 1997. Hardcover: Clarion. Ages 9–12.**

The impressive Louis Braille first demonstrated a working model of his reading system for the blind in 1824, when he was fifteen years old. He had lost his sight at age four in an accident, and attended France's only school for the blind, where he found the reading system slow and frustrating. Building on a military message system of punched dots, Braille changed it until it provided fast, efficient reading and writing. Although his system was clearly superior to the old one, it was a struggle to persuade authorities to adopt it. Ultimately, though, the Braille system prevailed and spread throughout the world. This well-written biography presents a sympathetic young man who persisted until he had succeeded in his quest. Occasional black-and-white pictures accompany the short chapters.

Fritz, Jean. *The Double Life of Pocahontas*. Illustrated by Ed Young. 1983. Hardcover: Putnam. Paperback: Puffin. Ages 9–12.

This fine biography, which provides a welcome antidote to the Disney version of Pocahontas, combines verified information about her life with speculation about its unknown aspects, offering a sense of a real person. The "double life" refers to her roles in her tribe and among the English. As the favored, intelligent daughter of a chief, Pocahontas was sent to negotiate with English settlers for captured tribe members. Later, when the English kidnapped her and her father refused to pay ransom, Pocahontas quickly learned the English language and customs. She married Englishman John Rolfe and bore a son, but died in England in 1617 at the age of twenty-one. Best known for saving the life of John Smith, Pocahontas was a more complex, accomplished person than many realize.

Huynh, Quang Nhuong. *The Land I Lost*. Illustrated by Vo-Dinh Mai. 1982. Hardcover: Peter Smith. Paperback: Harper. Ages 9–13.

The author of this entertaining memoir grew up in Vietnam in a small riverside village with a jungle on one side and mountains on the other. Many of the fifteen chapters, which read like related short stories, concern dangerous encounters with four wild animals—the tiger, wild hog, crocodile, and horse snake. Tank, the family's fierce water buffalo, also plays a large role. In one incident, Tank fights a huge tiger, while the other buffaloes look on. In another, the men in the village chase and finally kill a wild hog, after it has killed a farmer and several dogs. A black-and-white watercolor of each story adds to the reader's sense of place. Although sadness comes through in the introduction—"But war disrupted my dreams. The land I love was lost to me forever."—the stories themselves are exciting rather than nostalgic. A wonderful way to be transported to another time and place.

Adventurers and Explorers

Martini, Teri. *The Secret Is Out: True Spy Stories.* **Illustrated by Leslie Morrill. 1990. Paperback: Avon. Ages 10–12.**

Each of the eleven chapters in this collective biography introduces a famous spy, moving chronologically from the Revolutionary War to 1960. The stories about men and women have exciting plots, occasional dialogue, and a pencil sketch of each spy. Some of the spies come across as heroes, such as those who saved Abraham Lincoln from an 1861 assassination plot. Others are viewed as despicable traitors, particularly double agents like Kim Philby, a British agent whose loyalty was to Russia. Readers will enjoy the details of the intrigues—codes, disguises, complex schemes—and the suspense that builds in some of the stories. An undemanding book with high appeal.

Reef, Catherine. *Jacques Cousteau: Champion of the Sea.* **Illustrated by Larry Raymond. 1992. Hardcover: Twenty-First Century Books. Ages 10–13.**

With an emphasis on his role as an environmentalist, this biography, written before his death in 1997, describes the life and work of diver and filmmaker Jacques Cousteau. In his childhood, Cousteau swam to improve his health. As an adult, he joined the French navy and invented the Aqua-Lung, a portable oxygen device for divers. In the 1940s he began producing films and writing books about the marvelous underwater world he and his colleagues saw when they dived. Later, he moved into television and expanded his message to alert viewers to the effects of pollution on the ocean. Illustrated with pencil drawings, this is a lively account of an unusual man.

Szabo, Corinne. *Sky Pioneer: A Photobiography of Amelia Earhart.* 1997. Hardcover: National Geographic Society. Ages 9–13.

Numerous black-and-white photographs, including many of planes, are the highlight of this biography of the famous aviator who was the first woman to fly solo across the Atlantic. Earhart bought her first plane when she was twenty-five and earned her pilot's license the next year, 1923. In an era of setting distance records, she was the first woman to make a solo round-trip flight across the United States, and in 1930 she set three women's world speed records. Despite the common belief that flying was too dangerous for women, Earhart loved the challenge. Like many male aviators, she died while trying to set a record, hoping to take the longest route ever flown around the world. This eye-catching biography emphasizes Earhart's feats as a flier and her spirit of adventure.

Van Meter, Vicki, with Dan Gutman. *Taking Flight: My Story.* 1995. Hardcover: Viking. Paperback: Penguin. Ages 10–13.

Vicki Van Meter will engage readers with the story of how she became a pilot and broke an aviation record, flying the farthest distance any child had flown. Her unflagging interest convinced her parents to support her ventures, which took hours of hard work on Vicki's part. In a conversational manner, she describes learning to fly and her preparations to fly coast to coast with an instructor in 1993. Careful planning, which entailed a lot of technical information, was the key to her success; she credits her love of math for helping her with the many mathematical aspects of flight plans. The grueling flight across the country tested her determination, but she succeeded despite illness and bad weather. She also flew accompanied across the Atlantic in 1994. Although she acknowledges that flying can be dangerous, Vicki emphasizes the many precautions she and her flight instructor take. The many photographs expand this intriguing story, which has strong child appeal.

Wadsworth, Ginger. *John Muir: Wilderness Protector.* **1992. Hardcover: Lerner. Ages 10–13.**

In 1867, when naturalist and adventurer John Muir was twenty-nine, he walked from Wisconsin to Florida, more than a thousand miles, taking the "wildest, leafiest, and least trodden way." All his life, he took long walks in the natural settings where he felt most at home. He moved to California in 1868, where he immersed himself in the Sierras, and began a lifelong mission to try to preserve the wilderness. The first president of the Sierra Club, he was instrumental in making Yosemite a national park. Muir's writings about wilderness and conservation had a profound impact in his own time and continue to be published and read. This readable biography includes many quotes from Muir and his contemporaries, as well as a fine assortment of black-and-white pictures. An inspiring story for all nature lovers.

Sports Stars

Dolan, Sean. *Michael Jordan: Basketball Great.* **1994. Hardcover: Chelsea House. Paperback: Chelsea House. Ages 9–13.**

This sixty-four-page biography, illustrated with well-chosen black-and-white photographs, presents Michael Jordan's rise to superstardom. In clear prose, the seven chapters describe his childhood, his college record at UNC, and his play on Olympic teams, with the greatest emphasis on his career with the Chicago Bulls. Quotes from Jordan, other players, and sportswriters are combined with apt anecdotes to balance the descriptions of specific games and plays. Jordan emerges as a great player whose intense competitive spirit is his strength and his weakness, on and off the court. His gambling is mentioned, as are his public complaints about his teammates, but an appreciation of his greatness dominates this readable biography.

Gutman, Bill. *Troy Aikman: Super Quarterback.* **1996. Hardcover: Millbrook. Ages 9–13.**

In this short, statistic-packed biography, Troy Aikman comes across as a quarterback who has encountered difficulties but has also enjoyed great success. The author spices the text with the sort of jargon sports announcers use, such as "really came through in the clutch" and "shook off the cobwebs." Detailed descriptions of games fill many pages, with stats about passes completed and number of touchdowns and interceptions. Aikman's childhood is described briefly, as is his college career. Drafted by the Dallas Cowboys, he joined a weak team that quickly improved. His victories at the 1993 and 1994 Super Bowls get ample coverage, followed by a brief discussion of the charities with which he is involved. Illustrated with photographs, this is an enjoyable, undemanding biography of a star quarterback.

Rappoport, Ken. *Sports Great Wayne Gretzky.* **1995. Hardcover: Enslow. Ages 10–13.**

Hockey fans call him The Great One, and this short biography shows why. Growing up in Ontario, Gretzky excelled on the ice from childhood on, with 378 goals in the 1971–72 season—during which he turned eleven years old. At seventeen, he began his amazing professional career with the Edmonton Oilers. Hockey fans will enjoy the detailed descriptions of games and seasons as the Oilers worked toward winning the Stanley Cup. After four such wins, the Oilers stunned Gretzky by trading him to the L.A. Kings. Occasional black-and-white photographs supplement the text, which focuses almost exclusively on hockey, with little about Gretzky's personal life. A fast-moving story about one of hockey's legends.

Torres, John A. *Home-Run Hitters: Heroes of the Four Home-Run Game.* **1995. Hardcover: Macmillan. Ages 9–13.**

Between 1900 and 1994, only ten major league baseball players hit four home runs in one game. After a general chapter about baseball, home runs, and the influence of Babe Ruth, this collective biography devotes a chapter to each of those ten players. The chapters start with a black-and-white photograph and end with a page of the player's statistics. With only a little about the player's personal life and childhood, each story concentrates on his career and specifically on the game in which he hit his four home runs. Opening with Lou Gehrig and closing with Mark Whitten in 1993, this book, with its peppy sports-page style, will appeal to baseball fans.

Wadsworth, Ginger. *Susan Butcher: Sled Dog Racer.* **1994. Hardcover: Lerner. Ages 8–10.**

Susan Butcher is a dominant force in the traditionally male sport of sled-dog racing. She is a four-time winner of the 1,049-mile Iditarod Trail Sled Dog Race, a grueling, dangerous trial through snow and ice that requires yearlong training, top physical condition, a keen understanding of the terrain, and an excellent ability to work with dogs. As the biography shows, Butcher's life centers around the race and her dogs. She is described as thriving on the physical and mental challenges of the sport, not content to rest on her laurels. After providing a brief personal background, the text details the races she has competed in and the challenges they presented. Although the black-and-white photographs are disappointing, readers will be intrigued by this story of a famous sled-dog racer.

Wright, David K. *Arthur Ashe: Breaking the Color Barrier in Tennis.* 1996. Hardcover: Enslow. Ages 9–13.

The death of Arthur Ashe in 1993 deprived the world of more than a great tennis player. Ashe had proven himself to be an articulate activist for civil rights and a supporter of education for blacks, especially athletes. This serviceable biography describes his upbringing in Virginia, where he experienced racial segregation throughout his childhood. He was also unwelcome at tennis tournaments and in tennis clubs elsewhere in the United States when he began to compete, but he continued with his powerful game and became a tennis superstar. After his stellar career on the court, ended by heart surgery, he went on to coach the U.S. Davis Cup team. With an equal emphasis on his athletic career and his public accomplishments, this short biography will introduce readers to a distinguished American.

Nonfiction

Brooks, Bruce. *Boys Will Be.* **1993. Paperback: Hyperion. Ages 9–14.**

What if a smart male writer, who remembers what it was like to be a boy, decided to defend boys and their habits in writing? That's what these thirteen essays do, while they also offer advice and reassurance. The essays, written in a conversational style, are quirky and opinionated, but full of thoughts that will ring true to many boys. For example, the final essay points out that boys get no respect and that adults always assume boys will do the wrong thing. Another chapter talks about why boys care so much about winning and why that's okay. A funny essay discusses why baseball caps are important to boys. Not everyone will agree with Brooks's views (mothers come across as obsessed with cleanliness), but his writing will spark ideas, confirm feelings, and make some readers laugh with recognition.

History

Byam, Michele. *Arms and Armor.* **1988. Hardcover: Knopf. Ages 8–13.**

Each double-page spread of this history of arms and armor intersperses short paragraphs of information with clear photographs of many objects. The chronological sequence moves from the Bronze Age and Celtic tools, with flint arrowheads and bronze helmets, through the Middle Ages, with crossbows, longbows, and knights' armor. It ends with a look at weapons used during the Westward Expansion, including those of Native Americans. Although the print in the captions is small, the photographs will captivate readers who are interested in the topic. The dozens of other "Eyewitness Books" provide enjoyable introductions to different aspects of nature, history, and technology.

Dolan, Edward F. *The American Revolution: How We Fought the War of Independence.* **1995. Hardcover: Millbrook. Ages 10–13.**

This volume offers a solid introduction to the Revolutionary War, from start to finish. It opens with the fighting in Lexington and Concord, then goes back to explain the roots of the war. It lays out the campaigns and battles chronologically, in clear, straightforward writing. Important individuals are introduced, including the British military leaders, often in sidebars with extra details and portraits. Many pages include a painting, etching, or map, although more maps would have been useful. The large design and frequent section headings keep the information from overwhelming the reader in this attractive volume.

Goor, Ron, and Nancy Goor. *Pompeii: Exploring a Roman Ghost Town.* **1986. Hardcover: Crowell. Ages 10–13.**

Buried by a volcano in A.D. 79, the Roman town of Pompeii became frozen in time until it was excavated in the 1860s. It offers unparalleled information about life in 79 because so much of the town was preserved—loaves of bread, snack bars, swimming pools. The clear text, beautifully organized, discusses Pompeii's burial and excavation, then takes the reader on a fascinating tour of the town, explaining what archaeologists have learned. Well-chosen details abound, such as the photos of graffiti reading "Samius to Cornelius: Go hang yourself." Numerous black-and-white photographs show the excavated town, with pictures of the streets, the houses, the public places, and the artwork. An exemplary introduction to a fascinating place, full of eye-opening facts about the past.

Stanley, Jerry. *Children of the Dust Bowl: The True Story of the School at Weedpatch Camp.* **1992. Paperback: Crown. Ages 10–12.**

Imagine building your own school—laying pipes, pounding nails, building bookshelves, even digging a swimming pool. In 1940, a group of children built the "Weedpatch" School in California, which began because local residents refused to finance a school for the children of "Okies," newcomers from Oklahoma who were seeking work during the Depression. In building their own school, the children, poor and often hungry, gained self-confidence from doing something so important. They learned the necessary skills as they went along from teachers and volunteers. Supplemented by a fine array of black-and-white photographs, the lively text describes the children and their families, their hardships, and their impressive accomplishments. This outstanding book brings an era alive in a way that readers will appreciate.

Wood, Ted, with Wanbli Numpa Afraid of Hawk. *A Boy Becomes a Man at Wounded Knee.* **1992. Hardcover: Walker. Paperback: Walker. Ages 8–10.**

In 1890, American soldiers killed 360 unarmed Lakota Sioux at Wounded Knee Creek. The men, women, and children had just made a harsh journey in temperatures below zero, trying to reach protection. In recent years, modern-day Lakota have duplicated that long journey by horse to "heal the Lakota nation and bring the suffering of the massacre to an end." This photo-essay follows eight-year-old Wanbli Numpa

Afraid of Hawk, an Oglala Lakota, on the journey through the December snow. Told in the first person, the narrative records the six days of hard, cold riding, and the final solemn ceremony, also shown in vivid photographs. At the end, Wanbli Numpa Afraid of Hawk is sad about his people's history but proud of his own accomplishment.

Nature and Science

Brandenburg, Jim. *To the Top of the World: Adventures with Arctic Wolves.* **1993. Hardcover: Walker. Paperback: Walker. Ages 9–13.**

Extraordinary color photographs of an Arctic wolf pack make this an unusually memorable nature book. Brandenburg, who spent months camping on Ellesmere Island at the top of North America to take his photographs, narrates his adventures in a conversational style, explaining how the wolves reacted to him and how he got certain unusual shots. Through text and photo, he introduces the wolf pack, including the six puppies that he photographed during their second and third months. He discusses wolf behavior and explains how they adapt to their harsh environment. Brandenburg's warm feelings for these social animals, who rarely seemed to mind his presence, is contagious. Highly recommended.

Brown, Mary Barrett. *Wings Along the Waterway.* **1992. Hardcover: Orchard. Ages 9–12.**

In this quietly beautiful nonfiction book, large watercolors enhance well-written information about twenty-one waterbirds. Two to four pages describe birds such as egrets, herons, ospreys, and loons, which live in wetlands. The text briefly covers habitat, nests and reproduction, eating habits, camouflage, and environmental concerns. Delicately colored illustrations, well integrated with the text, also occasionally fill wordless double-page spreads. This outstanding informational book is a pleasure in every way.

Cerullo, Mary M. *Sharks: Challengers of the Deep*. Photographs by Jeffrey L. Rotman. 1993. Hardcover: Cobblehill. Ages 9–12.

This well-written book starts off with a quiz of true-or-false statements, such as "Most sharks are man-eaters" and "Sharks have no bones." Although the reader can check the answers in the back, the best approach is to read the information-rich text that provides the answers and much more. The color photographs show different sharks, close-ups of their features, and underwater scenes. Readers learn about the shark's habitats, eating habits, reproduction, how they breathe, why they need to keep moving, their phenomenal sense of smell, and shark attacks. The striking close-up of a shark's teeth on the jacket will draw in readers, who will devour the book's fascinating facts.

Lasky, Kathryn. *Surtsey: The Newest Place on Earth*. Photographs by Christopher G. Knight. 1992. Hardcover: Hyperion. Paperback: Hyperion. Ages 9–12.

On November 14, 1963, an extraordinary event occurred: an island erupted into being in the Atlantic Ocean. This exemplary photo-essay traces the geological history of the island, called Surtsey, and follows its changes since 1963. Because Surtsey is seventy miles from Iceland, Lasky incorporates well-chosen quotes from Icelandic mythology to complement the host of scientific facts. She also explores social aspects, such as how the island was named. Most of the attention focuses on how the island grew, what flora appeared, and how seals and birds began to populate it, which makes a remarkable story. Outstanding color photographs, including many of spectacular eruptions, are integral to the story. Don't miss reading about this remarkable new place.

Lauber, Patricia. *Flood: Wrestling with the Mississippi.* 1996. Hardcover: National Geographic Society. Ages 9–13.

Why does a river like the Mississippi flood? What exactly happens, and could it be prevented? These are some of the questions answered in this short study of the river, with a focus on its worst floods, in 1927 and 1993. Powerful photographs show the magnitude and effects of the 1993 flood, with diagrams and maps to explain the causes and how engineers have dealt with them. The role of humans in changing the course of the river is presented in precise prose that makes the technical issues easy to understand. This well-crafted, well-illustrated nonfiction book will hold the attention of readers who didn't know they were interested in the topic. Look for other books by the same well-regarded author.

Technology

Ballard, Robert D. *Exploring the Titanic.* Illustrated by Ken Marschall. 1988. Hardcover: Scholastic. Ages 9–14.

This popular volume combines history and technology as it reviews the tragic voyage of the *Titanic* and describes exploring its remains. The section on the sinking uses cross-section diagrams, photographs, and paintings to show what happened when an iceberg hit the ship in 1912. The text draws on the vivid accounts of a few survivors to make the scene come to life. Oceanographer and adventurer Ballard then relates the story of his expeditions to find the ship and photograph its remains. Diagrams depict the equipment and vehicles used, and eerie underwater photographs show their findings. The excellent interaction of text, photographs, and diagrams makes the information in this account easy to grasp.

Jones, Charlotte Foltz. *Mistakes That Worked.* Illustrated by John O'Brien. 1991. Paperback: Doubleday. Ages 9–12.
This diverting book explores the origins of forty modern inventions—including new recipes—that resulted from mistakes. Who made the first potato chip? Paper towels? Blue jeans? Silly Putty? These parts of modern life all have intriguing stories attached to them that may inspire future inventors. Post-it notes, for example, used a glue that wasn't strong enough for its original purpose, but worked for a scientist who needed to post temporary notes. The inventor of Velcro was struck with his idea when burrs stuck to his clothing. Quirky cartoonlike drawings add humor to the interesting anecdotes. Written with contagious enthusiasm, these stories make a good nonfiction read-aloud. A companion book is *Accidents May Happen.*

Lindblom, Steven. *Fly the Hot Ones.* 1991. Paperback: Houghton. Ages 10–13.
Have you ever wanted to be in the cockpit of a fighter plane? Or an ultralight? Or an old-fashioned biplane? This exciting guide to eight planes puts the reader at the controls, using second-person narration to make the experience immediate. After learning on a Piper Cub, the reader advances to a more powerful Pitts S-2B Aerobatic Biplane, to try a loop: "You put the Pitts into a shallow dive, then, at 170 mph, pull back on the stick and start climbing." In an F-16 Fighting Falcon, the trip entails "hog popping," practicing combat maneuvers against other planes. Among the nonmilitary

planes are the innovative Quicksilver Sport Ultralight and the Janus Sailplane. Photographs, including a color insert, and diagrams add to the pleasure that this exhilarating book will give to airplane fans.

Platt, Richard. *Stephen Biesty's Incredible Cross-Sections.* **Illustrated by Stephen Biesty. 1992. Hardcover: Knopf. Ages 8–14.**

Boys who pass up other books cannot keep their hands off this popular volume that shows cross-sections, including interiors and structural details, of a castle, submarine, tank, coal mine, oil rig, jumbo jet, ocean liner, and more. A general paragraph describes each structure, while the rest of the text is in small paragraphs connected by a line to something in the picture. Sidebars give additional information, like an explanation of walking in space on the space shuttle pages. The detailed pictures often show a tiny figure using a toilet—in a castle, for example—a sight that interests children. For those who like to know how things are made, this crowded oversized volume will provide hours of close study. See Biesty's other cross-section books, too.

Zubrowski, Bernie. *Wheels at Work: Building and Experimenting with Models of Machines.* **Illustrated by Roy Doty. 1986. Hardcover: Morrow. Paperback: Morrow. Ages 9–14.**

This outstanding book explores six basic wheel-related machines: the pulley, the windlass, the gear, the water wheel, the windmill, and the paddle wheel. In each case, Zubrowski begins with a general introduction to the machine and its history, then moves into how to construct a model of it. Each numbered step is clearly explained in words and demonstrated in well-labeled line drawings. After constructing the machine, the reader is given "experiments to try," followed by a section titled "What's happening?," which explains the principles involved. The machines and experiments get progressively more complicated but can be accomplished by carefully following directions. Similar excellent science-activity books by Zubrowski include *Balloons*, *Messing Around with Pumps and Siphons*, *Bubbles*, and many others.

Hobbies and Sports

Ames, Lee J. *Draw 50 Monsters, Creeps, Superheroes, Demons, Dragons, Nerds, Dirts, Ghouls, Giants, Vampires, Zombies, and Other Curiosa.* **1983. Paperback: Doubleday. Ages 6–11.**

In this popular, nearly wordless book, each page demonstrates the steps in drawing a particular person or monster. Starting with just a few lines, each of the six or eight drawings per page adds lines and shading in a way that is easy to imitate. The drawings are mostly of famous characters from movies, literature, and the artist's imagination, from Darth Vader and the Phantom of the Opera to Medusa and Hercules. Children looking for less fanciful figures to draw will find them in *Draw 50 Animals*, *Draw 50 Athletes*, *Draw 50 Airplanes, Aircraft and Spacecraft*, and the many other drawing books by Ames.

Friedhoffer, Bob. *The Magic Show: A Guide for Young Magicians.* **Illustrated by Linda Eisenberg. 1994. Hardcover: Millbrook. Ages 9–13.**

This handy guide gives directions for eighteen magic tricks and explains in detail how to put on a show with a sense of theater. It covers creating a stage personality, adding music, publicizing a show, and using a magician's table, with a diagram for constructing one. The tricks are divided into three categories: opening an act, the middle of the act, and tricks for a strong finish. The author offers five routines composed of three tricks that work well together. Directions for each trick include the goal, props needed, setup, routine, and suggested "patter." An unusually useful book for the young magician.

Hughes, Dean, and Tom Hughes. *Baseball Tips*. Illustrated by Dennis Lyall. 1993. Hardcover: Random House. Ages 8–13.

This solid handbook teaches the basics of baseball using clear instructions, diagrams, and pencil drawings. The first of the three main categories is "Up to Bat," with chapters on hitting, bunting, baserunning, and stealing and sliding. The next section addresses fielding, catching fly balls, and throwing, while the last category discusses the different positions in some detail. A final chapter addresses the importance of a good attitude. Beginning players and those who want to review information will find this a useful, enthusiastic guide.

Irvine, Joan. *Build It with Boxes*. Illustrated by Linda Hendry. 1993. Hardcover: Morrow. Paperback: Morrow. Ages 8–12.

Anyone who likes crafts will enjoy this idea-packed book. Each project is carefully explained with detailed written instructions and pictures of each step. A note lists the materials needed, with a boxed exclamation point for those steps that require adult supervision. The first chapter shows how to make boxes, followed by ideas of things to put in them, like dioramas and pop-ups. Next come crafts using cereal boxes and bigger cardboard boxes, like a pinhole camera, a mini golf course, and an obstacle course. "Boxes You Can Wear" features an airplane, a dinosaur, and a moon suit, while the final chapter discusses how to put on performances using boxes. This excellent craft book will lead to hours of fun using simple, inexpensive materials. Also see Irvine's books on making pop-ups.

Mullin, Chris, with Brian Coleman. *The Young Basketball Player.* **1995. Hardcover: Dorling Kindersley. Ages 9–14.**
Photographs of six children demonstrate many basketball moves in this popular sports book in which each double-page spread addresses part of the game, such as "Shooting," "Rebound Play," "Fast Break," and much more. Step-by-step instructions accompany the photographs, with captions to point out useful details and diagrams to expand the information. General topics include a short history of the game, a guide to the court and officials, and a page on "Leagues," written before the current women's professional leagues started. Useful for beginning and slightly advanced players, this is one in an attractive series that includes many other sports.

Sullivan, George. *In-Line Skating: A Complete Guide for Beginners.* **1993. Hardcover: Cobblehill. Paperback: Puffin. Ages 9–13.**
Fifteen chapters cover all aspects of in-line skating, with color photographs to demonstrate specific tips. After a short history, the book gives detailed advice on picking out skates and how they should fit, followed by information about safety equipment. Several chapters address technique for the very beginner, explaining how to start and stop, and the safest ways to fall. With an encouraging tone, the text moves on to more advanced maneuvers, roller hockey, and racing. Two final chapters talk about taking care of skates and rules for avoiding injuries. A helpful guide with straightforward information and good advice.

Winston, Mary, editor. *American Heart Association Kids' Cookbook.* Illustrated by Joan Holub. 1993. Hardcover: Random House. Ages 10–13.

The thirty-plus recipes in this cookbook were tested by children to make sure they are easy to follow. A brief discussion of kitchen use and safety precedes the recipes for snacks, soups and salads, entrées, vegetables, breads, desserts, and beverages. Each recipe, labeled with a skill level, lists ingredients and equipment, followed by numbered instructions, with a red sign for steps that require adult help. Although the cookbook emphasizes healthful food, chefs with a sweet tooth will find directions for scones, cake, and cookies. Extensive cooking and nutrition information fills the last twenty pages, including nutrient analyses of each recipe. Bright illustrations add to the attractiveness of this useful book.

Poetry

Frost, Robert. *You Come Too: Favorite Poems for Young Readers.* Illustrated by Thomas W. Nason. 1959. Hardcover: Henry Holt. Paperback: Henry Holt. Ages 9–14.

This classic among poetry collections for children provides an excellent introduction to America's best-loved poet, Robert Frost. The selection of fifty-one poems includes many of his most well known, such as "Birches," "Mending Wall," "The Road Not Taken," "Fire and Ice," and "Stopping by Woods on a Snowy Evening." A few longer poems, including "The Death of the Hired Man" and "Two Tramps in Mud-Time," are interspersed with the many short ones. They are grouped loosely by topics of interest to children—for example, trees, flowers, animals, and children. The poems read aloud well and lend themselves to memorizing. With a small number of lovely woodcuts, this is an exceptional poetry book.

Hopkins, Lee Bennett, selector. *Opening Days: Sports Poems*. **Illustrated by Scott Medlock. 1996. Hardcover: Harcourt. Ages 8–12.**

Eighteen poems, accompanied by energetic paintings, pay tribute to the joy and excitement of sports. Sports fans will particularly enjoy the selections about their favorite sports, while poetry lovers will savor the images. Among the topics included are karate, running, biking, swimming, baseball, and basketball, focusing on both male and female athletes. In Lillian Morrison's "The Spearthrower," a girl can hear the roar of the crowd as she practices, while Gary Soto's "Ode to Weight Lifting" describes a boy who lifts weights alone in his garage, with a "roar red as a lion's." The collection ends on a fitting note, with a poem titled "Final Score."

Larrick, Nancy, editor. *Piping Down the Valleys Wild*. **Illustrated by Ellen Raskin. 1968. Paperback: Dell. Ages 9–13.**

This fine volume brings together more than two hundred poems, accessible to readers in middle grades but also good for reading aloud to younger children. Drawn mainly from American and British poets, most of the poems are shorter than a page and spaciously laid out so as not to overwhelm the reader. The only illustrations are on the chapter title pages, leaving pictures to the reader's imagination. The poems are in sixteen loose categories, such as animals, birds, weather, and cities, as well as funny poems, spooky poems, and dreamy ones. This is a collection to be enjoyed again and again.

Prelutsky, Jack. *Something Big Has Been Here*. Illustrated by James Stevenson. 1990. Hardcover: Greenwillow. Ages 8–12.

Prelutsky, a master of light verse, and Stevenson, an outstanding comic illustrator, combined their talents to produce this amusing volume. Most of the poems are short and funny, with pictures that enhance the humor. They bounce along rhythmically, often starting with a straight description and ending with a funny twist. Now and then, strange characters appear, such as the Disputatious Deeble and the Smoking Yokadokas. As a change of pace, a few verses deal with children's problems such as wishing they were bigger, while other poems celebrate the joy of language. But for the most part, children will chuckle over the silliness and clever wordplay, and want to read the poems aloud. One of Prelutsky's many popular volumes of light verse.

Worth, Valerie. *All the Small Poems and Fourteen More*. Illustrated by Natalie Babbitt. 1994. Hardcover: FSG. Paperback: FSG. Ages 8–14.

In this exquisite book, each page contains a short, deceptively simple poem, accompanied by exactly the right small black-and-white illustration. The subjects come from everyday life: a safety pin, turtle, slug, cat bath, lawn mower, mosquito, and more. The poems, which number more than one hundred, play with language and ideas, relying on concrete images delivered in well-chosen words. For example, one poem describes a garden hose, "muzzled/Tighter by/The nozzle,/Can rain/Chill diamond/Chains/Across the yard." Beautifully arranged in a small, sturdy volume, these gems will have the reader looking at the world in a fresh way.

Fact or Fiction? Probably Fiction

Marsh, Carole. *Unidentified Flying Objects and Extraterrestrial Life.* **1996. Hardcover: Twenty-First Century Books. Ages 9–13.**

Many aspects of UFOs and other extraterrestrial topics are covered in an evenhanded manner in this slim book. It includes stories about flying saucers and alien abductions, the history of UFOs, and references to these mysteries in popular culture, with sidebars on early science fiction movies, comic books, *Star Trek*, and more. On a more scientific note, the book discusses attempts by NASA to find evidence of life on other planets through radio telescopes and space exploration. The author, who is skeptical but not close-minded about UFO sightings, does hold out hope for finding life on another planet. Appendices list related organizations and on-line sites, suggested reading, and a UFO telephone reporting line.

McKissack, Patricia C. *The Dark-Thirty: Southern Tales of the Supernatural.* **Illustrated by Brian Pinkney. 1992. Hardcover: Knopf. Paperback: Knopf. Ages 9–13.**

"While I was growing up in the South, we kids called the half hour just before nightfall the dark-thirty. We had exactly half an hour to get home before the monsters came out," explains the compiler of these spine-tingling stories. Notes at the beginning of each of the ten tales, which are drawn from African-American traditions, explain their origin and add useful information. For example, in one story a girl doesn't get quite what she wants when she goes to a conjure woman, whose supposed powers are explained in the note. The stories, from the past and present, involve magic and ghosts, evil and justice. The dark illustrations suit the collection's haunting tone perfectly. A Newbery Honor Book.

Schwartz, Alvin, collector. *Scary Stories to Tell in the Dark*. Illustrated by Stephen Gammell. 1981. Hardcover: Harper. Paperback: Harper. Ages 9–14.

Children who cannot get enough of scary stories love this collection of spooky stories from American folklore. One chapter offers "jump stories," tales that end with a shouted line or scream meant to make the listener jump. Another chapter brings together urban legends, stories often told at camp or slumber parties, such as "The Hook," about a couple in a car who hear a scratching sound and later find a hook from an escaped murderer on the door. In the final chapter, humorous stories provide a chance to laugh at scary things. Most of the stories are illustrated with creepy black-and-white drawings. This is a well-documented folklore collection with unrivaled child appeal. Also see *More Scary Stories to Tell in the Dark* and *Scary Stories 3: More Tales to Chill Your Bones*.

Walker, Paul Robert. *Bigfoot and Other Legendary Creatures*. Illustrated by William Noonan. 1992. Hardcover: Harcourt. Ages 8–13.

Is there such a creature as Bigfoot? Or the Loch Ness monster? This appealing book looks at those creatures that some people believe in, as well as the Almas, Yeti, Lusca, Mokele-Mbembe, and Kongamato. Each chapter describes a fictional encounter with one of the creatures, followed by a discussion of evidence, and the opinions of scientists. The story about Bigfoot, for example, concerns a boy who is camping with his father and gets carried away by the beast, only to be found unharmed the next morning. Informational paragraphs discuss footprints that have been found, as well as a short, inconclusive film of what may be a Bigfoot. Colorful, dreamlike pictures offer the artist's interpretation of these legendary creatures that intrigue many children.

5

Books for Older Readers

Fiction writers who specialize in books for older children are among the most creative and empathetic of authors. They care deeply about adolescent concerns and emotions and, as a consequence, have written insightful novels, some of them brilliant, some brilliantly funny. The older child who likes to read has a remarkable selection available. These books are more sophisticated in theme and construction than the books in the previous chapter, with more complex characters and more ambiguity. The annotations indicate those books with themes and topics that are also emotionally accessible to younger readers. The age ranges go only to fourteen, but some of the books would appeal to older teenagers, too.

At this age, many children start reading books written for adults, a few of which are listed here. Fantasy and mystery fans are particularly likely to supplement their reading with adult fiction. But all adolescents should be encouraged to include in their reading the "young adult" literature written for them, which speaks directly to their concerns and interests.

As in Chapter 4, the list below is divided into Fiction, Biographies, and Nonfiction. Within Fiction are Adventure and Survival Stories, Historical Fiction, Contemporary Life, Humorous Stories, Sports Fiction, Mysteries and Ghost Stories, and Fantasy and Science Fiction. Biographies are divided into Leaders and Activists; Artists, Musicians, and Writers; Scientists and Inventors; Men and Women in History; Adventurers and Explorers; and Sports Stars. Nonfiction sections are History; Nature and Science; Technology, such as computers and engineering; Hobbies and Sports; and Poetry.

Be sure to check for more suggestions in Chapter 4 and in the collections of folklore in Chapter 2. And keep in mind that the picture-story books associated with younger children can offer excellent examples of writing and art, and a kind of comfort to readers on the verge of growing up.

Fiction

Adventure and Survival Stories

Alexander, Lloyd. *The Illyrian Adventure.* 1986. Paperback: Dell. Ages 10–14.

Legendary treasures and magical warriors, lots of danger, and a courageous heroine characterize this fast-paced story. Professor Brinton Garrett relates the adventures of his ward, sixteen-year-old Vesper Holly, who goes to visit the mythical country Illyria and becomes involved in a rebellion. Vesper thrives on danger, and always triumphs, at least temporarily, against her deadly enemies. Each of the exciting chapters ends with a cliff-hanger like a kidnapping, a near stabbing, or the sound of rifle fire. Like a female Indiana Jones, Vesper has a nose for trouble but is equipped with the brains, physical strength, and ingenuity to bounce back every time. This entertaining tale is followed by *The El Dorado Adventure* and others.

Alexander, Lloyd. *Westmark.* 1981. Paperback: Dell. Ages 10–13.

Theo, a printer's apprentice who loves honor, has his beliefs tested when his life is plunged into danger. Orders from Westmark's evil Prime Minister Cabbarus ruin Theo's place of work, kill his beloved employer, and leave Theo a fugitive. Running away, he falls in with the likable rogue Count Las Bombas and his sidekick Musket, who rely on fraud to make a living, as well as a street-smart girl named Mickle. Theo, who can't reconcile himself to tricking people, leaves his new friends and takes up with young revolutionaries who share his hatred of Cabbarus. Finally reunited with Mickle, Bombas, and Musket, Theo enters his strangest and most hazardous adventure of all. This first book in the *Westmark* trilogy, laced with violence and difficult questions, is a thoroughly satisfying tale.

Avi. *The True Confessions of Charlotte Doyle*. 1990. Hardcover: Orchard. Paperback: Avon. Ages 10–14.

This seafaring adventure about mutiny and murder is a favorite with both male and female readers. Charlotte Doyle expects a quiet, chaperoned trip from England to America in 1832, but instead finds her life drastically changed by the perilous voyage. She must choose sides between a furious crew and a cruel captain, then prove her worth. But her unconventional choice and actions almost cost Charlotte her life when she is tried for a murder she didn't commit. The experience transforms her from a proper young lady to someone who can survive on her own and control her own fate. A Newbery Honor Book, this thrilling firsthand account of her voyage will grip readers from the opening lines to the wonderfully satisfying conclusion. Highly recommended.

Cole, Brock. *The Goats*. 1987. Hardcover: FSG. Paperback: FSG. Ages 11–14.

In this brilliant, popular novel, a boy and a girl who don't know each other are stripped naked by their fellow campers and abandoned together on an island. Utterly miserable, the two "goats," as camping tradition calls them, swim across the lake and break into a summer cottage to spend the cold night. At first wary of each other, they unite over the idea of disappearing and not returning to camp, at least for a few days. They resign themselves to stealing a little, get help from unexpected sources, and learn to depend on each other as their friendship grows. A realistic picture of the harsh side of summer camps, this taut adventure will stir the sympathy of readers while keeping them in suspense until the end.

Dickinson, Peter. AK. 1990. Paperback: Dell. Ages 12–14.

Paul, who is about twelve, has been fighting as a guerrilla in his African country for as long as he can remember. With no family of his own, he has been adopted informally by his commando leader, Michael. When the war ends and Michael starts to work in the new government, Paul goes to school far from the capital city. But the precarious government topples, Michael is imprisoned, and Paul vows to free him. With his friend Jilli, Paul flees from school, recovers his buried AK rifle, and travels through rough country to the city. The two Warriors, as they call themselves, get involved in political protests and, at the inspiring climax, help stir the people of the city to fight for freedom. Full of suspense as the two try to survive in the wilderness, and then in the dangerous city, this is an extraordinary adventure about the challenges of war and of peace.

George, Jean Craighead. *Julie of the Wolves*. 1972. Hardcover: Harper. Paperback: Harper. Ages 11–14.

In this memorable survival story, an Inuit girl named Miyax has run away from home and is lost without food in the Alaskan wilderness. Because it is the season when the sun never sets, she must wait months for the North Star to appear in the sky before she can get her bearings. Until then, she learns how to survive by watching a wolf pack and remembering what her father had taught her about outdoor skills. Despite frustrating mistakes, she overcomes the problems of food and shelter. The wolves grow more used to her presence, and Miyax starts to feel more at home on the tundra than in her former life. As the time approaches when she can leave, she faces the question of where she belongs. Winner of the Newbery Medal, this brilliant novel remains popular with boys as well as girls. Followed by *Julie* and *Julie's Wolf Pack*.

Hinton, S. E. *The Outsiders*. 1967. Hardcover: Viking. Paperback: Dell. Ages 11–14.

"What kind of world is it where all I have to be proud of is a reputation for being a hood, and greasy hair? I don't want to be a hood, but even if I don't steal things and mug people and get boozed up, I'm marked lousy." The compelling voice of fourteen-year-old Ponyboy Curtis tells this story about the close bonds among his gang of greasers and their rumbles—large fights—with the Socs, arrogant upper-class kids. Ponyboy, whose parents have died, lives with caring older brothers. While Ponyboy can handle rumbles, he and his friend Johnny get into serious trouble one night and must flee from the police. In the end, Ponyboy learns what really matters in his life, but the price is painfully high. Written by a sixteen-year-old, this story, told in unpolished prose, captivates even the most reluctant readers.

Hobbs, Will. *Bearstone*. 1989. Hardcover: Atheneum. Paperback: Avon. Ages 11–14.

Cloyd, who is part Ute and part Navajo, feels alive only outdoors. He has spent four years wandering in Utah canyons, herding his goats, with so little education he can hardly read. Now, after a year back in school, Cloyd goes to spend the summer on a remote ranch with an old man named Walter. Walter knows how to give Cloyd chores he enjoys and the space he needs, but what Cloyd wants most is to climb the nearby mountains. The boy and the man work out a friendship, despite some painfully angry moments, and ride into the mountains together to an old gold mine. While each pursues his dream, they seal a relationship that echoes a father-son bond that neither of them ever had. A dramatic adventure story, beautifully written.

Mikaelsen, Ben. *Rescue Josh McGuire.* **1991. Hardcover: Hyperion. Paperback: Hyperion. Ages 10–14.**

After Josh's father Sam kills a bear, Josh sees its cub and knows his father has illegally shot a mother bear. But Sam, who is often drunk and belligerent, not only denies it, he ends up striking Josh. Miserable and frightened, Josh resolves to save the cub by running away with it and trying to survive in the snowy mountains of Montana. Action alternates between Josh on the mountainside and the search that is mounted to find him. He has left a note demanding that bear hunting be outlawed, and his disappearance publicizes his cause. In the end, Josh finds that he has made a difference but that most of his problems are not solved. Although the writing is uneven, this powerful story will strike a chord with many readers and keep them hooked until the end.

O'Brien, Robert C. *Z is for Zachariah.* **1975. Paperback: Aladdin. Ages 11–14.**

A nuclear holocaust has turned the United States into a wasteland in this suspenseful futuristic thriller. On a family farm protected by its valley microclimate, seventeen-year-old Ann Burden believes she may be the only person left alive. Her life is endangered when she finds out she is wrong. John Loomis, who appears one day in a radiation-resistant suit, has a dark secret that sets him screaming when he is ill. Increasingly disturbed, he wants to dominate Ann, taking over operation of the farm and then invading her bedroom one night.

She escapes unharmed but retreats to the hills to protect herself from John and his gun. After a high-stakes game of hide-and-seek, Ann takes her fate in her own hands and gambles on the future. Readers will be completely absorbed in this disturbing battle for survival.

Paulsen, Gary. *Canyons*. **1990. Hardcover: Peter Smith. Paperback: Dell. Ages 11–14.**

Two boys meet across time in this riveting novel set in Texas. Modern-day Brennan, a fifteen-year-old who lives with his mother, is spending his summer mowing lawns for money and running for pleasure. Coyote Runs, an Apache in 1864, is going on his first raid for horses, an event that he believes will turn him into a man. On a camping trip in a canyon, Brennan comes across a skull and starts to hear Coyote Runs's voice from the past. Secretly taking the skull home with him, Brennan becomes obsessed with tracing its history and quieting the voice, a quest that ends back in the canyon with a dramatic final scene. The first ten of twenty-four chapters alternate between Coyote Runs and Brennan, with the rest of the book in Brennan's time. A quick-paced tale of two boys who test their courage as never before.

Paulsen, Gary. *Hatchet*. **1987. Hardcover: Simon & Schuster. Paperback: Simon & Schuster. Ages 11–14.**

Brian Robeson is flying to the Canadian wilderness to visit his father when the pilot of the single-engine plane suffers a fatal heart attack. In a fearful panic, with the words "Gonna die" screaming in his head, Brian manages a crash landing, which by chance he survives. But now he is stranded in the wilderness, with a hatchet as his only tool for survival. How he struggles alone for months, encountering snakes, porcupines, wolves, and other hazards, makes for a mesmerizing story. The reader gets inside Brian's head, where desperate thoughts about survival mix with confusion about his parents' divorce. The taut writing made this a Newbery Honor Book, while the gripping adventure has made it a great favorite, especially among boys. Brian also appears in *The River* and *Brian's Winter*.

Temple, Frances. *Grab Hands and Run.* 1993. Hardcover: Orchard. Paperback: Harper. Ages 10–13.

Twelve-year-old Felipe likes his life in El Salvador with his parents and younger sister Romy, but he knows his country is in turmoil. One day his beloved father, a political activist, is missing, presumably taken by the brutal authorities. Felipe, Romy, and their mother must follow their father's earlier advice: "Grab hands and run. Go north, all the way to Canada." Danger besets their every move, as they make their way by bus and on foot through El Salvador, Guatemala, Mexico, and into the United States. If they get caught entering the countries illegally, they will be sent back to El Salvador, where they are no longer safe. Keeping up their strength and spirits, the three plod on through their difficult journey to its equally difficult end. Their family ties and the help from strangers offer the only hope in this forceful modern novel of survival.

Historical Fiction

Collier, James Lincoln, and Christopher Collier. *My Brother Sam Is Dead.* 1974. Hardcover: Macmillan. Paperback: Scholastic. Ages 11–14.

Tim Meeker knows from the start that the Revolutionary War won't be easy on his family. His adored older brother,

Sam, enlists in the Patriot army against the wishes of their father, who hates war. At the family's Connecticut tavern, Tim and his parents remain loyal to the king, while their neighbors split into two factions. Tim is torn, and longs for the glory that he imagines soldiers receive. But as the years pass, and tragedies strike his family and their friends, he changes his mind about what truly matters and what constitutes courage. An afterword explains that many of the details and characters are historically accurate, although the main characters are fictional. An excellent historical novel that raises important questions about war while it tells an exciting story. A Newbery Honor Book.

Fleischman, Paul. *Bull Run*. Illustrated with woodcuts by David Frampton. 1993. Hardcover: Harper. Paperback: Harper. Ages 10–14.
Sixteen people from the North and South tell their personal versions of the Civil War battle of Bull Run and the days leading up to it. In narratives of one to two pages, the speakers describe the sights, sounds, smells, and emotions of war. A horse-lover joins the Southern cavalry, then grieves for all the dead and wounded horses on the battlefield. A slave accompanies her master to battle, then flees across the stream of Bull Run to escape slavery. Voice after voice gives vivid details from different vantage points: a young fifer, a Northern general, the sister of a boy who never comes home from Bull Run. Although the chapters are short and easy to read, putting the facts and characters together will challenge the reader. Endpapers show a map of the battleground, and small woodcuts grace each narrative. A thoughtful, innovative novel.

Levoy, Myron. *Alan and Naomi.* **1977. Paperback: Harper. Ages 11–14.**

Alan Silverman wants to be out playing stickball and flying his model Spitfire, not inside trying to help the strange new girl in their apartment building. Naomi Kirshenbaum, recently arrived from war-torn Europe, watched the Gestapo kill her father and has never fully recovered. But Naomi's mother hopes Alan can help her by trying to be friends. Hopeless as it seems, he reluctantly visits her, talking through a ventriloquist's dummy when she won't respond any other way. He worries about being labeled a sissy, but when Naomi turns out to be smart and funny at times, Alan quits dwelling so much on his image. But just when things seem much better, he has to face the heartbreaking fact that Naomi's pain is something that love and friendship cannot cure. One of the most powerful Holocaust stories written for young people, this is highly recommended.

Mazer, Harry. *The Last Mission.* **1979. Paperback: Dell. Ages 12–14.**

Fifteen-year-old Jack Raab, who is Jewish, hates Hitler. Set in 1944, this is the gripping story of how he enlists in the Army Air Corps by lying about his age and flies bombing missions over Europe. Thrown suddenly into the world of older men, Jack swears and smokes with the rest of them, but secretly misses his family and worries that the army will learn his true age. Vivid prose describes the frightening missions to bomb Germany, flown in formation through air filled with deadly flak. The war is almost over when a mission goes tragically wrong. Jack's life, if he survives, will be changed forever. Full of details about the B-17 and the men who fly it, this war novel will keep readers absorbed from its hopeful beginning to its wrenching end.

Myers, Walter Dean. *Fallen Angels*. 1988. Hardcover: Scholastic. Paperback: Scholastic. Ages 12–14.

It is 1967 when Richie Perry, just out of high school, enlists in the army, knowing he can't afford college and hoping to use his income to help his younger brother. Despite a bad knee, he ends up in Vietnam, in the boonies, fighting a war he doesn't fully understand. His buddy Peewee, a quick-witted fellow black from Chicago, helps Richie survive, literally and figuratively. But every day brings the possibility of death, a bewildering reality that changes the men in Richie's platoon. Riveting prose conveys jungle sounds and stench, fear, racial tensions, and the strange excitement of fighting. Myers develops a fully realized cast of characters, and brings the reader deep inside Richie Perry, to share his harrowing experiences. A remarkable novel about war, its intense friendships, and its pain. Not to be missed.

Paterson, Katherine. *The Master Puppeteer*. 1976. Paperback: Harper. Ages 11–14.

A talented storyteller, Paterson draws readers into the world of eighteenth-century Japan in this powerful historical novel. During a famine, thirteen-year-old Jiro apprentices himself to the famous puppeteer Yoshida to ease the burden on his parents. He becomes good friends with Yoshida's son, Kinshi, and settles into life with the other apprentices, slowly learning the art of manipulating large puppets. As the famine worsens, rumors abound about a Robin Hood–like figure named Saburo who is robbing rich merchants to help the poor. Jiro believes he knows the bandit, and debates betraying him for a reward to help his starving parents. Meanwhile, he worries about Kinshi, who wants to help the hungry masses fight the merchants. Exciting scenes build to a surprising climax in which Jiro tests his courage and loyalty.

Paton Walsh, Jill. *Fireweed.* **1969. Paperback: FSG. Ages 12–14.**

During World War II, when London was heavily bombed, children were sent away from the city for safety. In this riveting novel, fifteen-year-old Bill, who was sent to Wales, has sneaked back to London, where he is surviving on his own, sleeping in bomb shelters and wandering the streets. Just as he runs out of money, he meets a girl his own age named Julie, who had been sent to Canada but returned when her ship was torpedoed. Joining forces, they pick up odd jobs and move into a partly collapsed house abandoned by Julie's aunt. They ignore the risks, even when bombs hit nearby, but the excitement of surviving without adults wanes as the war continues. Tragedy strikes in a breathtaking scene, followed by a bittersweet conclusion. An unusually vivid story of friendship and survival during wartime.

Paulsen, Gary. *Nightjohn.* **1993. Hardcover: Delacorte. Paperback: Dell. Ages 12–14.**

In painfully realistic terms, twelve-year-old Sarny, who bears witness to the evils of slavery and the courage of her fellow slaves, describes the owner's cruel pleasure in whipping the old, young, and especially the strong. Sarny's life is changed when John, later known as Nightjohn, is brought to the farm and offers to teach her to read, an act that is punishable by law. Knowing that reading gives power and the ability to record the truth, he risks his life to bring this gift to others. He is brutally punished for helping Sarny, but it doesn't stop him from teaching and doesn't stop her from learning. Readers may find this short novel hard to read because it is told in dialect, and emotionally challenging because it refuses to gloss over the brutality of slave life. A deeply disturbing and moving story. A companion novel is *Sarny*.

Sutcliff, Rosemary. *The Shining Company.* **1990. Hardcover: FSG. Paperback: FSG. Ages 12–14.**

The Shining Company was a group of three hundred highly trained warriors in A.D. 600 who fought Saxon invaders. As the story opens, the son of a minor lord, Prosper, turns twelve and his father gives him Conn, a bondservant his own age, as an unwanted present. Soon the boys become friends, and several years later they travel to what is now Scotland, where Prosper serves as a shieldbearer to one of the Shining Company. Trained in fighting, he and his compatriots grow strong and fierce. They confidently set off to defend their land against the Saxons, but when the horrendous fighting begins, losses mount as the three hundred warriors and their six hundred shieldbearers face hordes of thousands. Although Prosper lives to tell his story, he is stunned by the death of his friends and the brutal pain of war. Written in polished prose, this battle-filled adventure offers no easy answers about war and bravery.

Taylor, Mildred D. *Roll of Thunder, Hear My Cry.* **1976. Hardcover: Dial. Paperback: Puffin. Ages 10–14.**

Set in 1933, this gripping novel chronicles the life of the Logans, the only black family to own land in their Mississippi town. A white plantation owner wants the Logans' land, but for nine-year-old Cassie, the story's narrator, and her family, the land gives them an independence they will fight to keep. While her parents and grandmother deal with this problem, hot-tempered Cassie and her three brothers, who have grown up in as protected and proud an environment as their family could provide, come up with their own ways of dealing with the racial hate they face from white neighbors. This long, complex novel re-creates the South during the Depression in such vivid terms that readers will feel as if they share the troubles and joys of the Logans and their struggles with the evils of racial injustice. Winner of the Newbery Medal, this is one in a series about the Logans.

Yep, Laurence. *Dragonwings*. 1975. Hardcover: Harper. Paperback: Harper. Ages 10–13.

In 1909, a Chinese flier flew an airplane over the hills of Oakland, California, having improved on the design of the Wrights' plane. Inspired by that story, this novel tells of a Chinese boy named Moon Shadow, whose father, Windrider, dreams of flying. Shadow is eight when he leaves China to live in San Francisco with the father he has never met. He makes a place for himself in the hostile city, first at the laundry in Chinatown where his father and friends work, and then when he and his father work for "demons," as they call whites. Finally, when Shadow is fourteen, the father and son move to the hills of Oakland where Windrider hopes to launch the plane he has built. With richly detailed descriptions of the times, this Newbery Medal winner creates memorable, sympathetic characters who are pursuing a compelling dream.

Contemporary Life

Avi. *Nothing But the Truth: A Documentary Novel*. 1991. Hardcover: Orchard. Paperback: Avon. Ages 12–14.

In this original novel, told through documents, ninth-grader Philip Malloy gravely disrupts other people's lives through his thoughtless actions. When Miss Narwin gives him a "D" in English, Philip is shocked that it will keep him off the track team, which is his main interest. Then he is assigned to Miss Narwin's homeroom. To bother her, he hums during the national anthem in defiance of the rules, and after the third time, he is suspended. Embarrassed, Philip claims he was singing patriotically, a story that reaches a journalist. Suddenly Philip gains national attention as a patriotic student unfairly suspended. Told through Philip's diary entries, phone calls, administrative school memos, newspaper articles, and other documents, the engrossing story raises questions about honesty, loyalty, and hypocrisy, and about the media and politics. Extraordinarily thought-provoking, this is a Newbery Honor Book.

Bauer, Marion Dane. *On My Honor*. 1986. Hardcover: Clarion. Paperback: Dell. Ages 11–14.

This powerful short novel examines issues of courage, honor, and responsibility through a gripping story. Twelve-year-old Joel gets annoyed with his daredevil neighbor Tony, but he has to admit they have fun together. As the book opens, Tony is trying to persuade Joel to do some dangerous climbing. Joel gives in against his better judgment, and later agrees to another bad idea. Annoyed, Joel dares Tony to do something *he* isn't good at, and the consequences are shattering. How will Joel deal with the tragic results of his dare? He wishes his father could change what happened, but all he can do is give Joel the love he needs to keep going. Even those who avoid reading will be caught in the grip of this Newbery Honor Book, which combines page-turning suspense with difficult questions.

Cart, Michael. *My Father's Scar*. 1996. Hardcover: Simon & Schuster. Ages 12–14.

Andy Logan feels as if he will never fit in or find "a friend of the heart." He tells his story from two perspectives—the present, during his first year in college, and looking back at life from age twelve through high school. His alcoholic father could never stand the sight of his overweight son, who loves to read and doesn't care about sports: "Get off your lazy butt. Get outside and do something." Fortunately, Andy's great-uncle recognizes a kindred spirit and introduces him to the life of the mind. As a high school freshman, Andy faces more than loneliness when he realizes that he is gay, and it scares him. His story, told in a realistic voice and graced with effective images, will touch any reader who has been rejected by a parent or has felt like an outsider. The moving final scene offers hope that one may reach, at long last, a place that feels like home.

Cormier, Robert. *The Chocolate War*. 1974. Hardcover: Pantheon. Paperback: Dell. Ages 13–14.

At Trinity Catholic High School, a secret society called the Vigils runs the show, dominated by a cruel senior named Archie. He comes up with "assignments" that students can't refuse. The teachers, who are Trinity Brothers, want "peace at any price, quiet on the campus, no broken bones. Otherwise, the sky was the limit." When freshman Jerry Renault, who is recovering from his mother's death, defies Archie and refuses his assignment to sell chocolates, he becomes the target of psychological warfare. The Vigils realize they must humiliate and break him before he breaks them. Is he a hero or a fool? The adults are no better than the teenagers in this bleak commentary on human nature. Suspenseful and masterfully written, this modern classic fascinates readers with its strong plot and painful themes. Followed by *Beyond the Chocolate War*.

Crutcher, Chris. *Staying Fat for Sarah Byrnes*. 1993. Hardcover: Greenwillow. Paperback: Dell. Ages 13–14.

"For All Those Who Finally Stand Up for Themselves" reads the dedication of this book in which high school senior

Eric Calhoune looks back on his junior high friendship with Sarah Byrnes. Both of them were outsiders, due to his weight and her scarred face, but, smart and articulate, they got back at their enemies through an underground newspaper. When Eric started swimming competitively, his weight dropped, and by senior year in high school, they have grown apart. Now Sarah is in a psych ward and has quit speaking. Is her silence deliberate or the result of mental illness? Eric gets caught up in Sarah's problems with her brutal father while, at the same time, he is training for swim meets and pursuing his first girlfriend. He is not ready for the danger that enters his life, but his spirit is as strong as his friendship with Sarah. Notable for its original voice and excellent plot, this is highly recommended.

Fox, Paula. *The Eagle Kite*. 1995. Hardcover: Orchard. Paperback: Dell. Ages 10–13.

Liam Cormac is stunned to learn that his father is dying of AIDS. Although his mother claims it's from a contaminated blood transfusion, Liam knows she is lying. Three years earlier, he saw his father embracing a man on a beach, a memory that now haunts the thirteen-year-old. Liam and his mother both blame his father, who has gone to stay in a seaside cabin, for their pain. How can Liam come to terms with his father, who is getting weaker every month? Where do all the years when he and his father were friends fit into the painful present? Liam lies to himself and to his friends, as his parents have lied to him, but he knows he must make a connection with his father, soon. In this finely crafted novel, Fox has drawn a three-dimensional adolescent and his parents, characters who are realistically flawed yet struggling to keep their love for each other alive.

Hiçyilmaz, Gaye. *Against the Storm*. 1992. Hardcover: Little, Brown. Paperback: Dell. Ages 12–14.

Eleven-year-old Mehmet doesn't want to leave his Turkish village to move to Ankara, but his family insists life will be better there. At least Mehmet manages to bring along Korman, the dog of his brilliant best friend Hayri, who has already moved to Ankara to study. The big city, crowded with the poor and unemployed, is as bad as Mehmet expected. In the midst of depressing poverty, Mehmet nevertheless grows physically and emotionally, as he helps his friends and forges his own values. No simple answers make his life easy, but the end leaves the reader with hope for this courageous and caring boy. An outstanding novel that introduces another culture while it conveys the universality of human concerns.

Klass, David. *California Blue*. 1994. Hardcover: Scholastic. Paperback: Scholastic. Ages 12–14.

High school junior John Rodgers doesn't fit into his family or his small lumbering town in northern California. He runs track instead of playing football like his father and brothers, and he cares more about butterflies and other natural history than his classmates do. So when he stumbles across a butterfly that he has never seen before, John is excited and worried. Perhaps he has discovered a new kind of butterfly; if so, it will send the town into turmoil when environmentalists find out. John confronts family problems, including his father's bullying, while he makes a fateful decision that he hopes is right. Vivid characters, a quick-paced plot, and excellent writing will keep readers turning the pages till the final dramatic scenes.

Lipsyte, Robert. *One Fat Summer*. 1977. Hardcover: Harper. Paperback: Bantam. Ages 12–14.

What does it mean to be a man? Does it mean being tough

and strong, or could it mean standing up for what you believe in? During a long, hot summer, Bobby Marks wrestles with these questions, describing his ordeals in a witty, insightful voice. Overweight and unhappy, he lands a job doing yard work and resolves to keep it, even though he finds the work hard and his employer unreasonably demanding. Worse yet, an unbalanced ex-marine who wanted the job is hounding Bobby at every turn. At home, his father treats him with disdain and his mother stuffs him with food. He contrasts his failures with the macho success of lifeguard Pete Marino, his sister's boyfriend. Yet Bobby transforms himself as the summer progresses, and makes up his own mind about what he wants to be. Still timely and satisfying, this novel is followed by *Summer Rules* and *The Summerboy*.

Martinez, Victor. *Parrot in the Oven: Mi Vida.* 1996. Hardcover: Harper. Ages 12–14.

Manny Hernandez wants to be a *vato firme*, a guy to respect, not just a kid kicked around by his older brother, Nardo, and the other guys in the California projects where they live. A good student, but with no chance of going to a better school, he picks up extra money working, sometimes picking chili peppers in the fields. Now that his father is out of a job and drinking most of the time, life is tense and sometimes violent in their house. Scary as the violence is, something about it attracts Manny, and he is eager to pass the painful initiation rites to join a gang. Written in simple, lyrical prose, with vivid images of California Valley life, this original, perceptive novel won a National Book Award.

Paterson, Katherine. *Park's Quest.* 1988. Paperback: Puffin. Ages 11–14.

Eleven-year-old Park cannot remember his father, who

died in Vietnam when Park was young, nor has he met anyone in his father's family. Although he lives in Washington, D.C., he has never visited the Vietnam Memorial to see his father's name. In Park's imagination, full of fantasies about King Arthur, his father is a proud warrior, but his mother won't talk about him. Finally, she lets Park visit his father's family in Virginia, where he encounters not only his grandfather, who is incapacitated by a stroke, but also an uncle he didn't know he had. Park immediately dislikes the Vietnamese girl Thanh and her mother, Uncle Frank's new wife. Why would his uncle marry one of the "geeks," as Park cruelly puts it, who killed Park's father? Thanh doesn't like him either, but when a long-kept secret is revealed, they turn out to have something important in common. A stimulating novel about a believable boy and his quest to know his past.

Philbrick, Rodman. *Freak the Mighty.* **1993. Hardcover: Scholastic. Paperback: Scholastic. Ages 11–14.**

Max has always felt big and stupid, and realizes that people talk behind his back about his violent father. But when Kevin, known as Freak because of his undersized body, moves in down the block, the combination of Max's strength and Freak's brain seems unbeatable. They run into trouble in their rough neighborhood, which tests them to their limits. But they and their remarkable bond survive, until they have to face the biggest trouble of all. Written from Max's point of view, and full of Freak's whimsical use of words, this is a powerful story of two misfits who together make a place for themselves in a difficult world. Don't miss it.

Salisbury, Graham. *Blue Skin of the Sea: A Novel in Stories.*
**1992. Hardcover: Delacorte. Paperback: Yearling. Ages
12–14.**

Eleven stories span Sonny Mendoza's life from age six until
he leaves high school in 1966. Since his mother died when he
was a baby, he has been living with his aunt Pearl, his uncle
Harvey, and his cousin Keo, who is a year older than Sonny.
But after the first story he moves to his father's house in the
same village on a Hawaiian island. His father and his uncles
are fishermen, but Sonny isn't sure he wants to be one, or that
he is as much like his father and Keo as he would like to be.
He struggles with his fears, especially of the ocean, and with
what it means to be a man. Encounters with a huge shark and
a vicious moray eel provide exciting stories, while his interest
in several girls over time adds romance. Beautifully written,
with vivid images, these stories offer an unusually strong combination of adventure and insight.

Spinelli, Jerry. *Maniac Magee.* **1990. Hardcover: Little,
Brown. Paperback: Scholastic. Ages 11–14.**

Hector Street divides the town of Two Mills in half, with
only blacks in the East End and only whites in the West. In
this exaggerated tale, Maniac Magee is a legendary white boy
who astounds everyone by feeling at home in both parts of
town. Orphaned Jeffrey Magee, known as Maniac, has run
away from his aunt and uncle, who no longer speak to each
other, and keeps running until he reaches Two Mills, where
his extraordinary athletic skills create a mythic reputation.
Kind as he is, bad things happen to everyone who befriends
him, and he himself is hunted by two macho boys who are
angry because he beat them in contests. Maniac runs for hours
a day, sleeps at the zoo, and never goes to school. What will
become of this extraordinary boy in such a strange town? And

how much of his legend can the reader believe? Winner of the Newbery Medal.

Voigt, Cynthia. *A Solitary Blue*. 1983. Hardcover: Atheneum. Paperback: Scholastic. Ages 11–14.

When Jeff Tillerman was seven, his mother, Melody, left him and his father, the Professor, a distant man who has no idea how to care for a child. Worried that his father will also leave if his rigid routine is disturbed, the boy takes care of the house and otherwise effaces himself. Melody reenters Jeff's life when he is eleven, with a warmth that comes and goes, bewildering Jeff and throwing his tightly controlled inner world off-kilter. When his father is shocked into noticing his son's needs, Jeff starts to appreciate the steady, if unemotional, love his father offers. He also learns to play the guitar, discovers his love of the ocean, and makes friends, including the straightforward Dicey Tillerman. A companion book to *Homecoming* and *Dicey's Song*, this Newbery Honor Book creates such an authentic character in Jeff that readers will feel they know him and will care deeply about his fate.

Zindel, Paul. *A Begonia for Miss Applebaum*. 1989. Hardcover: Harper. Paperback: Bantam. Ages 11–14.

"Something terrible has happened," declares Henry Zedniz who, with his friend Zelda, narrates alternating chapters of this intriguing novel. Their favorite high school teacher, Miss Applebaum, is ill and won't be teaching them science again. The two visit Miss Applebaum in her apartment near Central Park and start exploring the park with her, learning science in the most enjoyable ways possible. In his chapters, Henry includes a few illustrations of their activities, such as launching hydrogen balloons and puzzles they solve. But along with the fun is the pain of watching Miss Applebaum get sicker and trying to help her in ways that sometimes backfire. In the end, Henry and Zelda do something they could never have imagined doing before their lives were changed by this remarkable woman.

Humorous Stories

Adams, Douglas. *The Hitchhiker's Guide to the Galaxy.* 1980. Hardcover: Crown. Paperback: Ballantine, Pocket. Ages 11–14.

"Inspired lunacy" is how one reviewer described this funny novel about a wacky trip across the galaxy. One morning Englishman Arthur Dent finds that his house is being bulldozed to make way for a bypass. Oddly enough, Earth itself is about to be eliminated to make way for a hyperspatial express route. Arthur's friend Ford, who is from another planet and is on Earth to gather information to revise the reference book *The Hitchhiker's Guide to the Galaxy*, escapes destruction by hitching a ride on a spaceship, and takes the confused Arthur with him. They bounce from danger to danger, and adventure to adventure as they go hurtling through space, encountering some truly strange characters. For those who like their humor fast and offbeat, this wild intergalactic journey is highly recommended. Followed by several sequels, starting with *The Restaurant at the End of the Universe*.

Clarke, J. *The Heroic Life of Al Capsella.* 1988. Paperback: Henry Holt. Ages 11–14.

The narrator, fourteen-year-old Al Capsella, would just like to be normal, but his parents, whom he refers to as Mr. and Mrs. Capsella, make that difficult. "The Capsellas are a real liability," he writes, especially his mother. "She's like an alien who's dropped in from another planet and doesn't know the customs—and she doesn't even try to learn." Dressed in her biker and hippie outfits, she likes to visit Al's school to complain about how things are run. He muses on this and his other problems in a hilarious voice, speaking for many kids his age as he deals with bizarre teachers and fellow students, and tries to get by without drawing attention to himself. But he also learns a valuable lesson in why being "normal" might not be everything it's cracked up to be. A comical, insightful novel, followed by *Al Capsella and the Watchdogs* and *Al Capsella Takes a Vacation*.

Danziger, Paula. *Can You Sue Your Parents for Malpractice?* 1979. Paperback: Dell. Ages 11–14.

Paula Danziger draws in readers year after year with her funny dialogue and her understanding of adolescents. Ninth-grader Lauren and eighth-grader Zack, who both want to be lawyers, meet in a junior high elective, "Law for Children and Young People." Because they like each other, classmates tease Lauren relentlessly for cradle-robbing. Trying to ignore the teasing, they get to know each other, and talk about their family problems. Lauren's father acts so tyrannical that she wonders if she can sue him for malpractice, while Zack has a personal reason for doing a class project about physical abuse of children. Despite their problems, the tone is so funny and hopeful that it will have readers chuckling and thinking at the same time.

Fine, Anne. *Flour Babies*. 1994. Paperback: Dell. Ages 11–14.

Simon and his classmates at an all-boys school only agree to do a science project about "flour babies" because they think the final class will include a wonderful explosion of flour. Each boy is to take care of a six-pound bag of flour for three weeks as if it were a baby, keeping it clean, safe, and always supervised by an adult. To his own surprise, the large, clumsy Simon, who has little interest in school, becomes attached to his flour baby, talking to it and thinking about how much work he must have caused his mother over the years. He also finds himself wondering about his father, who walked out when Simon was a baby. Serious thoughts notwithstanding, the tone of the book is hilarious, full of absurd situations caused by the flour babies and Simon's carefree approach to life.

Koertge, Ron. *Confess-O-Rama*. 1996. Hardcover: Orchard. Ages 12–14.

Fifteen-year-old Tony has moved so often, due to the deaths of his father and three stepfathers, that he no longer bothers to make new friends. But when he enrolls at Paradise High, an artistic girl named Jordan and her offbeat pals insist on befriending the reluctant newcomer. Confused about his attraction to the outspoken Jordan and worried about his grieving mother, Tony calls Confess-O-Rama, a telephone number he saw on a poster, and talks into a tape. He also seeks relief through cooking, his favorite hobby. When the outrageous Jordan gets in trouble for a good cause, Tony has to make a choice about his new friends. Meanwhile, he has made a disturbing discovery about Confess-O-Rama. Dry, witty dialogue will have readers laughing at this story about art, love, and growing up.

Lynch, Chris. *Slot Machine*. 1995. Hardcover: Harper. Paperback: Harper. Ages 12–14.

Elvin Bishop has a highly developed sense of humor, which he needs to get through his three weeks at the Christian Brothers Academy's camp for incoming freshman. He is flanked by his best friends, Mikie and Frankie, but their good-will is not enough to save him from the menacingly macho camp philosophy. The aim is for each boy to find his athletic "slot," something overweight Elvin doesn't have and doesn't really want. Nevertheless, he is slotted into one activity after another, and even makes a stab at succeeding at one. While Elvin is floundering, Mikie makes a place for himself on the basketball court and Frankie seeks popularity with the older athletes. In the end, Elvin defies the notion of slots, keeps his wits about him, and lands on his feet. A darkly funny look at a male rite of passage, narrated by an observant teenager.

McCants, William D. *Anything Can Happen in High School (And It Usually Does)*. 1993. Hardcover: Harcourt. Paperback: Harcourt. Ages 12–14.

As this novel opens, T. J. Durant, who is about to begin his sophomore year, is miserable. He dated Janet all summer and socialized with her friends in the school's most prestigious clique, but now she's dumped him for the arrogant student council president. T.J. hopes to win her back by starting the Radical Wave, a service club for less wealthy, "outsider" students such as surfers. But the Wave clashes with the school council, and soon it's a clear struggle of outsiders against insiders. His old friend Vivian, who is strong, smart, and attractive, shows a romantic interest in T.J., but he still pines for Janet and her glitzy friends. Beach parties, volleyball, and surfing give a southern California flavor to this appealing combination of humor, romance, and high school politics.

Pinkwater, Daniel. *The Snarkout Boys and the Avocado of Death*. 1982. Paperback: Dutton. Ages 11–13.

Genghis Khan High School students Walter Galt and Winston Bongo, and their new friend, a girl called Rat, "Snark

Out" whenever they can, sneaking out at night to go to the Snark Theater. When they start looking for Rat's missing uncle, their unlikely adventures have the zaniness of the movies that they watch at the Snark, like *The Attack of the Mayan Mummy* and *Invasion of the Bageloids*. They explore an underworld they never knew existed in their town, and join forces with a famous detective as well as the famous wrestler Mighty Gorilla to reach the wild ending, which features an evil orangutan and the strange Avocado of Death. For those who like their humor surrealistic and fast-moving, this thriller cannot be beat. Followed by *The Snarkout Boys and the Baconburg Horror*.

Pinkwater, Jill. *Buffalo Brenda*. 1989. Paperback: Aladdin. Ages 11–14.

If your Long Island high school team is the Buffaloes, and they need a mascot, what would be better than a live buffalo? That's what Buffalo Brenda thinks as she tries to break up her suburban school's tedium with outrageous plans. She begins stirring up trouble when she joins the school newspaper, but the principal soon puts a stop to her disruptive articles. So she and her friends launch an underground paper, causing chaos in the cafeteria with their exposé on what the kitchen is really serving the students. But that turmoil is nothing compared to the reaction when the football team finds their field inhabited by a buffalo. Anyone who has found school boring will cheer on Brenda and her friends in their series of madcap schemes.

Salassi, Otto R. *On the Ropes*. 1981. Paperback: Morrow. Ages 11–14.

When Squint's virtuous but repressive mother dies, he tracks down his errant father Claudius, who, to Squint's delight, turns their Texas farm into the Claudius Gains Wrestling

College. Claudius's colorful troupe, which includes the Masked Marvel, the Steel Claw, Badlands Betty, and others, revamps the bleak farmhouse until "There wasn't a high-rolling gambler or a lowlife bandit in Texas who wouldn't feel at home there." Claudius plans three days of high-profile wrestling that he hopes will raise enough money to save the farm from the bank. When the goal seems to be thwarted by the massive Angel of Sorrow, who appears and challenges all the fighters, Squint and his father have to scheme their way out of the threat. A rollicking adventure full of dry Texas humor.

Sleator, William. *Oddballs*. 1993. Hardcover: Dutton. Paperback: Puffin. Ages 12–14.

Sleator's stories, based on his childhood, will delight those who like a dose of "grossness" in their humor. His easygoing parents—a professor and a pediatrician—give Bill, his sister, Vicky, and their two much younger brothers, Danny and Tycho, lots of leeway. Bill's mother is "unconcerned about things like hygiene, foul language, and personal appearance," to the shock of some of his friends' mothers. As Bill and Vicky get older, they define themselves as "oddballs" who don't fit into the popular cliques. Instead, they devise offbeat ways to have their own fun with their group of male and female friends, who love to give elaborate parties and play practical tricks on strangers. Many adolescent readers will identify with their disdain for the popular crowd and hoot at their funny escapades.

Sports Fiction

Baczewski, Paul. *Just for Kicks*. 1990. Hardcover: Harper. Ages 11–14.

Be prepared to laugh at the voice of Brandon, the narrator of this sports story, who draws an unforgettable picture of the high school football team he manages. All that his team needs to dominate is a kicker, and Brandon knows that his sister, Sarah, could do a great job. When Sarah tries out, the coach, who runs the team like a boot camp, is sure he can break her. But Sarah, an excellent athlete, is unimpressed with his tough talk and more than holds her own. Brandon supports her all the way, but when a girl he likes mentions her plans to try out for the boys' basketball team, he loses his cool and has to reassess his biases. Hilarious descriptions of the coach's driving approach to football are the highlight of this entertaining story.

Brooks, Bruce. *The Moves Make the Man*. 1984. Hardcover: Harper. Paperback: Harper. Ages 12–14.

Narrator Jerome Foxworthy is a very smart thirteen-year-old from a caring family. He loves basketball but isn't welcome on the school team when he is the only black student to integrate a junior high in his North Carolina town. So he perfects his moves by playing on his own. When his mother is hospitalized and then at home recuperating, Jerome takes home ec to learn to cook, and meets Bix, the only other boy in the class. Narrated in Jerome's distinctive voice, this is the story of their friendship, which they solidify through basketball, and the story of Bix's struggle with his family's problems. Sports fans will enjoy the lyrical descriptions of basketball moves and maneuvers, while anyone who appreciates excellent writing will also want to read this memorable Newbery Honor Book.

Crutcher, Chris. *Ironman.* **1995. Hardcover: Greenwillow. Paperback: Dell. Ages 13–14.**

Have you ever heard the words "It's for your own good" or "This will hurt me more than it hurts you" as a justification for punishment? The high schoolers in Anger Management class, including Bo Brewster, know those phrases as the prelude to physical or psychological pain. Bo's father, who has convinced himself that making life hard for Bo will teach the boy responsibility, banished Bo to his room for months when he was young. Now a high school senior, Bo can't control his anger at a teacher who sounds like his father. He channels some of the anger into his triathlon training, and finds a refuge in Anger Management, where kids he thought were thugs turn into allies. Alternating between third-person narrative and letters Bo writes to talk-show host Larry King, the story culminates in the Ironman race, which Bo's father tries to sabotage. Sports, romance, and serious questions about family relationships are woven together in this witty, compelling novel.

Deuker, Carl. *Heart of a Champion.* **1993. Paperback: Avon. Ages 12–14.**

Seth never had baseball fever until he became friends with Jimmy Winter in sixth grade. Seth, whose father is dead, meets Jimmy and his dad at a park and starts practicing baseball with them. Jimmy's father, who drinks too much, pushes Jimmy by yelling at him, but he also teaches the boys a lot about ball. When Jimmy's parents split up, he moves away for a while, but he is back for high school, joining Seth on the JV baseball team freshman year. Jimmy sparks the team into life and advances quickly in baseball, with Seth lagging behind. United during senior year on the varsity team, they have a good chance of winning the championship, if drinking doesn't get in the way. Play-by-play baseball combines with serious themes in this well-written, quick-paced novel.

Dygard, Thomas J. *Running Wild*. 1996. Hardcover: Morrow. Ages 12–14.

Pete Holman believes that "Nobody does anything for nothing," so he can't understand why a police officer lets him go one night instead of calling his mother, on the condition that Pete go out for football. The high school senior reluctantly keeps his promise, despite the jeers of his drinking buddy Jimbo. To his own surprise, Pete keeps returning to football practice, even though his muscles ache and he is sure his teammates look down on him. When he shows a natural talent for finding the holes in the defense and makes some key plays, Pete is thrilled to be successful at something for once. His life just keeps improving, until Jimbo purposely jeopardizes his old friend's success. Detailed descriptions will satisfy football fans, while Pete's realistic transformation will appeal to anyone who likes a good story.

Lipsyte, Robert. *The Brave*. 1991. Paperback: Harper. Ages 12–14.

Seventeen-year-old Sonny Bear has a monster inside of him that he can't always control. When he does, he's a good boxer, who could be great. But when the rage overcomes him, he does stupid things and loses fights. Fate keeps giving him new chances, though, thanks to the people who care about him. His uncle Jake, who lives on the Moscondaga Reservation, believes in Sonny and gets him in shape, while policeman Albert Brooks, from Lipsyte's earlier book *The Contender*, tries to steer Sonny clear of drug dealers when the teenager comes to New York City, and introduces him to a good boxing gym. But Sonny struggles, knowing most people look down on him as an Indian and his tribe rejects him because his father was white. Don't miss this tautly written, suspenseful novel that is not just for boxing fans. Followed by *The Chief*.

Murrow, Liza Ketchum. *Twelve Days in August*. 1993. Hardcover: Holiday House. Paperback: Avon. Ages 12–14.

In this gripping novel, sixteen-year-old Todd O'Connor just wants to play soccer, now that he is on the varsity team. But as practice begins, the team is torn apart by the hatred of one top player, Randy, for Alex, another talented player newly arrived in Vermont from California. Angry that Alex may get the position he considers his own, Randy labels Alex a "fag" and baits anyone who likes Alex or stands up for him. While Todd's discomfort with homosexuality, learned from his father, keeps him from befriending Alex, the team divides into two camps with Todd trying to avoid a choice. Nothing seems to be going right for Todd, who alienates his girlfriend by driving recklessly and exchanges blows with Randy. In twelve long August days, Todd confronts his own prejudices and cowardice, and changes his view of life. A powerful novel that combines soccer and important social issues.

Myers, Walter Dean. *Slam!* 1996. Hardcover: Scholastic. Ages 12–14.

"Basketball is my thing. I can hoop. Case closed. I'm six four and I got the moves, the eye, and the heart"—so opens this outstanding novel about a seventeen-year-old Bronx ballplayer called Slam. Nothing comes easy to Slam, even with his talent and skill on the court, and his grades at an arts magnet school are slipping. When he's not thinking about basketball, he's daydreaming about the smart girl he likes and worrying about his best friend, Ice, who suddenly has a lot of money. As Slam makes a video of his neighborhood for a class, the reader sees it through his eyes as rough but his home. His mother wants something better for him, and so does he, but some days the way out seems impossibly blocked. Exciting basketball games combine with convincing scenes from Slam's life in this absorbing sports book.

Soto, Gary. *Taking Sides*. 1991. Hardcover: Harcourt. Paperback: Harcourt. Ages 11–14.

Lincoln Mendoza, a star basketball player on his junior high team, and his mother have moved from San Francisco's Mission District to a safer suburb. But as Lincoln complains to his old friend Tony, "There's no brown people here. Everyone's white, except for one black dude on the team." Despite Lincoln's excellent playing, his new coach doesn't like him. To add to his troubles, Lincoln has a fight with Tony and feels awkward around Monica, the new girl in his life who is also Hispanic American and plays basketball. Lincoln injures his knee before the game against his old school, yet the game becomes a turning point in adjusting to his new life. Lots of dialogue, including Spanish words defined in a glossary, convey Lincoln's likable character, his good relationship with his mother, and his growth as he tackles problems on and off the basketball court.

Spinelli, Jerry. *There's a Girl in My Hammerlock*. 1991. Hardcover: Simon & Schuster. Paperback: Aladdin. Ages 10–13.

Popular novelist Jerry Spinelli turns his observant eye toward wrestling, asking, How would a junior high boys' wrestling team react if a girl went out for the team? When a talented athlete named Maisie does just that, the team members are disbelieving. Okay, maybe she could be good, but they don't want to find out. In fact, they don't want to touch her, much less have the kind of body contact wrestling entails. Boys on opposing teams default rather than wrestle a girl, so Maisie has no chance to compete in a sport she genuinely loves. Although wrestling matches start drawing hostile students and townspeople who are furious with Maisie, she finally earns the team's respect with her courage and perseverance. Realistic dialogue, lots of laughs, and enough wrestling lore to satisfy fans make this a winner.

Wallace, Rich. *Wrestling Sturbridge*. 1996. Hardcover: Knopf. Paperback: Knopf. Ages 12–14.

Narrator Ben, a high school senior, lives in a small Pennsylvania town where the wrestling team matters to everyone. Since most boys will end up working at the cinder block factory with their dads, wrestling offers their main chance for fame. But Ben wrestles best at 135, the same weight as his friend Al, the school's top wrestler. At important meets, Al gets to wrestle while Ben looks on. For Ben, who believes he has a chance at displacing Al, it all comes down to one match, the week before the state championship. But Ben isn't sure that his single-minded sports focus is worth jeopardizing his romance with Kim, and he knows that it doesn't offer a way out of the stifling small town that hardly anyone leaves. A perceptive novel, with well-drawn characters and plenty of sports action.

Mysteries and Ghost Stories

Bellairs, John. *The House with a Clock in its Walls.* **1973. Hardcover: Peter Smith. Paperback: Puffin. Ages 10–14.**

Black magic and white magic clash in this eerie story about a boy whose attempts at casting a spell cause a catastrophe. Lewis, whose parents have died, feels welcome living with his uncle Jonathan and doesn't mind that Jonathan and his neighbor Mrs. Zimmerman practice white magic. But he isn't happy at school, where being overweight and not athletic makes it hard to gain friends. When he tries to impress a possible new friend by performing magic in a cemetery at midnight, things get out of hand and Lewis has to deal with the scary consequences. The first in a satisfying series.

Cross, Gillian. *On the Edge.* **1984. Hardcover: Holiday House. Ages 12–14.**

The son of an investigative journalist, Tug is kidnapped by terrorists one day as he comes in from running. A man and woman take him to a small cottage, and insidiously try to convince him that he is their son, while demonstrating that family life is a terrible thing—the main tenet of their terrorist group. Jinny Slattery, who lives near the cottage, suspects something odd is going on when she hears one of the terrorists tell a deliberate lie. She starts spying on the cottage and pieces the story together when she hears news reports about the kidnapping. Just when it seems that Jinny has enlisted the help she needs to rescue Tug from the gun-wielding terrorists, her plan goes badly wrong and Jinny herself is thrown into grave danger. A well-crafted, intriguing thriller.

Doherty, Berlie. *The Snake-Stone*. 1996. Hardcover: Orchard. Paperback: Penguin. Ages 11–14.

Fifteen-year-old James, who loves to dive, could be the junior British diving champion if he puts his mind to it. But he can't concentrate on diving once he starts wondering about his birth mother. He's always known that he was adopted, but only lately has it intrigued him. He has an ammonite, a "snake-stone," that was with him when his parents adopted him, and now he comes across a torn envelope with a partial address on it that came with the snake-stone. The discovery sets him on his way to seek his birth mother on a secret trip across England that proves more challenging than he expected. James is a believable, sympathetic teenager whose parents love him and trust him to find out what he needs to know. Readers will be sorry to reach the end of this memorable novel.

Duncan, Lois, editor. *Night Terrors: Stories of Shadow and Substance*. 1996. Hardcover: Simon & Schuster. Paperback: Simon & Schuster. Ages 11–14.

Eleven short stories by outstanding writers explore themes about the dangers of the night. In a tale by Richard Peck, a boy who is new in town climbs out his window at night with a mysterious girl—or is she a ghost?—who keeps appearing in his room. "The Dark Beast of Death" by popular mystery writer Joan Nixon tells about a girl in a gang who has to choose between her gang members and avenging a murdered friend. In another story, a strange visitor to an isolated house starts his stay by sharpening an ax, the first step toward murder. Ghosts, killers, coffins, mysterious voices, writhing snakes, and encounters with the dead make this collection satisfying to readers who enjoy well-written, creepy stories.

Goldman, E. M. *Getting Lincoln's Goat: An Elliot Armbruster Mystery.* **1995. Hardcover: Delacorte. Paperback: Dell. Ages 12–14.**

When the Lincoln High School mascot, a goat called Linc, goes missing twelve days before the season's biggest football game, tenth-grader Elliot Armbruster, an aspiring detective, volunteers to solve the mystery. Elliot teams up with three other students to find the goat, which proves nearly impossible. Funny, understated dialogue, a parody of tough-guy detective stories, keeps the tone light. One night, when they think they may find the goat, Elliot lists the evening's plan of action, which includes "Don Combat Attire" (they all dress in fatigues), "Commandeer Vehicle" (one student hot-wires his uncle's car), and "Liberate Goat," which doesn't turn out as expected. An amusing mystery full of wry observations about the life of an insecure high schooler, this has a bit of romance and a good plot twist at the end.

Haddix, Margaret Peterson. *Running Out of Time.* **1995. Hardcover: Simon & Schuster. Paperback: Aladdin. Ages 10–13.**

It is 1996, but a group of people in an experimental village live as if it is 1840, secretly observed at their work and play by tourists. The adults know they are part of an experiment, but the children don't. When villagers begin to sicken and die of diphtheria, the adults, who until then had access to medical care, realize the experiment has gone awry. Someone must secretly escape to the modern world and get help without getting caught by the villains now running the experiment. Thirteen-year-old Jessie agrees to try, and sneaks out into a dangerous world where she is immediately pursued. Everything is new to her—telephones, televisions, and cars. But once she has overcome her shock and thinks she has found help, people she thought she could trust turn on her. Can she outwit her opponents and make enough sense of the modern world to save her family and friends? A clever, well-written page-turner.

Hamilton, Virginia. *The House of Dies Drear*. 1968. Hardcover: Simon & Schuster. Paperback: Macmillan. Ages 11–14.
Twelve-year-old Thomas loves the idea of moving into a house that was part of the Underground Railroad. When he discovers a button that opens a tunnel in the house, he ventures in, but his flashlight goes out and strange sounds scare him. More strange events beset Thomas and his family in the large Ohio house. Much as Thomas and his father love history, and are proud of their African-American heritage, the hostility in the community and from the house's caretaker, the mysterious old Mr. Pluto, starts to bother them. But they persist in trying to unravel the strangeness, and are rewarded in a most remarkable way. A wild, ghostly evening in the woods serves as a climax to this historically accurate mystery. Followed by *The Mystery of Drear House*.

Hayes, Daniel. *The Trouble with Lemons*. 1991. Hardcover: Godine. Paperback: Fawcett. Ages 11–13.
Tyler McAllister, a likable twelve-year-old with a talent for getting in trouble, considers himself a "lemon," like a car that should be turned in for a better one. New to a small New York town, he immediately swims into a dead body at the local quarry and starts a disastrous chain of events. He and his friend Lymie suspect two high school students of putting the corpse there, but they doubt the police would believe them. Meanwhile, Tyler is dealing with a bully at school and defend-

ing his unusual family arrangement of living with a beloved housekeeper and a helpful groundsman while his mother and brother star in movies. His father, who always found fault with Tyler, has recently died, adding to his problems. Tyler is watching his back every minute, while trying to come up with a plan to unmask the culprits. A popular, funny, and fast-paced mystery. Followed by *Eye of the Beholder* and *No Effect*.

Howe, James. ***What Eric Knew: A Sebastian Barth Mystery.*** **1985. Hardcover: Atheneum. Paperback: Avon. Ages 11–13.**

Sebastian Barth likes to pit his mind against mysteries, so he is immediately intrigued when his friend Eric, who has moved away, sends him a letter with this short message: "S.I.S." Sebastian, his old friend David, and Corrie, a strong-spirited girl new to the neighborhood, no sooner start puzzling it out than a ghostlike figure appears to Corrie in the cemetery next to her house. Eric's second letter starts them wondering about the strange actions of two boys in their neighborhood. The ghost keeps appearing, and the questions pile up, but all the strands come together at the end to solve two mysteries. The first in an undemanding, entertaining mystery series.

Kerr, M. E. *Fell.* 1987. Paperback: Harper. Ages 12–14.

Combining suspense and romance, this novel introduces John Fell, whose dead father was a detective and who seems destined to follow in his footsteps. During the summer after his junior year in high school, Fell receives a strange, lucrative offer to attend a fancy boarding school under an assumed name, where he gets involved with a powerful, possibly dangerous school clique known as the Sevens. The explanations he's been given for the secrecy cease to make sense, but what are the real reasons, and how much danger is he in? He also wonders why the mysterious girl he is beginning to love is so elusive. This first installment in a popular series is a quick read that promises more excitement in its sequels *Fell Back* and *Fell Down.*

Nixon, Joan Lowery. *Spirit Seeker*. 1995. Hardcover: Delacorte. Paperback: Dell. Ages 11–14.

When Cody Garnett's parents are found knifed to death at home, the police suspect teenager Cody, who had argued with them that evening about a new car. But his friend Holly, whose father is the police detective on the case, believes in Cody's innocence, even when the facts seem to be stacked against him. Although her father forbids Holly to see Cody, she keeps in touch and starts searching for evidence in his favor. She digs into his father's business records, visits Cody's lawyer, and even spends time with a clairvoyant who claims that Holly herself has unknown powers. But it is the power of deduction and Holly's courage that win in the long run in this tense, fast-moving mystery by a popular author.

Patneaude, David. *Someone Was Watching*. 1993. Hardcover: Albert Whitman. Paperback: Albert Whitman. Ages 11–14.

Nobody saw Chris's little sister, Molly, drown in the river, but her coloring book was on the pier, and search crews never found her body. Three months after the tragedy, thirteen-year-old Chris watches a videotape he made on the day she disappeared and sees things that don't seem right. With his close friend Pat, he starts to investigate and embarks on a search that leads them across the country to find the truth about what happened that day at the river. Chris, who is smart and brave, misses Molly deeply and isn't ashamed to show it, while Pat, a six-foot-tall football player, also misses Molly and worries about Chris. A suspenseful story with likable heroes and a dramatic conclusion.

Peck, Richard. *The Ghost Belonged to Me.* **1975. Paperback: Penguin. Ages 10–13.**

When his classmate Blossom Culp tells thirteen-year-old Alexander that he is psychic, Alexander scoffs. But then, to his shock, Alexander starts seeing eerie lights in his barn that thrust him into events he had never imagined could happen. His new powers do not sit well with his overly respectable mother and sister, but his old uncle Miles understands the psychic world and helps Alexander in his ghostly tasks. In the end, the scrappy Blossom Culp pitches in as well. Alexander's dry observations about the people around him and small-town life in 1913 add humor to this popular ghost story. The first in a series.

Fantasy and Science Fiction

Cooper, Susan. *Over Sea, Under Stone.* **Illustrated by Margery Gill. 1965. Hardcover: Harcourt. Paperback: Macmillan. Ages 10–14.**

When Barney, Jane, and Simon visit their great-uncle Merry, they get caught up in a perilous struggle against evil forces. First they find a map that seems to lead to the Holy Grail nearby on the coast of Cornwall. With Great-Uncle Merry's help, the children seek the Grail, while enemies try to steal the map and reach the treasure first. The climax pits the boys, with some help from Jane, against the forces of nature and the enemy. Ancient stones on cliffs, moonlight excursions, and references to King Arthur flavor this mythological fantasy, the first in a complex series of five books, which do not all feature the same children. The fourth book, *The Grey King*, won the Newbery Medal.

Farmer, Nancy. *The Ear, the Eye, and the Arm*. 1994. Hardcover: Orchard. Paperback: Puffin. Ages 11–14.

In this highly original novel, thirteen-year-old Tendai, who longs for adventure, is cooped up in his well-to-do family's Zimbabwe home in the year 2194. Because his father is the country's head of security, Tendai, his sister, Rita, and their younger brother, Kuda, are not allowed to wander around the city. When they do manage to sneak out, they are kidnapped, then escape, only to be trapped again by several bizarre characters. Their parents hire the Ear, the Eye, and the Arm, three likable detectives who each have a superpower due to genetic mutations. The detectives are hot on the trail of the children and their enemies but are never quite close enough until the gripping climax, in which all of the main characters must test their courage against the threat of enormous evil. An absorbing, fast-paced story with wonderful humor and lots of excitement. A Newbery Honor Book.

Jones, Diana Wynne. *Archer's Goon*. 1984. Hardcover: Greenwillow. Ages 11–14.

In this complex, entertaining fantasy, thirteen-year-old Howard Sykes comes home one day to find a huge man with a small head sprawled on a kitchen chair. Nicknamed the Goon, the visitor plans to stay until Howard's father, who is an author, writes two thousand words for him. As it turns out, several strange people want Mr. Sykes's writing, and Howard wants to know why. He learns that their city is run by seven wizardly siblings, each of whom controls different aspects, such as housing, electric power, education, music, crime, and police. After the wizards start plaguing his family, Howard and his stubborn younger sister, known as Awful, visit each sibling in turn, trying to figure out why their family has been thrust into the absurd power struggle. By one of today's most talented fantasy writers, this imaginative novel is highly recommended.

LeGuin, Ursula K. A *Wizard of Earthsea*. Illustrated by Ruth Robbins. 1968. Hardcover: Atheneum. Paperback: Bantam. Ages 11–14.

When the bronzesmith's son, Ged, realizes his strong talent for magic, he wants to use it quickly to gain power and glory. He voyages across the Archipelago to the island of Roke, where the wizards of Earthsea are trained. But the path to becoming a mage is painfully slow, and his poor background embarrasses him. Spurred by pride, Ged experiments with powers beyond his control and calls up a dark spirit from the dead. Although he survives the encounter, he must give up his dreams of glory and leave Roke. In his wanderings, he fights dragons and other enemies, but ultimately his quest requires him to face the darkness again. LeGuin has created a richly detailed world with its own history, languages, and magic, which will fully engage readers. A sophisticated fantasy, this is the first book in the outstanding Earthsea series.

Lipsyte, Robert. *The Chemo Kid*. 1992. Paperback: Harper. Ages 12–14.

At his junior prom, Fred Bauer discovers a lump in his neck, which turns out to be a rare form of cancer. He has always felt like a wimp, a nobody, and now, he thinks, he will be a wimp without hair and with a puffy, greenish face from chemotherapy. But a computer game called Cyberpunk Rovers that he once played takes on new meaning as Fred faces real dangers and seems to develop superpowers. Could he be as strong as he thinks he is? Or is he just creating a new persona to fight the cancer, as other teenagers at the hospital have done? While he is fighting his personal battles, he also gets involved in his girlfriend's protests against chemical dumping in a local reservoir. Realistic gallows humor among his friends with cancer combines with cyberspace fantasy to create a highly original story about a boy who discovers unknown strengths.

Lowry, Lois. *The Giver*. 1993. Hardcover: Houghton. Paperback: Dell. Ages 11–14.

In this brilliant novel set in the future, a boy named Jonas is assigned to train with The Giver, the one person in their conformist society who studies history and holds the painful and pleasurable memories of the past. In his new role, Jonas starts to question the ways of his society, which provides for everyone's basic needs but gives people very few choices. He experiences a range of emotions and sensations for the first time, which sets him apart from his friends and family. When a crisis arises in his family, Jonas has to make a painfully difficult choice before he feels ready for it. Jonas's actions lead to an ambiguous conclusion that may frustrate some readers, while others will find it as thought-provoking as the rest of the book. A Newbery Medal winner.

McKinley, Robin. *The Hero and the Crown*. 1984. Hardcover: Greenwillow. Paperback: Ace. Ages 10–14.

Dragons, which have always been a problem in Damar, are getting worse—small dragons plague the countryside, and a fearsomely large dragon lies in wait. Aerin, misfit daughter of the king of Damar, has rehabilitated her father's injured warhorse, Talat, and concocted a salve that protects against dragon fire. Riding Talat, supplied with her salve, and skilled at swordplay, Aerin first kills small dragons, then fights the most dangerous dragon seen in years. Having survived this almost fatal encounter, Aerin the Dragon-Killer must face an even more difficult foe, an evil sorcerer who threatens all of Damar. A terrific adventure in the spirit of high fantasy, this won the Newbery Medal. It is a prequel to *The Blue Sword*, in which Aerin appears but another heroine plays the central role.

Pearce, Philippa. *Tom's Midnight Garden*. 1959. Hardcover: Harper. Paperback: Harper. Ages 10–13.

Tom resents being sent to stay with his aunt and uncle in their boring apartment, banished by his brother's measles. But his attitude changes when he sneaks out one night and finds a huge garden behind the house, with countless hidden places to explore. The next day he realizes that the garden doesn't exist—except at night. So each night he runs free and soon becomes friends with Hatty, a girl in old-fashioned clothes who shares his games, builds a tree house with him, and enjoys herself despite her otherwise miserable life. Tom wonders why Hatty is young on some nights, and much older on others. Is she a ghost or, as she argues, is he? And how can he avoid being sent home, now that he has found the garden? This enchanting fantasy is a book that readers hope will never end.

Pierce, Tamora. *Wild Magic*. 1992. Hardcover: Atheneum. Paperback: Random House. Ages 11–14.

Daine, who has always lived near the wilderness, is an outstanding archer and woodswoman who can communicate with animals through magic. When she lands a job caring for the queen's horses, the queen and her followers appreciate Daine's powers more than she does herself. With the help of a mage, she expands her abilities, despite the danger of becoming a wild animal in the process. Her increased powers prove vital when the country must defend itself against an invasion of immortal monsters. The first of four books in the Immortals series, this swashbuckling adventure offers a mix of magic and battle in a mythical land. Fantasy fans will also enjoy *Alanna*, and the other books in the Song of the Lioness series, which shares characters with *Wild Magic*.

Pullman, Philip. *The Golden Compass*. 1996. Hardcover: Knopf. Paperback: Ballantine. Ages 11–14.

In this long, original fantasy, Lyra Belacqua and her animal companion Pantalaimon go on a quest to free her father from prison and rescue the many children who have been kidnapped from her country. As she journeys north to a dangerous land where cruel scientists are experimenting on the missing children, she makes friends with witches, an armored bear, and other children. An adventurer at heart, Lyra takes risks without fear and discovers her talent for planning strategies against her enemies. But little does she know how important her success will be—and not just to herself. This complex, absorbing novel with a surprisingly inconclusive ending will have readers eager to read its sequel, *The Subtle Knife*.

Sleator, William. *Interstellar Pig*. 1984. Hardcover: Peter Smith, Dutton. Paperback: Puffin. Ages 12–14.

Barney, who is staying at a summer cottage with his parents, finds the renters in the only nearby cottage to be strange but appealing. The woman, Zena, and the two men, Manny and Joe, speak English with an accent Barney can't identify and spend most of their time playing a board game called Interstellar Pig. They seem oddly obsessed with the cottage he is staying in, and barge in to search it when his parents are gone. Barney is flattered when Zena invites him to join the game and finds it more compelling than he expected. It revolves around aliens from different planets trying to find and keep The Piggy, no matter the cost to others. It isn't long before Barney realizes that it is more than a game and far more dangerous than anything he has ever encountered. An imaginative adventure that will hold readers in its grip.

Stevermer, Caroline. *River Rats.* **1992. Hardcover: Harcourt. Paperback: Harcourt. Ages 12–14.**

Science fiction meets Mark Twain in this adventure about six orphaned teenagers on a riverboat. Set in the twenty-first century, the story takes place after the Flash, when most cities have been destroyed. The River Rats travel the lethally polluted Mississippi River on a paddle wheeler that was once a museum, performing rock and roll at small towns to earn money. Their problems increase when they rescue an older man called King from angry pursuers with hounds, who then start following the boat. King is a great musician, but his presence leads the River Rats into peril in a nearly deserted city. The narrator, Tomcat, who longs to prove his courage, learns in the process how much he loves the river and their boat. Especially fun for those who know Huck Finn, this is a terrific, futuristic thriller.

Tolkien, J. R. R. *The Hobbit, or, There and Back Again.* **1932. Hardcover: Houghton. Paperback: Ballantine, Houghton. Ages 10–14.**

"In a hole in the ground there lived a hobbit"—so begins this rich fantasy classic. Hobbits, who are smaller than humans and inclined to be stout, know how to enjoy themselves. Bilbo Baggins, who is around fifty, has led a respectable life, but now the wizard Gandalf talks him into taking an adventure. Against his better judgment, Bilbo sets off with thirteen dwarfs, who believe he is a burglar, to recover treasure stolen by a dragon long ago. On the journey, they encounter nasty trolls, vile goblins, and magical elves. They engage in a dreadful battle, and Bilbo more than proves his worth to his new friends. Tolkien creates a complete world with its own languages and history, one that readers will not want to leave. Fortunately, *The Hobbit* is followed by the incomparable *Lord of the Rings* trilogy, in which Bilbo's nephew Frodo goes on a longer, darker adventure of his own.

Turner, Megan Whalen. *The Thief.* 1996. Hardcover: Greenwillow. Ages 12–14.

Gen's bragging about what a good thief he is has landed him in the king's prison in a country that resembles ancient Greece. When the king's minister takes Gen on a journey to steal a magic stone, the thief is happy to be out of prison, even if he is not always well treated by the minister and his three underlings. The pace of the journey and the story are leisurely until they reach their destination, where the thief pits himself against magical forces. Then, as the story moves toward the end, the plot takes some unexpected, fascinating turns. For any reader who enjoys a challenging plot, this book is a must. A Newbery Honor Book.

Biographies

Leaders and Activists

Beals, Melba Pattillo. *Warriors Don't Cry.* **1995 abridged edition. Paperback: Pocket. Ages 13–14.**

In 1957, fifteen-year-old Melba Pattillo was one of nine African-American students to integrate Central High School in Little Rock, Arkansas. She tells her painful story in a matter-of-fact voice, but the events themselves will grip readers and stir their anger. The hatred that the white citizens directed toward the students was unrelenting. Pattillo relied on her remarkably strong mother and grandmother but worried about the suffering that the integration caused them. Guarded by soldiers, the black students were still in danger from dynamite, threats of lynching, and acid sprayed in their eyes. Beals's suspenseful, well-written story brings an immediacy to this shameful chapter in our history, which every reader should know about. Highly recommended.

Bober, Natalie S. *Thomas Jefferson: Man on a Mountain.* **1988. Paperback: Aladdin. Ages 12–14.**

"Author of the Declaration of Independence, Of the Statute of Virginia for Religious Freedom, and Father of the University of Virginia" is the description Jefferson himself chose for his gravestone. He also served as president, vice president, and diplomat to France, and wrote in various fields. This 250-page biography's strength is the subject himself, whose life and achievements, personal and public, are described in a readable manner. Excerpts from his many daily notes and letters as well as other contemporary writings add interesting details. With its admiring tone, the biography doesn't adequately deal with the discrepancy between Jefferson's writings against slavery and his own reliance on slaves. Nevertheless, this biography provides a serviceable portrait of an impressive man.

Freedman, Russell. *Lincoln: A Photobiography.* **1987. Hardcover: Clarion. Paperback: Clarion. Ages 10–14.**

This photobiography paints a vivid picture of Abraham Lincoln through strong writing and a fine array of photographs. After a compelling introductory chapter, the book follows Lincoln from his childhood, distinguishing myth from fact, through his years of manual labor to his career as a lawyer and politician. Much of the book covers his presidency and the Civil War that raged during it. The most photographed man of his time, Lincoln can be seen to age visibly through the war years. Newspaper cartoons, paintings and etchings, and reproductions of his handwritten speeches round out the richly researched picture. Although Lincoln's ambition and his moodiness are not ignored, a sense of his compassion and courage permeates the text. A memorable Newbery Medal winner.

Harrison, Barbara, and Daniel Terris. *A Twilight Struggle: The Life of John Fitzgerald Kennedy.* **1992. Hardcover: Lothrop. Ages 12–14.**

This effective biography offers a balanced view of John F. Kennedy, tracing his path to the presidency and in the White House. Beautifully organized, it opens with Frost's poem "Birches," and uses quotes from it to set the mood for each chapter. One chapter covers Kennedy's childhood and schooling, followed by six chapters on his political career. Personal and professional problems are acknowledged, while Kennedy's strengths, presented with a liberal bias, come across clearly, including his support of the arts and his commitment to public service. The well-crafted text and many black-and-white photographs give a sense of Kennedy's charm and the country's fascination with him and his family. Also look for the authors' biography of Robert Kennedy.

McKissack, Patricia, and Fredrick McKissack. *W.E.B. DuBois*. 1990. Hardcover: Franklin Watts. Ages 10–14.

Anyone who believes the civil rights struggle began in the 1960s will find this biography enlightening. It describes the life and work of the remarkable African-American leader W.E.B. DuBois, who was born in 1868 and died in Ghana at the age of ninety-five. His fine mind earned him a scholarship to Fisk University, study at the University of Berlin, and a doctorate from Harvard. He taught at Atlanta University, published widely, edited the NAACP magazine *The Crisis*, and worked untiringly for the rights of blacks. This even-handed biography takes note of DuBois's conflicts with other leaders, including Booker T. Washington, and clearly describes his disillusionment with the United States and its policies toward blacks. Although the text appears dense on the page, the writing is accessible and the story of DuBois's accomplishments is one all Americans should know.

Myers, Walter Dean. *Malcolm X: By Any Means Necessary*. 1993. Hardcover: Scholastic. Paperback: Scholastic. Ages 12–14.

In this appreciative biography, Myers looks at the life and accomplishments of the controversial black leader Malcolm X. Born Malcolm Little, the future leader was the son of parents who worked for civil rights and suffered for their courage. An excellent student but discouraged from aiming high, Malcolm ended up in prison at age twenty, where he learned about the Nation of Islam, a religious movement that became the focus of his life. It provided the path Malcolm followed to become a leader who voiced the anger that many blacks felt, while also working to improve conditions for blacks. Before his assassination at age thirty-nine, Malcolm X embraced a wider vision of black world unity. This well-written biography incorporates relevant history about African Americans and the civil rights movement into its thoughtful portrait of an outspoken leader.

Severance, John B. *Gandhi: Great Soul*. 1997. Hardcover: Clarion. Ages 11–14.

Mohandas Gandhi, one of the most influential men of the twentieth century, led a life of both action and thought. This attractive volume, filled with black-and-white photographs, concentrates on his political activities and his philosophy, while only briefly discussing his personal life. Because Gandhi's life was intertwined with India's struggles to become independent from England, useful background and incidents from that history are included. Although largely admiring, the biography does allude to Gandhi's difficulties with some of his colleagues and with his wife. Overall, this well-focused biography depicts a courageous man who promoted nonviolence as a means of change.

Artists, Musicians, and Writers

Cox, Clinton. *Mark Twain: America's Humorist, Dreamer, Prophet.* **1995. Hardcover: Scholastic. Ages 11–14.**

With an emphasis on Twain's struggles with racism, this biography offers a fair-minded portrait of a complex man. It explores the many roads Twain took on his way to becoming one of America's greatest writers, with apt details about his adventures on the Mississippi River and in the West. Twain's writings are described briefly for those who haven't read them, as are the reactions of critics and the public. The main focus is Twain's expansive, many-sided personality with its strengths and weaknesses. The forthright look at his racism shows its origins, how much he overcame it and spoke out for blacks eventually, but also how he never completely abandoned his prejudices. A variety of illustrations enhance this fluent biography about a significant writer.

Duggleby, John. *Artist in Overalls: The Life of Grant Wood.* **1996. Hardcover: Chronicle Books. Ages 10–14.**

Grant Wood, the Iowan who painted "American Gothic," the famous painting of a somber rural man in overalls holding a pitchfork next to a woman in an apron, originated the American style of painting known as Regionalism. This elegant biography tells about Wood's childhood and education, and the many obstacles he faced on his way to becoming a well-respected artist. Large reproductions of his works in color and black-and-white show the range of his talent, while the landscapes give a sense of the Iowa countryside where Wood grew up. The book is beautifully designed from the dust jacket to the endpapers, with the attention to visual detail appropriate to a book on art. An unusually good biography of an artist.

Mühlberger, Richard. *What Makes a Picasso a Picasso?* 1994. Paperback: Metropolitan Museum of Art/Viking. Ages 11–13.

This useful book focuses on Picasso's artwork, although it touches briefly on his personal life. The artist's originality is stressed as well as his impact on the art world. In discussing the paintings, reproduced in color, the text talks about color, line, shape, composition, subject matter, and brushwork. Often one area of a painting is enlarged for special discussion. The paintings highlight his different styles and eras, such as his Blue period, Circus period, cubism, and collage. Readers will gain a better understanding of how to view Picasso's work and art in general. One in a long series that includes Brueghel, Cassatt, Monet, and others.

Osofsky, Audrey. *Free to Dream: The Making of a Poet: Langston Hughes.* 1996. Hardcover: Lothrop. Ages 11–14.

Many excerpts from his writing grace this biography of the famous African-American poet Langston Hughes. Supplemented by occasional photographs of him, his family, and the places he lived, the text spans Hughes's life from his unhappy childhood through his illustrious career to his death in 1967. Social history about African Americans is woven into the story as well. Hughes faced enormous challenges in the literary world, where it was difficult for blacks to get published and make a living. Yet through extraordinary talent and determination, he did succeed, writing forty-six books, plus plays and even operas, giving a voice to the hopes, dreams, and struggles of fellow African Americans. This admirable biography may inspire readers to seek out more of Hughes's poetry.

Reef, Catherine. *Walt Whitman*. 1995. Hardcover: Clarion. Ages 11–14.

Walt Whitman, who lived from 1819 to 1892, pioneered a style of poetry that has influenced the generations after him. This biography sets his life in the context of nineteenth-century America, discussing factors that affected him, such as the growth of New York, abolitionism, and the Civil War. A balanced assessment emerges of the poet's personality, from his unwillingness to work hard at a job to his intense love of nature and language. Drawing effectively from Whitman's poetry and prose, and from the writings of those who knew him, the text describes a complex man. His homosexuality is mentioned briefly, but far more emphasis is put on his relationship with his parents and siblings, and on his work. Photographs, etchings, and other artifacts enhance this well-designed, effective book.

Thompson, Wendy. *Joseph Haydn*. 1991. Hardcover: Viking. Ages 12–14.

This unusually rich biography features bars of music from some of Haydn's well-known compositions, including an entire early sonata. The many paintings and drawings of the composer and his times integrated into the text create an attractive collage. The biography combines information about Haydn's accomplishments with interesting details about his personal life, amplified by quotes from his own writings and those of his contemporaries. His character flaws are fairly noted, but the focus is on his great talent and originality, with reference to specific works and how they were received. Readers will be eager to listen to the musical works described, to add yet another layer to this fine volume. Also look for books by the same author about Mozart, Beethoven, and Schubert.

Wilson, Janet. *The Ingenious Mr. Peale: Painter, Patriot and Man of Science.* 1996. Hardcover: Atheneum. Ages 11–14.

"Ingenious" is the perfect word for Charles Willson Peale, who lived from 1741 to 1827, and pursued an impressive range of interests such as art, natural history, and inventing. In a time when few made a living as painters, Peale was well known for his portraits of prominent men, including many of George Washington. He established the first public American picture gallery, and opened the country's first scientifically organized museum of natural history. Black-and-white reproductions of Peale's paintings complement the lively writing in presenting an exceptional man.

Scientists and Inventors

Freedman, Russell. *The Wright Brothers: How They Invented the Airplane.* Illustrated with Original Photographs by Wilbur and Orville Wright. 1991. Hardcover: Holiday House. Paperback: Holiday House. Ages 10–14.

As amateur photographers who knew they were making history, the Wright brothers documented their progress in aviation with extraordinary photographs, which are used to great effect in illustrating this biography. The text provides fascinating details about the brothers and their work, as well as background about aviation and their contributions to it. Their personalities and their intense enjoyment in inventing come through clearly. "We could hardly wait for morning to come to get at something that interested us. *That's* happiness," said Orville. Even those not interested in aviation will be pulled in by the well-told story and the starkly beautiful photographs. This Newbery Honor Book is not to be missed.

Haskins, Jim. *Outward Dreams: Black Inventors and Their Inventions.* **1991. Hardcover: Walker. Ages 11–14.**

Haskins pays tribute to an impressive array of black inventors from colonial times through the present, taking note of the racial bias many of them faced. He devotes a chapter to Benjamin Banneker, a mathematician who, in the 1790s, produced a highly accurate almanac based on his own astronomical observations. James Forten, who was born in 1766, made a fortune from a device to improve sailing ships and ran his own sail factory. The list continues: Lewis Latimer, Granville T. Woods, Madame C. J. Walker, George Washington Carver, and many others. Haskins uses clear prose and apt anecdotes, with occasional photographs, to present the little-known, intriguing stories.

Kittredge, Mary. *Barbara McClintock: Biologist.* **1991. Hardcover: Chelsea House. Ages 12–14.**

In 1983, eighty-one-year-old Barbara McClintock received the Nobel Prize for her groundbreaking work in genetics. She had revealed her most important findings thirty years earlier, but other scientists had rejected her innovative theories, which are explained in simplified terms and diagrams throughout the text. When gender bias prevented McClintock, a brilliant graduate student, from getting a good teaching job, she secured a permanent research position at a research center where she spent most of her career. "It was fun," she explained about her work. "I couldn't wait to get up in the morning." This engaging biography conveys McClintock's determination to follow her own direction in her personal life as well as her work. Her perseverance and independence will inspire all readers, whether they hope to be scientists or not.

McPherson, Stephanie Sammartino. *Ordinary Genius: The Story of Albert Einstein.* **1995. Hardcover: Carolrhoda. Ages 10–13.**

In this readable biography, Einstein comes across as always excited about ideas. As a boy, he was fascinated by the force of magnetism in a compass; on his deathbed, he was still making notes about a scientific interest. McPherson explains his theories of relativity, noting that the explanations are greatly simplified, and paints a picture of Einstein's private and public lives, including his troubled first marriage, his growing fame, and his commitment to Jewish causes. The reader receives an impression of a man for whom thinking about the workings of the universe was his greatest joy, but who also took time to try to make a difference in the world. Black-and-white photographs of this distinctive-looking scientist add a personal note.

Pasachoff, Naomi. *Alexander Graham Bell: Making Connections.* **1996. Hardcover: Oxford. Ages 12–14.**

This biography for older readers skillfully introduces one of the world's great inventors, conveying Bell's keen excitement at solving problems and his commitment to improving the world, especially for the deaf. Although he had little formal education, he followed his father and grandfather into the field of speech therapy, from which he branched out to all aspects of sound, which led to designing the telephone. Bell also had strong interests in genetics and early aviation, and helped start the National Geographic Society and *Science* magazine. His work with the deaf, including his friend Helen Keller, gave Bell his greatest satisfaction. This elegant biography, illustrated with black-and-white photographs and diagrams, features several useful sidebars about technological information.

Men and Women in History

Atkinson, Linda. *In Kindling Flame: The Story of Hannah Senesh, 1921–1944.* 1985. Paperback: Morrow. Ages 13–14.

How many people who have escaped from enemy-occupied territory would be willing to parachute back in to help others? Hannah Senesh was a brave young Jewish woman who fled from Hungary to Palestine during World War II, only to join the Resistance Movement and return to rescue Allied prisoners and her compatriot Jews. She amazed her colleagues with her prowess at parachuting and with her fearlessness. A person of strong character, Senesh died for her beliefs at an early age. Drawing from her own prolific writings and the testimony of friends, this moving biography presents a courageous freedom fighter.

Frank, Anne. *Anne Frank: The Diary of a Young Girl.* Translated by B. M. Mooyaart. 1967. Hardcover: Doubleday. Paperback: Bantam. Ages 11–14.

While hiding from the Nazis in Amsterdam, the adolescent Anne Frank expressed her hopes and fears in a remarkably vivid diary that still speaks to readers. She faced the news of the death of many friends, and the fact that she and her family might die. Nevertheless, she also dwelt on everyday pleasures and problems, keeping her sense of humor intact, and tried to view her family's confinement as a "dangerous adventure." A talented writer, she chose effective anecdotes and slices of conversation to draw a picture of her surroundings. Her ability to bring the reader into her world is so extraordinary that the final note about her death in a Nazi concentration camp feels like a personal loss. An intensely powerful work that everyone should read.

Freedman, Russell. *The Life and Death of Crazy Horse.* Illustrated with drawings by Amos Bad Heart Bull. 1996. Hardcover: Holiday House. Ages 11–14.

When the Sioux war leader Crazy Horse was thirteen, he had a sacred vision that showed he could not be hurt by his enemies if he always acted for the good of his people. His life seemed to confirm the vision, for he was a daring fighter who survived many battles and was killed off the battlefield. This finely crafted story of his life also provides a picture of the Sioux and related tribes during the second half of the nineteenth century, and bears testimony to the unconscionable way the U.S. government treated them. Freedman describes Crazy Horse's childhood and coming-of-age, then recounts his deeds as a warrior fighting for his people's independent way of life, with descriptions of specific battles. Memorable drawings by a cousin of Crazy Horse illustrate this dynamic book.

Hamilton, Virginia. *Anthony Burns: The Defeat and Triumph of a Fugitive Slave.* 1988. Hardcover: Knopf. Paperback: Knopf. Ages 12–14.

This gripping biography does more than record the life of Anthony Burns, who was tried under the Fugitive Slave Act of 1850. It draws a picture of the bleak indignities of slave life, and the despair of returning to slavery from freedom. Burns, who had escaped from Virginia to Boston, became a focus for abolitionists when his "owner" had him arrested and planned to take him back. Author and lawyer Richard Dana defended Burns, while pro-slavery president Franklin Pierce authorized federal troops to guard Burns and prevent rioting. The text follows the trial closely, while also conveying Burns's painful memories of his childhood and teenage years as a slave. An emotionally charged story about an important historical figure.

Murphy, Jim. *A Young Patriot: The American Revolution as Experienced by One Boy.* **Illustrated with prints. 1996. Hardcover: Clarion. Ages 11–14.**

In 1776, Connecticut farm boy Joseph Martin enlisted to fight the British, and served almost continuously until the war ended in 1783. Many years later, he wrote a book detailing his experiences. Drawing heavily on Martin's own words, this exemplary history book, illustrated with occasional prints, follows Martin's war years while giving general information about the Revolution. Martin encountered important military leaders such as Washington, Lafayette, and Steuben, and fought in major battles. He wintered at Valley Forge, and took part in a minor mutiny when troops were nearly starving. His words cut through any romantic view of the soldiers' lives, yet he retains his sense of courage and patriotism throughout. A vivid picture of the Revolution.

Sullivan, George. *Mathew Brady: His Life and Photographs.* **1994. Hardcover: Cobblehill. Ages 12–14.**

History and photography buffs will find this biography of great interest. Mathew Brady pioneered the role of photography in recording history, consciously making a record of the Civil War for posterity. Before the war, Brady had established himself as an important daguerreotypist, specializing in photographs of famous people. Photographs taken by his employees of battlefields and the dead soldiers brought the Civil War home to people in an immediate way never experienced before. This well-organized volume, amply illustrated with photographs from Brady's studio, looks at the war through photographs and offers a historical perspective to photography as a field.

Adventurers and Explorers

Andronik, Catherine M. *Prince of Humbugs: A Life of P. T. Barnum.* 1994. Hardcover: Atheneum. Ages 11–14.

P. T. Barnum, founder of the Barnum & Bailey Circus, was the consummate showman. He concocted new ways to promote his enterprises and loved to be in the limelight. In fact, he was the first person to use "limelights," the forerunners of modern spotlights, to draw crowds. With a partner, he introduced the extra rings that created a three-ring circus to give viewers more to watch. This absorbing biography reveals his shortcomings and his willingness to twist the truth for profit. But his colorful life and pioneering use of advertising make him a notable historical figure, one whose life reads like a fast-moving novel. Black-and-white pictures, including some of his ornate mansions, give a sense of the era.

Ayer, Eleanor H. *Margaret Bourke-White: Photographing the World.* 1992. Hardcover: Silver Burdett. Ages 11–14.

Photographer Margaret Bourke-White risked danger again and again to take crucial photographs of historic events. During World War II, she stood on the roof of the American embassy to photograph Germany's bombing of Moscow. She went on an Allied bombing raid and took photographs from the lead plane, and accompanied General Patton to Buchenwald, where she bore witness to concentration camp atrocities. Bourke-White was also a pioneer in the areas of photo-essays, which she published in *Life* magazine, and industrial photography, where her shots of factories and steel mills changed the way people viewed industry. Black-and-white photographs from her extensive work illustrate different stages in her career in this exciting biography.

Reit, Seymour. *Behind Rebel Lines: The Incredible Story of Emma Edmonds, Civil War Spy.* 1988. Paperback: Harcourt. Ages 10–13.

During the Civil War, a remarkable woman named Emma Edmonds disguised herself as a man to serve in the Union Army, one of about four hundred women who passed as male soldiers. For two years she fooled everyone around her except for a chaplain's wife. A skillful spy, she went on eleven missions behind Confederate lines to collect information on troop size and plans, passing at various times as an old black man, a handsome Confederate sympathizer, and a matronly Irish peddler. Her army career ended when she was hospitalized and her secret discovered. This dynamic biography intrigues male and female readers alike.

Stefoff, Rebecca. *Marco Polo and the Medieval Explorers.* 1992. Hardcover: Chelsea House. Ages 13–14.

More than a biography, this book describes an era when Europeans expanded their horizons, none farther than the famous traveler Marco Polo. In 1275, when he was twenty, Marco Polo left Venice on a journey to the Far East, returning only after twenty years of traveling and service to the Mongol leader Kublai Khan. When he published the story of his travels, it inspired explorers such as Columbus to seek an ocean route to China. This well-written account details the routes Polo took, and some impressive achievements of the Mongol empire such as their advanced transportation and postal systems. With many prints, including a color inset, this history captures the spirit of an exciting time and a venturesome traveler.

Woog, Adam. *Harry Houdini.* 1995. Hardcover: Lucent. Ages 11–14.

This substantial biography chronicles the life and career of the famous magician Houdini. Packed with information, the book includes many black-and-white photographs, reproductions of posters, and sidebars on topics such as straitjackets and the disappearing elephant trick. It follows Houdini's progress, from performing on Coney Island to his emergence as an international star, and explains how he did some of his tricks. Houdini's forceful self-confidence and large ego are clear, as is his capacity for endless work. Despite the dense format and overabundance of quotes, this biography of Houdini's colorful life is an exciting read.

Sports Stars

Krull, Kathleen. *Lives of the Athletes: Thrills, Spills (And What the Neighbors Thought).* **Illustrated by Kathryn Hewitt. 1997. Hardcover: Harcourt. Ages 9–14.**

Baseball great Roberto Clemente liked to drink grape juice mixed with raw eggs. Kung fu expert and movie star Bruce Lee kicked and punched in his sleep. When Gertrude Ederle swam across the English Channel, she coated her skin with olive oil, lanolin, and lard mixed with petroleum jelly. These are among the quirky facts that readers will learn along with career highlights of twenty significant athletes. A few are household names like Babe Ruth and Jackie Robinson; others, like Babe Didrikson and Sonja Henie, were better known in their time. Three to five pages of vibrant text are each accompanied by a colorful caricature. This entertaining volume covers a century of athletic prowess. Also look for companion books on musicians, artists, and writers.

Lewin, Ted. *I Was a Teenage Professional Wrestler.* 1993.
Hardcover: Orchard. Paperback: Hyperion. Ages 10–14.

To finance his art school education and get launched in a
career, noted children's book illustrator Ted Lewin worked
evenings as a professional wrestler. This memorable autobiography highlights the unusual juxtaposition of his "double
life: Renoir, Rubens, and Picasso by day; headlocks, hammer-
locks, and flying tackles by night." He brought the two areas
together by sketching and painting the world of professional
wrestlers; some of those works are reproduced in the book.
Lewin describes the wrestling life, with its camaraderie, adula-
tion, injuries, and occasional riots, in a conversational tone.
Even the reader with no interest in professional wrestling will
find this creative book fascinating.

Lipsyte, Robert. *Jim Thorpe: Twentieth-Century Jock.*
1993. Hardcover: Harper. Paperback: Harper. Ages 10–14.

In 1950, the Associated Press voted Jim Thorpe "the Male
Athlete of the Half-Century" for his remarkable accomplishments, which included playing outstanding football, winning
Olympic Gold medals in the decathlon and pentathlon, and
playing pro baseball. A Native American, Thorpe grew up
poor in Oklahoma and was forced to attend Indian boarding
schools dedicated to teaching students "civilized white ways."
He encountered prejudice against Native Americans all his
life, as this short biography documents. Lipsyte presents a
smoothly written, balanced account of Thorpe, with many
descriptions of athletic events. Anyone who cares about sports
should read about this early superstar.

Macy, Sue. *Winning Ways: A Photohistory of American Women in Sports.* **1996. Hardcover: Henry Holt. Ages 11–14.**

A woman boxing in 1912? A woman rodeo rider from the first half of this century? A female weight lifter from the 1930s? Readers will be surprised by the range of sports women have participated in over the years, shown in page after page of fascinating photographs. In one noteworthy series of photos, officials are tearing the number off a woman running in the Boston Marathon, which was still restricted to men in the early 1970s. Interviews and newspaper stories are incorporated into the well-crafted text, which notes the prejudices and controversies that female athletes faced. An absorbing social history, this unique photo-essay is a real eye-opener.

Morgan, Terri, and Samuel Thaler. *Steve Young: Complete Quarterback.* **1996. Hardcover: Lerner. Paperback: First Avenue. Ages 9–14.**

As a freshman at Brigham Young University, Steve Young was the eighth-string quarterback. But he went on to prove himself in college and in the 1995 Super Bowl, when he was quarterback for the winning 49ers. This straightforward biography recaps that victory, then goes back to look at Young's childhood, education, career, and Mormon values. Although his gifts to charity and his hard work to earn a law degree while playing pro ball are mentioned, the book's emphasis is on his football career, with detailed descriptions of games and winning plays, and lots of color and black-and-white photographs. Certain to please sports fans, who will also enjoy other sixty-four-page entries in the Sports Achievers series.

Rivers, Glenn, and Bruce Brooks. *Those Who Love the Game: Glenn "Doc" Rivers on Life in the NBA and Elsewhere.* 1993. Hardcover: Henry Holt. Paperback: Harper. Ages 12–14.

Imagine sitting around with an analytical, articulate NBA player talking about what it's like to play pro ball and go to the NBA finals. This book offers that experience in print as "Doc" Rivers reflects about basketball as a pro sees it. He gives his candid opinion about many of the great players: Jordan, Magic, Bird, Ewing, and others. He muses about how his job affects his family life and about the painful thought of retiring. Readers will also get specific tips about basketball from an experienced player. Award-winning writer Brooks weaves Rivers's words into a well-organized whole, adding comments and facts but letting Rivers's voice dominate. With a far richer take on the game than any ordinary sports biography, this book is a gift to basketball fans.

Nonfiction

History

Bachrach, Susan D. *Tell Them We Remember: The Story of the Holocaust.* 1994. Hardcover: Little, Brown. Paperback: Little, Brown. Ages 10–14.

Written in conjunction with the U.S. Holocaust Memorial Museum, this fine book bears witness to the children and teenagers, more than a million total, who died in the Holocaust. To make the story personal, an opening page shows twenty "identity" photographs of young people, labeled with their names, and dates and places of birth. Throughout the text, the photos reappear with more information about their fates. Many other photographs document the Nazis' rise to power, the ghettos, and the death camps. After sections on Nazi Germany and the "Final Solution," a third section discusses resistance fighters and others who risked their lives. It ends with eleven of the "identity" photographs—those who survived. An extraordinarily moving account told in clear prose with powerful photographs. Highly recommended.

Giblin, James Cross. *When Plague Strikes: The Black Death, Smallpox, AIDS.* Illustrated by David Frampton. 1995. Hardcover: Harper. Paperback: Harper. Ages 12–14.

This thoughtful book looks at the Black Death, smallpox, and AIDS, three of the worst diseases ever, and explores the effect on society of the plague, a term that means an epidemic with no cure. The Black Death, which started in the fourteenth century and spread across Europe, is described in excerpts from gruesome contemporary accounts. Smallpox dates back to ancient times and wasn't considered to be eliminated until 1977. The story of how a vaccine was developed and reluctantly accepted is fascinating. The section on AIDS reviews its social history and medical advances through early 1995. This is a well-written, compassionate account of the diseases and reactions to them, illustrated with dramatic woodcuts.

Marrin, Albert. *The Yanks Are Coming: The United States in the First World War*. 1986. Hardcover: Atheneum. Ages 12–14.

This 225-page book about the U.S. involvement in World War I will engage history buffs. After a look at the war's origins and particularly at the war at sea, the book moves to April 1917, when the United States entered the war. It follows the training of the American soldiers and their introduction to trench warfare, a method of fighting conveyed in effective, gruesome detail. Battles such as Belleau Wood are described at length, and a whole chapter is devoted to the flying aces and their dangerous missions. Black-and-white photographs, apt quotations, descriptions of important figures, and a chapter on the Home Front round out this highly readable history book. Look for Marrin's many other fine histories and biographies.

Murphy, Jim. *The Great Fire*. 1995. Hardcover: Scholastic. Paperback: Scholastic. Ages 10–14.

In this exciting history, Murphy re-creates the Great Fire of 1871, which burned for thirty-one hours and destroyed central Chicago. To paint the picture in human terms, Murphy uses the vivid writings of four people who encountered the fire firsthand: a newspaper reporter, a visitor from New York, the

Chicago Tribune editor in chief, and a twelve-year-old girl who almost died. Through their eyes, the reader experiences the incredible sounds and sights of a city burning, the panic of the citizens, and the relief at surviving a tragedy that killed perhaps three hundred people. The readable text lays out the origins of the fire, the path it took and the damage it did, and its aftermath, during which the city was rebuilt. Maps, etchings, photographs, and numerous quotes from primary sources add to the sense of immediacy in this excellent Newbery Honor Book.

Myers, Walter Dean. *Now Is Your Time! The African-American Struggle for Freedom*. 1991. Hardcover: Harper. Paperback: Harper. Ages 11–14.

Award-winning author Walter Dean Myers brings together many strands of history in this study of African Americans from colonial times through the 1960s. He uses his skills as a storyteller to bring the facts to life and focuses on certain people to illuminate a whole era in history. One chapter follows the fate of Abd al-Rahman Ibrahima, a Muslim and member of the Fula people, who was taken from Africa and sold into slavery in Mississippi. Myers illustrates his stories and chronological record with etchings, posters, newspaper ads, and black-and-white photographs. Quotations from letters, diaries, and other writings add to the effectiveness of the text, which even includes some poetry. A lively volume packed with powerful information and images.

Nature and Science

Cobb, Vicki, and Josh Cobb. *Light Action! Amazing Experiments with Optics.* Illustrated by Theo Cobb. 1993. Hardcover: Harper. Ages 12–14.

This fine book explains different aspects of optics, using easy-to-follow experiments to demonstrate the principles. Readers start by blocking light and bending it in simple experiments. Bouncing light comes next, with the entertaining task of turning off a television from another room using mirrors. After a look at light and color, readers turn to making waves using a ripple tank. Other topics include polarized light and breaking up light, with procedures using prisms, electric eyes, and doorbells. Experiments come complete with a list of materials and equipment, an explanation of the procedure with diagrams and pictures, and a section labeled "Here's What's Happening." This is only one of many excellent experiment books by Vicki Cobb, which include *Science Experiments You Can Eat, The Secret Life of Cosmetics,* and *Chemically Active!*

Eyewitness Visual Dictionary of the Universe. **1993. Hardcover: Dorling Kindersley. Ages 11–14.**

This oversized volume concentrates on astronomy, with a few forays into space exploration. Each double-page spread looks at one topic, starting with "The Universe," "Galaxies," and "The Milky Way." Although each page presents a lot of information in word and picture, the clean design keeps it from seeming overwhelming. Appendices supply details on size, distance, magnitude, and more. Sure to appeal to anyone with an interest in our galaxy and beyond. One in a popular series.

Jackson, Donna M. *The Bone Detectives: How Forensic Anthropologists Solve Crimes and Uncover Mysteries of the Dead.* Photographs by Charlie Fellenbaum. 1996. Hardcover: Little, Brown. Ages 10–14.

Crime detection and science merge in the field of forensic anthropology, in which old bones are studied for clues to a crime. This book describes a real criminal investigation that began in 1987, when a skull, other bones, and some clothing remnants were uncovered on a Missouri ranch. A "bone detective" was called in to investigate, a process followed in detail in the text and photographs. In the end, the case was solved and the murderer convicted. Sidebars offer additional information about investigation techniques such as identifying fingerprints and analyzing teeth. Final pages describe studies of bones one hundred to several thousand years old. While some readers will find the subject grisly, others will be fascinated by it.

Lauber, Patricia. *Summer of Fire: Yellowstone 1988.* 1991. Hardcover: Orchard. Ages 10–14.

In 1988, powerful forest fires swept through Yellowstone Park, leaving more than two and a half million acres seemingly devastated. This well-crafted book, full of spectacular photographs, describes the fire and its aftermath, in which the land began to renew itself immediately after the fires subsided. Gripping prose describes how the fires started, how they spread, and the valiant efforts to control them, finally accomplished by rain and snow. Most interesting is how different flora and fauna reacted to the conditions created by the fire. This thought-provoking book by an outstanding nonfiction writer challenges conventional thinking on forest fires, while telling a fascinating story. Highly recommended.

Patent, Dorothy Hinshaw. *Biodiversity*. Photographs by William Muñoz. 1996. Hardcover: Clarion. Ages 10–14.

Respected science writer Patent turns to the timely topic of biodiversity, focusing on North America and Costa Rica. She begins by explaining what biodiversity is, how it evolves, and why it is important. Beautiful color photographs extend the text with examples of the flora and fauna discussed. Patent addresses the problems presented when humans change animal habitats through development, lumbering, and pollution. She highlights Costa Rica's efforts and various U.S. efforts to preserve biodiversity. Her tone is grave but not without hope, as she calls for more efforts to save the natural world. An attractive book that makes a complex subject accessible. For a look at a related subject, see Patent's longer book *The Vanishing Feast: How Dwindling Genetic Diversity Threatens the World's Food Supply*.

Technology

Billings, Charlene W. *Supercomputers: Shaping the Future*. 1995. Hardcover: Facts on File. Ages 12–14.

This factual book describes the supercomputer centers in the United States, followed by a history of computers in general and supercomputers in particular. Technical terms such as "LAN," "CPUs," and "gigabytes" are explained in the text and also defined in a glossary. The final chapters look at many applications of the supercomputer, including its use for weather prediction, medical research, astronomy, and design of aircraft and cars. The last topic is virtual reality, how it works and what it is used for. Black-and-white photographs and many diagrams help make the complex information easier to understand. A solid introduction to an increasingly important part of technology.

Bortz, Fred. *Catastrophe! Great Engineering Failure—and Success*. 1995. Hardcover: W. H. Freeman. Paperback: W. H. Freeman. Ages 12–14.

A hotel skywalk that collapses, a bridge that twists apart in the wind, a space shuttle that explodes—these monumental disasters and several others are analyzed in this intriguing book on engineering. Because engineers learn from their mistakes, they study catastrophes to see what went wrong and to learn how to keep the disasters from being repeated. The author takes readers through such analyses, using helpful diagrams and photographs, and talks about the implications for the future. For example, he links the 1965 electrical blackout in the Northeast to potential problems on the information superhighway, because both systems rely on interconnections. A stimulating look at catastrophes, large engineering projects, and the uses of failure, written by a knowledgeable, enthusiastic guide.

Collins, Michael. *Flying to the Moon: An Astronaut's Story*. 1994 revised edition. Paperback: FSG. Ages 12–14.

It is an unexpected gift that one of the Apollo 11 astronauts is such a good writer. Collins, who piloted the command module while Armstrong and Aldrin took the first moon walk, describes the path that prepared him for that mission, from his air force career as a fighter and test pilot to his training as an astronaut starting in 1964. This readable 160-page account focuses on the technology of space launches as well as on his flights. Even knowing that Apollo 11 was a success, the reader feels suspense build as the astronauts enter the command module before blasting off. Collins conveys genuine enthusiasm for his work and for the broader issue of space exploration. A great read.

Isaacson, Philip M. *Round Buildings, Square Buildings, and Buildings That Wriggle Like a Fish.* **1988. Hardcover: Knopf. Paperback: Knopf. Ages 11–14.**

In this beautifully designed book about architecture, Isaacson discusses buildings around the world, shown in excellent color photographs. He starts with the Taj Mahal, the Parthenon, and the cathedral at Chartres, comparing and contrasting them in several ways, then looks at elements of architecture such as harmony, color, material, and shape, using many examples. His articulate, sometimes lyrical, comments and descriptions will prompt the reader to look at buildings in a new way, more carefully and appreciatively. Also see Isaacson's other elegant book, A *Short Walk Around the Pyramids and Through the World of Art.*

Macaulay, David. *The Way Things Work.* **1988. Hardcover: Houghton. Ages 10–14.**

For the person with a thirst to know how machines work, this massive volume packs information on every page, using drawings, diagrams, and explanations. Macaulay demystifies technology by adding playful woolly mammoths, who appear frequently in the illustrations. The book, which has four main parts, starts with "The Mechanics of Movement," about simple machines like levers, pulleys, screws, and more. "Harnessing the Elements" includes floating, flying, and power from pressure, heat, and nuclear processes. Light, photography, printing, sound, and telecommunications fall under "Working with Waves," while the final section deals with aspects of electricity and automation. Readers will find this good for browsing as well as a valuable reference book.

Hobbies and Sports

Coleman, Lori. *Fundamental Soccer*. Photographs by Andy King. 1995. Hardcover: Lerner. Ages 10–14.

After giving a short history of the game, this book gets down to basics with descriptions of dribbling, passing, shooting, and more. Each move is demonstrated in a series of clear color photographs that show enthusiastic teenagers on a soccer field. After a discussion of the game itself, with a look at rules and fouls, several pages describe a specific game in some detail. Conditioning exercises and drills and skills training are covered, followed by razzle-dazzle moves like sliding tackles and scissors kicks. This is useful as a detailed introduction to soccer or as a review for experienced players. Other books in the series include *Fundamental Tennis*, *Fundamental Volleyball*, and *Fundamental Golf*.

Keene, Raymond. *The Simon & Schuster Pocket Book of Chess*. 1989. Paperback: Simon & Schuster. Ages 11–14.

Written by an International Chess Grandmaster, this guide takes a serious, lucid approach to the game, with instruction for beginners and more advanced information for current players. More than a hundred diagrams extend the text, illustrating and clarifying rules and specific moves. After a short history of chess, the book sets forth the basic rules and explains standardized chess notation. One chapter looks at each piece and how it moves, followed by chapters on the opening moves, the middle game, and the endgame. Review quizzes, with answers on another page, allow readers to check their comprehension. Final sections, now out of date, discuss chess champions, and computers and chess. Written with an admirable thoroughness, this is an excellent, information-packed guide.

McKissack, Patricia C., and Fredrick McKissack, Jr. *Black Diamond: The Story of the Negro Baseball Leagues.* **1994. Hardcover: Scholastic. Ages 10–14.**

Some of the best baseball players who ever lived were excluded from the national baseball leagues because they were African American. Until 1947, when Jackie Robinson integrated the Brooklyn Dodgers, talented black players joined the Negro Leagues. This entertaining book introduces such great players as Josh Gibson, "Cool Papa" Bell, "Smoky" Joe Williams, Satchel Paige, and many more as it describes the different Negro Leagues and the problems they faced. Although social history is woven into the story, the main focus is baseball, with enough details to satisfy fans. Newspaper quotes, comments from surviving players, legendary anecdotes, and black-and-white photographs add to this account of a fascinating part of baseball history.

Pinkwater, Jill and D. Manus. *Superpuppy: How to Choose, Raise, and Train the Best Possible Dog for You.* **1976. Paperback: Clarion. Ages 12–14.**

If you have a dog, plan to get a dog, or just like reading about dogs, this is the book for you. Written by a wife and husband who run a dog training school (and write novels and picture-story books), it covers a huge amount of information in an easy-to-follow way. The first chapters go through the decision to get a dog, with a look at how feasible it is, depending on family circumstances. Readers are advised on where to find a dog and what to look for. Many aspects of owning a dog are addressed: health care, food, housebreaking, grooming, and obedience training. The instructions are clear and thoughtful, aided by simple illustrations. Although slightly outdated in parts, the book still serves as an excellent, enjoyable guide for new and experienced dog-owners.

Rossiter, Sean. *The Basics: Hockey the NHL Way.* **1996. Hardcover: Sterling. Ages 10–14.**

With an enthusiastic tone and clear instructions, Rossiter explains the basic skills that hockey players must master. Color photographs show top players as well as young players, including a few girls, demonstrating skills. The topics include skating, offense, defense, goaltending, equipment, and fitness. In teaching skills like passing and shooting, the book describes specific maneuvers, then suggests practice drills. Tips and quotes from stars appear frequently. Rossiter's excitement comes across in this useful guide to learning and improving hockey skills.

Schmidt, Norman. *Best Ever Paper Airplanes.* **1994. Paperback: Sterling. Ages 11–14.**

Combining the fun of crafts with information on how airplanes work, this colorful book gives instructions for making eighteen paper airplanes out of ordinary bond paper. An introduction offers tips about safety and construction, and discusses the theory of flight, including lift, gravity, drag, and thrust. The detailed instructions, which include ideas for decorating, progress from simple to complex, with the first airplane requiring six simple steps and the final design, sixteen intricate steps. The designs have been tested for flight. The instructions call for careful work and dexterous fingers to make the impressive planes shown in color photographs. A fine, advanced craft book.

Scobey, Joan. *The Fannie Farmer Junior Cookbook.* **Illustrated by Patience Brewster. 1993. Hardcover: Little, Brown. Ages 10–14.**

For those who like to cook or who would like to learn, this is an excellent guide, with over one hundred recipes. The first thirty-five pages discuss types of food, tools, and safety, and define cooking terms. The recipes cover a wide range of dishes from soups and breads to many desserts. Nicely laid out, the recipes list ingredients and equipment clearly, then give step-by-step instructions. Small black-and-white drawings decorate the spacious pages. The emphasis is on basic dishes, including hamburgers, chili, microwaved fish, lasagna, salads, brownies, and other popular sweets. Family and friends will benefit from the reader who puts this fine book to use.

Poetry

Carlson, Lori M., editor. *Cool Salsa: Bilingual Poems on Growing Up Latino in the United States.* 1994. Hardcover: Henry Holt. Paperback: Fawcett. Ages 11–14.

More than three dozen poems by different writers convey feelings about growing up bilingual in the United States. Most are presented in English and Spanish, although a few combine the two languages, with a glossary at the back of the book to translate the Spanish words. Divided into categories such as "School Days," "Hard Times," and "Time to Party," the poems span a wide range of emotions. Some reflect a life of poverty and hardship, while others rejoice in a Latino heritage. A fine collection for Latino Americans, who will recognize their own voices, and for readers who don't speak Spanish but love good poetry.

Gordon, Ruth, selector. *Peeling the Onion: An Anthology of Poems.* 1993. Hardcover: Harper. Ages 12–14.

"Poetry is the onion of readers. It can cause tears, be peeled layer by layer, or be replanted to grow into new ideas. And it adds taste, zest, and a sharp but sweet quality that enriches our lives," says a note to the reader of this excellent anthology. Gordon has gathered together more than sixty poems about nature and people, some from well-known modern poets like Roethke and Pastan, others from less familiar poets. The poems, many in translation, offer fresh, evocative images that speak to adolescent readers. Very short poems are interspersed with longer ones in a well-designed format with large typeface and generous white space. Other anthologies compiled by Gordon include *Time Is the Longest Distance*, *Under All Silences: Shades of Love*, and *Pierced by a Ray of Sun: Poems About the Times We Feel Alone*.

Hughes, Langston. *The Dream Keeper and Other Poems*. Illustrated by Brian Pinkney. 1993. Hardcover: Knopf. Paperback: Knopf. Ages 9–14.

These thirty-six short poems range from celebrations of life to lamentations about injustice to black Americans. Exquisitely illustrated with swirling black-and-white artwork on every page, they provide an inspirational introduction to a great poet. While many of the poems will probably be new to readers, they may recognize the widely anthologized "Dreams," "April Rain Song," and "Poem," which begins, "I loved my friend./He went away from me." The poems speak about seasons, dreams, family, love, religion, and the pride of being black. Elegantly designed and printed on high-quality paper, this fine volume could well become a treasured family book.

Janeczko, Paul B. *Wherever Home Begins*: 100 Contemporary Poems. 1995. Hardcover: Orchard. Ages 12–14.

Anthologist Paul Janeczko has gathered one hundred contemporary poems about places and homes with topics such as small towns, deserted houses, bars and restaurants and stores, water, workplaces, city life, bus stations, and drifting. Some are nostalgic for a slower, friendlier time, while others look at the bleakness of certain places, sometimes childhood homes. Most of the poems are a page or less in length. They are loosely grouped by topic, but without headings to pinpoint the themes. This is a wonderful anthology that will evoke familiar feelings and offer new perspectives, while introducing a wide range of modern poets. Look, too, for Janeczko's other fine anthologies.

Knudson, R. R., and May Swenson, selectors. *American Sports Poems*. 1988. Hardcover: Orchard. Ages 11–14.
This is a masterful, seemingly exhaustive, collection of poems about different sports. Although baseball dominates, the topics include other team sports as well as swimming, skating, fishing, karate, sailing, and much more. Some poems offer tribute to specific athletes, while others use sports as a jumping-off point for broader ideas. The array of poets is impressive, including Carl Sandburg, John Updike, Linda Pastan, Lawrence Ferlinghetti, and Lucille Clifton. Notes in the back provide useful information about the poets and the poems' subjects. The collection conveys a palpable enthusiasm for all aspects of sports and the deep enjoyment they bring participants and spectators.

Resources for Parents

Locating Books

Libraries

Public libraries are a great resource for parents. They are free, and typically offer a broader and deeper range of books than are found in bookstores. Libraries are the best place to find books that are out of print, an important service because many children's books go out of print quickly. Libraries are also more likely than bookstores to carry books from smaller presses.

Good libraries are increasingly easy to use. Some public library catalogs can be accessed from home, using a computer and a modem. Many libraries are part of a branch system or a large cooperative system, so you can use your card at more than one library. In such cases you can usually return books to the library closest to you, even if you checked them out elsewhere. Most libraries have book drops so that you can return books when the library is closed.

Computerized catalogs may intimidate some library users, but most people get accustomed to them quickly. Like the traditional card catalog, the computerized catalog shows you whether your library owns a book, but it also tells you if it is on the shelf or checked out. Often computerized catalogs also show whether a nearby library has the book, which you could then borrow through interlibrary loan.

Interlibrary loan (ILL) is a convenient way to get access to many more books than your local library has in its collection. In many libraries, there is no charge to borrow a book through ILL, although some public libraries require a small fee per book. Some computerized catalogs allow you to input your library card number if you want to request a book from another library. Your local library will call you or send a notice when it arrives, often in a few days.

While you are signing out books, find out what other programs and services your local library offers. You may discover storytimes for younger children, summer reading programs for a wide range of ages, junior critic clubs for older children, programs on parenting, and more. Many libraries carry books on tape and videos, too.

School libraries come in all sizes, and the large ones will probably have many of the books in this guide. Some school libraries are open during the summer, although most are not. Whether parents can sign out books depends on the school.

Bookstores and Catalogs

Bookstores vary enormously in their selections of children's books. Some offer a wide array of books, usually with an emphasis on paperbacks. Others have only a small selection, or carry mostly books in popular series. Some cities have bookstores devoted just to children's books, a treat for children's book lovers.

It is important to realize that most bookstores will order a book for you at no charge if the bookstore doesn't carry it. If you don't see the book you want, ask about placing such a special order.

Bookstores are increasing the services they offer for families, adding storytimes, author book signings, and other programs. Several large bookstores now offer children's books by mail through the World Wide Web, and some give recommendations of children's books at their Web sites.

Most catalogs and book clubs offer very small selections of good children's books. One exception is *Chinaberry Books*, an outstanding catalog of more than five hundred children's books, with thoughtful descriptions of each title. It covers toddlers through adolescents, with a section on parenting books and a small selection of novels for adults. Write: Chinaberry Books, 2780 Via Orange Way, Suite B, Spring Valley, CA 91978. Call 1-800-776-2242.

Keeping Up with Children's Book Publishing

If you are interested in keeping up with what's new in children's books, here are some recommended magazines and review journals. Also keep an eye on your local newspaper, which may have regular or occasional articles on new children's books. Libraries often provide book lists that highlight recent recommended books. For example, each year the American Library Association publishes an annotated list of approximately seventy-five Notable Children's Books, a useful resource available in most libraries.

- *The Horn Book Magazine* is a well-established, bimonthly journal about children's books. It prints insightful reviews of recommended books and well-written articles about children's literature. Available at bookstores and libraries, and by subscription. Write: The Horn Book Magazine, 11 Beacon Street, Boston, MA 02108. Call: 1-617-227-1555.
- *Book Links* is an attractive, useful magazine of great interest to children's librarians and teachers, published by the American Library Association six times a year. It highlights books on selected topics and authors, geared toward curriculum needs. Available by subscription and in many libraries. Write: Book Links, 434 W. Downer, Aurora, IL 60506. Call: 1-630-892-7465.
- *Five Owls* is published bimonthly for "readers personally and professionally involved in children's literature." It includes articles, bibliographies, and reviews. Write: Five

Owls, 2004 Sheridan Avenue South, Minneapolis, MN 55405.

- *Parents' Choice: A Review of Children's Media*, published by the Parents' Choice Foundation, offers well-balanced reviews of books, television shows, movies, videos, software, music, toys, and games. Also includes bibliographies and educational articles. Issued quarterly. Write: Parents' Choice, P.O. Box 185, Waban, MA 02168.

Encouraging Your Son
to Read

- Let your son see you reading—books, newspapers, or magazines. Make reading part of your household. Read aloud to him and encourage him to read to you.
- Leave books lying around the house. Buy some books that are likely to appeal to your son, or get a stack for free at your public library.
- For those boys who fear being teased, reading may be essentially private. Respect that he may not want to talk about everything he reads or be praised for reading (depending, of course, on the child).
- Subscribe to a magazine that might interest him (see the list below).
- Encourage relatives and family friends whom your son loves and admires to give books as presents. When giving him presents, you might combine a book with another interest, such as a soccer ball and a soccer book.
- Let your child make choices at the library or bookstore, and *don't criticize his interests.* Let him pick books that are too easy but may be comforting, or books that are too hard but have interesting pictures or photographs. It's also important to let him explore various topics, even if they don't fit stereotypical male interests, without being teased.
- Recognize that reading about information is as legitimate as reading novels. Acknowledge this fact to your son when he follows written instructions for a hobby or reads the sports pages.

- Some children love acquiring facts or trivia, and especially enjoy the *Guinness Book of World Records*, the *World Almanac*, or sports almanacs, just for the fun of browsing through them.
- If he is interested in a particular sport, seek out fiction or informational books about that sport, or a biography of a famous athlete.
- Try reading nonfiction aloud, especially on a topic your child cannot yet read about alone but about which he wants to know more.
- Choose a book together to give in his name to his school or your public library.

Magazines

Here are recommended magazines for boys ages two to fourteen, including general-interest magazines and magazines geared to specific topics. Magazines offer the benefit of short articles, which will appeal to reluctant readers who may not want to tackle a whole book. Boys with specific interests in areas like nature or sports, for example, will find magazines with timely information, often supplemented with excellent photographs. Since most children enjoy getting mail, a magazine subscription is one more way to build excitement about reading. Check with your public library for current information about subscribing.

Calliope: World History for Young People
For ages 9 14. A forty-eight-page magazine, issued five times a year; each issue focuses on a theme in history.
Chickadee
For ages 3–8. A Canadian nature magazine published ten times a year by the Young Naturalist Foundation. Has articles, activities, puzzles, drawings, stories, and color photos on nature and science.
Cobblestone: The History Magazine for Young People
For ages 9–14. A forty-eight-page magazine issued nine times a year; high-quality articles focus on one aspect of American history, with photographs, games, activities, puzzles, and more.
Cricket: The Magazine for Children
For ages 9–14. Issued monthly. An unusually attractive general-interest magazine with high-quality stories, poems, and illustrations.

Faces: The Magazine About People
For ages 9–14. Published ten times a year in conjunction with the American Museum of Natural History. Offers articles, projects, and photographs on natural history and anthropology.

Highlights for Children
For ages 4–10. Issued monthly. This general-interest magazine, which continues to be popular, offers puzzles, articles, stories, activities, and more for a wide age range.

Kid City
For ages 6–10. Published ten times a year by the Children's Television Workshop. "For graduates of Sesame Street," this is a general-interest magazine on a variety of topics. Includes some advertising.

Ladybug: The Magazine for Young Children
For ages 2–6. Issued monthly. A companion magazine to *Cricket*, this also has unusually high-quality stories, poems, and illustrations as well as songs and games. Also contains an insert for parents.

Merlyn's Pen: The National Magazines of Student Writing
Middle school edition for ages 11–14. Published four times during the school year. This magazine consists of short stories, poems, essays, letters, and illustrations by middle school students.

Muse
For ages 8–14. Published bimonthly by the publishers of *Cricket* in conjunction with *Smithsonian Magazine*. A high-quality magazine about different aspects of science and the arts. Excellent photography and well-written, up-to-date articles. Includes some advertising.

National Geographic
For ages 10 and up. Published monthly by the National Geo-

graphic Society. This well-established magazine with beautiful photographs and lively articles appeals to children as well as adults.

National Geographic World

For ages 8–13. Published monthly by the National Geographic Society. An attractive magazine with articles, stories, and color photographs about science, people, and places of interest to children.

Odyssey: Science That's Out of This World

For ages 9–14. Published monthly September through May. A forty-eight-page magazine with articles and color photographs on a particular theme about astronomy and outer space. Includes sky charts.

OWL: The Discovery Magazine for Children

For ages 9–12. A Canadian nature magazine published ten times a year by the Young Naturalist Foundation. Has articles, activities, puzzles, contests, stories, and color photos on nature and the environment.

Ranger Rick

For ages 6–10. A nature magazine published monthly by the National Wildlife Federation. Excellent color photographs, short articles, and columns about animals, plants, and other aspects of the natural world.

Sesame Street Magazine

For ages 2–6. Published ten times a year by the Children's Television Workshop. Stories and activities, some related to characters from the Sesame Street television show. Includes an insert for parents.

Spider: The Magazine for Children

For ages 6–9. Published monthly. Another companion magazine to *Cricket*, with excellent stories, poems, articles, and illustrations, often by recognized children's writers and illustrators.

Sports Illustrated

For ages 12 and up. Weekly. Older children often prefer this version over *Sports Illustrated for Kids*.

Sports Illustrated for Kids

For ages 8–13. Published monthly. A popular glossy magazine with articles and photographs about sports, including amateur and professional athletes. Includes many advertisements.

Stone Soup: The Magazine by Young Writers

For ages 6–13. A forty-eight-page magazine with stories, poetry, book reviews, and illustrations by children up to age thirteen. With an insert for teachers.

3-2-1 Contact

For ages 8–14. A science magazine published by the Children's Television Workshop ten times a year. With articles, activities, and color photographs on a central theme.

Your Big Backyard

For ages 3–6. A nature magazine published monthly by the National Wildlife Federation. Excellent color photographs, short articles with big typeface, and simple activities about animals, plants, and other aspects of the natural world. Includes several pages for adults.

Zillions

For ages 8–14. Published bimonthly by the Consumers Union. This "Consumer Reports for Kids" evaluates products of interest to children, in terms of durability and price. Includes video, music, and book reviews by children and teenagers.

Tips on Reading Aloud

Reading aloud well does not come naturally to everyone. Here are techniques you can practice until they come easily. *The Read-Aloud Handbook* by Jim Trelease (Penguin, 1995, 4th edition) offers more ideas on how to go about it, as well as numerous reasons that reading aloud is beneficial.

- If you haven't read the book already, scan it to get a sense of its contents before you start reading aloud.
- Choose books you are excited about or your child is excited about. It is hard to read a book you don't enjoy, especially a long one.
- Read with expression. A monotone is hard to listen to. Children need to hear changes in your voice to indicate when you are reading dialogue. Vary your pace, too. Slow down to build up suspense, and speed up during exciting scenes.
- Create voices for different characters if you enjoy it, but it isn't necessary for a good reading. A story can be read effectively in a straightforward manner as long as you have expression and enthusiasm.
- Read at a moderate pace, not too fast. Listening is a challenge for many children, and you don't want to leave them behind as you speed ahead. Picture-story books require time for enjoying the illustrations.
- Feel free to stop and discuss the book if you and your listener want to. Answer questions as they come up. How much you want to stop and explain new words is up to you. If they can be understood in context, you may want just to

keep reading. Stopping too often to explain can undermine the story's impact.

- Keep in mind that children can look bored or restless and still be listening. Some children need to be moving around or fidgeting with something. The real question is, are they following the story? If so, let them squirm or even draw pictures as they listen.

- Sometimes a book will lead to conversations afterward, sometimes not. Play it by ear. Either way is fine.

- If your child wants to read to you sometimes, great. Beginning readers especially enjoy their new skills. You can trade off pages or chapters, or just sit back and listen.

- If your child is not enjoying a book, you are not obliged to finish it. This is most likely to come up with chapter books. You don't want to abandon a book quickly, but if a book has not sparked interest after several sessions, try another one. If this is a pattern, you may want to switch to shorter books and build up to longer ones.

- Try reading just a few poems together at a time. Start with light verse if you are uncomfortable with poetry. You may be surprised at how much fun you and your child can have with poems.

- Reading aloud has a host of educational benefits, but it works best if it isn't approached as an educational exercise. Parents have been known to have children repeat each word after them, as a device to teach reading. Such a tedious approach is more likely to dampen enthusiasm for books than to promote learning. Just enjoy the books together; the increased vocabulary, understanding of story structure, exposure to correct grammar, and other benefits will follow naturally.

Activities with Books

Books stand on their own as art and entertainment, and sometimes the best approach is simply to read a book and savor it. In other cases, discussing the book enriches the experience. But it can also be fun to pair books with activities such as crafts, trips, cooking, and more. Most of the following ideas are geared toward picture-story books and biographies, but reading a novel together can also lead to shared activities. Some of the nonfiction books, in fact, contain activities, such as science experiments, crafts, magic tricks, and more. Brainstorm with your child about other possibilities, with the goal, as always, to make reading a wonderful experience.

- Combine crafts and books. Read *Stringbean's Trip to the Sea*, then make some postcards and send them to friends and relatives. Read *Mouse Paint* and mix up some paints into new color combinations. Read *The Sea-Breeze Hotel* and make a kite together. Read *The Paper Crane*, then try some origami.
- Add props to your reading of a picture-story book. Get a squirt gun or set of Groucho Marx glasses for reading *Chester's Way*, or an eye patch for *Tough Boris*.
- Pair a picture-story book about an animal with a short nonfiction book. Read *Patrick's Dinosaurs*, then a factual book on dinosaurs. Read *The Mare on the Hill*, then a book on horses.
- Read *Eating Fractions*, then cook together. Cooking is a wonderful combination of math, such as fractions and measuring, and reading recipes. Try one of the recipes in *Pretend Soup and Other Real Recipes*.

- Take a low-key field trip in conjunction with a picture-story book. Read *Matthew's Meadow* and then take a walk in a meadow.
- If you live in a city, read *Alphabet City*, then go look for letters in your urban setting. With older children, read *Round Buildings, Square Buildings, and Buildings That Wriggle Like a Fish*, then take a walk and talk about the buildings you see.
- Read *Zin! Zin! Zin! A Violin* before going to hear instrumental music.
- Read *Owl Moon* and go out on an evening hike to look for birds.
- Read *The Airplane Alphabet Book* and visit a local airport.
- After reading a book illustrated with collage, try making a collage. Or paint with watercolors after seeing watercolor illustrations in a book. Read *The Big Orange Splot*, then each draw your dream house.
- Encourage your child to write and illustrate his own books. He can dictate the words to you if he doesn't know how to print yet. Remind him to add an "About the Author" paragraph.
- Read a biography together about an artist and take a trip to a museum. Paint a picture or make a sculpture together. Since children's books have a limited number of reproductions of paintings, find a book for adults with even more pictures to look at.
- Read about a musician in *Lives of the Musicians, Mozart Tonight*, or other biographies, and listen to music they have composed. It can also be fun to do free-form drawing to the music.
- Read a folktale from another country together and then locate the country on a map. Find a book with photographs of that country. Read *Nellie Bly's Monkey*, then trace her trip around the world on a globe.

- Read a folktale, then a parody of the tale, such as "Jack and the Beanstalk" and *Jim and the Beanstalk*, or "Little Red Riding Hood" and *Ruby*. Talk about the similarities and differences.
- Read about an athlete or sport, then go to a local sports event, such as a high school or college game or track meet.
- Read a novel together that has been made into a movie, such as *Harriet the Spy* or *James and the Giant Peach*. Watch the video and compare the two.
- Read a novel in conjunction with a trip to a geographic region: *Go Fish* for Florida, *Nekomah Creek* for Oregon, and so on.
- Pair a novel and a related history book. For example, middle readers could read *The Riddle of Penncroft Farm*, a novel concerning the Revolutionary War, and then *The American Revolution*, a factual account.
- Listen to a book on tape together on a long trip. A number of the novels in this guide have been recorded and are available at your library or for rent through the mail.

Books for Children on Sex and Growing Up

It is vital for children to understand the changes that will take place in their bodies when they become adolescents. They need accurate information about sex, and reassurances about puberty and its effects. Here are some recommended books with age guidelines.

Andry, Andrew C., and Steven Schepp. *How Babies Are Made.* **Illustrated by Blake Hampton. 1968. Paperback: Little Brown. Ages 5–8.**

Simple information for younger children about sexual reproduction in flowers, animals, and humans. Illustrated with cut-paper illustrations.

Cole, Joanna. *How You Were Born.* **Photographs by Margaret Miller. 1993 revised edition. Hardcover: Morrow. Paperback: Morrow. Ages 4–7.**

Color photographs and diagrams show the development of the fetus and the birth process, and the welcome arrival of newborn babies into several families.

Fenwick, Elizabeth, and Richard Walker. *How Sex Works: A Clear, Comprehensive Guide for Teenagers to Emotional, Physical, and Sexual Maturity.* **1994. Hardcover: Dorling Kindersley. Ages 12 and up.**

This attractive guide discusses the bodily and emotional changes at puberty, relationships, sexual feelings and intercourse, contraception, pregnancy and parenthood, sexual diseases, sexual abuse, sexual harassment, and rape. Diagrams and color photos supplement the text.

Harris, Robie H. *It's Perfectly Normal: Changing Bodies, Growing Up, Sex & Sexual Health*. Illustrated by Michael Emberley. 1994. Hardcover: Candlewick. Paperback: Candlewick. Ages 9 and up.

A well-crafted book that answers children's questions about their bodies and sexual reproduction. The straightforward text is balanced by funny, apt cartoon drawings, many of nude figures.

Madaras, Lynda, with Dane Saavedra. *The What's Happening to My Body? Book for Boys: A Growing Up Guide for Parents and Sons*. 1988 revised edition. Paperback: Newmarket. Ages 9 and up.

A comprehensive, readable handbook filled with useful information, mainly about males, although some facts about female puberty are included. Madaras has written a companion volume for girls.

Author Index

AUTHOR INDEX

Title Index

TITLE INDEX

TITLE INDEX

TITLE INDEX

TITLE INDEX

TITLE INDEX

Category Index

CATEGORY INDEX

377

CATEGORY INDEX

CATEGORY INDEX

CATEGORY INDEX

CATEGORY INDEX